Theory of Criticism

Murray Krieger

THEORY OF CRITICISM

A Tradition and Its System

THE JOHNS HOPKINS UNIVERSITY PRESS

BALTIMORE AND LONDON

The Johns Hopkins University Press, Baltimore, Maryland 21218
The Johns Hopkins University Press Ltd., London

Library of Congress Catalog Card Number 75–36935
ISBN 0-8018-1825-7

151214

IN MEMORIAM

Rosalie Littell Colie

Contents

Preface

I can think of three books I meant to write in the course of writing this one. Saying something about what each of them was to have been may help clarify the complex objectives I hope this book to serve.

My initial intention, rather ambitious if not vainglorious, was to write a general introduction to critical theory for advanced students of literature. It was to separate out and describe the basic problems in poetics and to use these, seen in relation to one another, as an index to help us define various theories of criticism. I thus hoped to provide methodological criteria for judging the various systematic solutions proposed to these problems through the history of criticism. Then, building on traditional positions, I wanted my study to reflect some of the varied notions abroad in the last two dozen years of theorizing. In effect, then, it was to be a *Theory of Literature* twenty or so years after. And I had hopes it would be found as useful as the Wellek and Warren had been, even to the point of serving as a text.

At the same time, I was anxious to establish the theoretical tradition by analyzing the positions of the major critics. This was in accord with the second book I originally had in mind: I had wanted to test the problems of poetics (as I conceived them) and their influence on critical practice by examining the theoretical difficulties into which these sample critics had stumbled. This work was not to be an exhaustive history, but rather an exploration of those inconsistent moments in each of our most distinguished older critics in which they struggled to accommodate their sense of poetic creativity to their fixed theoretical commitments. I saw that, with the best of our critics—those who will not permit their theoretical commitments to blind them to the unpredictable demands of the single literary work—critical discourse at certain points becomes a reasoned disorder, or a disordering of reason. Thus, I was ready to observe, often the critic's inner person asserts itself at the expense of his systematic allegiance, so that what confronts us is a theoretical inconsistency that we welcome in preference to the insensitivity and neglect produced by theoretical dogma uncontested. Concentrating on this necessary conflict between literary experience and literary theory, which leads to the conflict in the critic between his sensibility and his system, I wanted to produce a study of landmark critics (including Plato, Aristotle, Horace, Longinus, Mazzoni, Sidney, Pope, Young, Lessing, Wordsworth, Coleridge, Shelley, Arnold, and Croce), a study that would try to isolate and account for the place in the writings of each of them where the dislocation in the system occurs. As a result, I meant to break through the stereotyped categories in which histories of theory usually place these theorists in order to find the conjunction of contrary notions, systematic and otherwise, that characterizes the special contribution of each of them as a critical personality. Yet all of them together, with their internal conflicts, were to be seen as constituting a humanistic tradition of critical theory.

As I contemplated my hopes for these two books, I realized that both would be dominated, in ways that candor would require me to face up to, by my own theoretical commitments. I felt as I began to write that I could not avoid pressing these problems toward my own sense of solutions to them, or pressing these theorists to what use I could make of them: what was to be a text (or a pair of texts) for an introductory course became a pretext for pursuing the issues where I saw them to have led the tradition of critical theory, as I conceived that tradition. Though in my first intended book I meant to furnish a framework for the discussion of critical theory in general, and though in my second intended book I meant to furnish a framework for the placement of major critical theorists and theories, as I began them it became obvious that I was proceeding, defensively, from the perspective of the particular theory that is my own. My attempt to set forth guidelines for any critical theory or actual theorists constantly reflected my predisposition to make a single theory look good. Thus I was led toward a third book, in which I would put together a theory of my own. In it, I now acknowledged, the general criteria for theorizing about criticism would be forced to support this theory; and similarly, all too similarly, the theoretical tradition, in its variety, would be seen—with some embarrassment—to justify my own manifestation of it as its inevitable product, for which it would now be made to serve as a series of less complicated precedents.

So this volume uses its introductory section, in which I set up a general schema to account for a variety of theoretical undertakings, and its second section, in which I analyze exemplary theories drawn from the history of criticism, to move toward my own contribution. But in these earlier sections, too, my own theoretical interests are dominant, so that this third is the book I have written, though I hope the other two are still present, if only in the background. It is by reason of this development that the book, I believe, becomes progressively difficult—further and further from a textbook style—as it closes in from the more universalistic ambitions of its earlier sections to the more exclusive arguments of its final section. My general discussion of the problems of theory (though reduced to the specifications of my own preferred theory) and my analysis of the several theorists in the history of the discipline (though forced to serve as precedents for my own developments of their ideas) are addressed to the general student of literature, with as little as possible taken for granted. As my own position moves more self-consciously to center stage, my language and argument may seem more appropriate for the specialized study of theory. I hope that by then all my readers have been prepared to stay with me, so that I gain the less specialized ones without losing my peers.

There is always the danger, of course, that I will fail both audiences, instead of succeeding doubly: that the introductory textbook tone will slow down my proceedings and offend the advanced reader, while my fully developed argument may confuse the student who was beginning to follow my intention. Yet my several objectives—the introduction to the study of critical theory, the tracing of the history of criticism through the analysis of a few sample theorists, and the setting forth of my theory in a systematic way that reflects its own history—all seem to me worth serving. Since I am a committed theorist as well as a historian and an analyst of theory, candor would require me to admit that I cannot try to serve one of these objectives without serving all at once. Whatever my successes in this book, it has certainly taught me that I cannot succeed as a writer of elementary textbooks. But I still must hope that students as well as teachers can make use of my work.

As I realized that my ultimate objective was to make the fullest and most developed theoretical statement of which I am capable, I came to see this book as the consequence of my theorizing that has spanned twenty years and five books. I had to bring together into an explicit theoretical system what lay scattered through my writings, though I saw them as consistently pointing in a common direction. Others have seen this, too, as is evident in the several studies that have appeared of my work as a consistent body of theory. But the task of setting it all forth in one place forced me to discover gaps and shifts in emphasis, as well as unanswered questions, and these required nothing less than my rethinking the system from the ground. So I have come to believe that this is no mere gathering together for a restatement, but that it is an extension of my previous thought, an advance to the fullness of systematic expression. It has gained also from my need here to relate it to the general requirements for a theory and to see it as a reflection of the theoretical tradition, even if I have distorted the latter in order to find precedents for my own claims.

Yet, to a great extent, this systematic statement continues to depend upon those piecemeal discussions in my earlier works. Since they were partial statements only, they could often treat a single aspect of theory in greater detail than is possible in this more general study. This accounts for the frequency in this volume of footnotes to my own work, usually to places in it where lengthier discussions might lend support to claims being argued for more briefly here. This practice is especially useful when my argument stands in need of demonstration by being applied to literary texts. My varied tasks in this volume too often preclude the luxury of introducing examples from practical criticism (I finally break down toward the end of Chapter 6 and can no longer resist inserting, from there to my conclusion, a few brief samples of literary analysis); but, prevented from greater indulgence here, I sometimes relieve my frustration by referring to my earlier writings in which such demonstration can be found. I hope this is adequate justification for this recourse to citations of myself, a species of self-reference of another sort than that called for by E. H. Gombrich.

I am anxious to insist that the infrequency of my appeals to literary works is not meant to reflect any sense on my part that theory is a self-sufficient discipline. Quite the contrary. Indeed, I hope that my theoretical skepticism is evident from the very first of the pages that follow. My need to refer theory at once to what it can do for the criticism of specific works is, as I have said, what accounts for many of my references to my earlier writings. These days one's concern to keep applied literary criticism at the center of his interest in theory needs to be emphasized. Not long ago one could properly complain about the neglect of theory by those scholars who practice criticism in the academy. More recently, however, the academic obsession with methodology has risen even to the level of literary study: not only has theory come into its own, but it seems to be nourishing itself as a separate institution, to which literature sometimes seems almost irrelevant. Especially as it seeks to move literary study—via semiotics—toward the social sciences, current theory, largely under the impetus of structuralism, seems at times to be using its role to undermine its mistress. So, having been one of those who fought in departments of literature to increase the importance accorded critical theory, I find it ironic that I now am concerned about its flourishing, out of my fear that in its recent forms theory leads away from the unique powers of literature as an art, the center of our humanistic domain. It was this fear that led me to realize that I could not conclude this volume without confronting the structuralist challenge to poetics with my version of the theoretical tradition. I believe this challenge may help that tradition to discover its definition.

Of course, the tradition is *my* tradition, what I have created for myself out of the writers I have chosen to treat; and it is probably true that my selections out of the long history of criticism have been governed by my need to dwell upon those whom I found most cooperative in allowing me to use them to establish it. But I must believe also that it was their ideas that gave this tradition the shape that I try to make my own. Still, any reader must be concerned about how idiosyncratic my treatment of them has been. Where some may charge me with anachronistic distortion, imposing upon a writer theoretical notions he could not have held, I would claim to see a writer like Coleridge (or, for that matter, even Aristotle himself) struggling toward concepts that his terminology, limited by his philosophical heritage, was not yet capable of containing. But, less defensively, honesty requires me to acknowledge that every writer in a tradition must be changed by the later writer who uses him in order to constitute that tradition and to see himself as its latest member. That is the greater part of history's value to each of us who seeks to discover his place in it. I leave it to the reader to judge the degree of my distortions, the value of the tradition they permit me to construct and sustain, and—perhaps the central issue—the extent to which my tradition is also one that has served as the source and the justification of our most enduring literature.

I interpret this tradition as fundamentally humanistic, in that at its center is man as the creator of forms. This human genesis turns what is outside man and resistant to his order into symbolic terms susceptible of human manipulation and human meaning. It is this tradition whose history I trace and try to extend, and it rests on the assumption of forms constructed in accordance with humanly conceived teleologies. Now it is true that the dominant mood at the moment in the arts, as well as in criticism and its theory, no longer accepts such an assumption: that the source and end and value of arts rests on man's imposition of his forms upon recalcitrant and unformed materials. But this is hardly the only aspect of contemporary culture that is antihumanistic; and I must stick by my assumption if I am to make sense of what I see as the best of our aesthetic heritage and the best hope for its future. This is the point on which I rest my machine: for me the ubiquity of man's form-making—his capacity (and need) to make forms and of other men's capacity (and need) to respond to them—justifies a heuristic notion of the aesthetic experience as a unified act at once "intentional" and

xiii

fictional. It is this notion on which my version of the theoretical tradition rests and from which my development of it emerges.

For this notion I am obviously indebted to my teacher, Eliseo Vivas, although it has been modified in the direction suggested by my late theoretical ally, Sigurd Burckhardt, as I have made clear in citation after citation in the pages that follow. Another late theoretical ally has made a deep imprint on these pages: the dear colleague to whose memory this book is dedicated. The wit and learning of Rosalie Colie, even in her absence, have continued to civilize and educate me. With my wife, Joan, who with me cherished her specially among our friends, I still find the shape of our imaginations responding to the forms she left with us. For myself, my imagination remains blessed also by the forms still made available for it daily by the creative wit of my wife. Would that the zodiac of my own wit had the range and the variety of constellations that have been lent me by such as these.

There are more mundane debts of gratitude that must be acknowledged: to the National Endowment for the Humanities, under whose research grant this study was begun, and to the University of California, whose research and travel grants permitted me to carry it forward and bring it to completion. Debts are owed also to the editors and publishers who have permitted portions of this book to appear in their volumes and their journals, and who have permitted them to be refashioned for use here: William Conway of the William Andrews Clark Memorial Library, UCLA; Joseph P. Strelka and the Pennsylvania State University Press; Sheldon Sacks of *Critical Inquiry*; Ralph Cohen of *New Literary History*; and the editors of the *Southern Review*. I must thank my secretary, Betty Terrell, for services that were prompted by a profound fidelity, as she helped bring the manuscript to its finished form; and I must thank those classes of students, in year after year of my graduate introduction to critical theory, who helped show me why and how to begin it.

Laguna Beach, California   Murray Krieger
October 1975

Part One  The Problem: The Limits and Capacities
of Critical Theory

I

The Vanity of Theory and Its Value

 Literary theory is a vain discipline. I mean "vain" in both senses: it is prideful, even preening, in its glittering systematic displays, and it is—ultimately—fruitless. Its pride requires it to assume, not only that an airtight, wholly coherent aesthetic of poetry can be achieved, but that such an aesthetic can account for the awesome variety of things we honor with the name of "poems," by virtue of the special experience they afford us. However, each attempt at theoretical completeness is rendered fruitless by the teasing elusiveness of the entities and experiences for which it is to account, and each attempt to handle (I really mean to manhandle) the varieties of poetic experience—to reduce them to theoretical order— is thwarted by the inadequacy of the systematic instruments (or weapons) the theorist is obliged to employ. Nevertheless, despite this double sense of the vanity of its mission, literary theory has occupied and continues to occupy the best efforts of devoted and intelligent minds, both philosophic and poetic, whose fruits are not themselves vain. Like their work, literary theory—once stripped of its pretensions —is worthy of study. Indeed, the student of literature cannot afford *not* to study it, to worry its problems and its would-be solutions to them.

By literary theory or poetics or aesthetics of poetry (three ways of saying the same thing) I mean the systematic construct that accounts for and makes consistent the individual critiques of works of literature.[1] Thus we begin, as readers, with the literary work; the rationalization of our reading of and response to the work results in the individual work

---

[1] Works, that is, in verse or prose, provided they have about them the fiction-making quality that Aristotle included within his sense of *poesis*. When I refer to them as "poems," I still mean literary works in this broad sense. When I refer, more narrowly, to verse alone, I shall acknowledge it to the reader. A complication arises from the fact that I shall at times use examples from verse to reveal more obvious devices that, *mutatis mutandis*, have their counterparts (though less quickly demonstrable ones) in nonverse "poems."

3

of criticism; and, in time, the coherent attempt to rationalize our discrete commentaries grows into our literary theory. A properly modest defender of the study of literary theory must, then, begin by acknowledging the limitations of its promise, indeed of its very capacities. Most of all he must acknowledge that no theory can adequately account for the diversity of literary experiences we would accept as legitimate: its universal claims can hardly deal adequately with errant effects not created in accord with it, nor can it exhaust the meanings and values latent within even the single work, those "more things in heaven and earth" within every work than can be "dreamt of" in any man's literary philosophy. From these follows the further and most modest acknowledgment that no literary theory is likely to make any of us a good critic. Unlike Stanley Edgar Hyman, the properly modest defender would have to admit that our theory may disarm, rather than arm, our vision.[2]

In any area of human experience our instinct for system, for regularizing through analysis (and through the universalities of language) the jagged particularities that confront us, should be accompanied by our awareness that its reductions must belie the infinite variety of our experience that is its subject. This systematic reduction is what our philosophic urge is all about: to impose the coherence of mental and linguistic constructs upon the myriad of prelinguistic data (prelinguistic even if the only way we grasp them or know of them is via the languages of our symbolic structures). This philosophic urge necessarily leads to the problem that has to be as old as philosophy: granted our philosophic striving for a total coherence, what are the philosopher's obligations to the fullness of experience, his obligations to have his system in part correspond to what that prelinguistic data must have been? The conflict between coherence and correspondence is inevitable, together with the corollary that every advance in coherence can be achieved only at the cost of cheating yet more of those particulars to which our discourse was, in the first place, created to correspond. (Or does the system maker's language finally refer only to itself? Or, for even the rest of us, are all our experiences reduced, as the solipsist would have it, to what our languages permit them to be, so that there are no prelinguistic data?) At least, this sense of give-and-take between coherence and correspondence—so that any gain in one comes with a loss to the other—is an inevitable accompaniment of those who do not hold to a philosophical realism, the naïve notion that universals have an ontological status and that sufficient wisdom can reduce all particulars to them without residue. I suspect this metaphysically happy cosmology

[2] Stanley Edgar Hyman, *The Armed Vision: A Study in the Methods of Modern Literary Criticism* (New York, 1948).

is rejected by most of us. The price of that rejection is our awareness of the war between coherence and correspondence, between mind and reality, that leads to the properly empirical distrust of our philosophy, even as we yield to the urge that keeps creating more of it.

But if propositional systems in general reveal their inadequacy to the data for which they pretend to account, we find them far more presumptuous when they seek to deal with literature, whose objects are expressly created to capture the complex nuances that make up human existence on the level of its utter singularity, its endless contingencies. Perhaps even more problematic is the fact that the literary theorist deals with experiences whose source is itself in language; so his own language can deceive him because it appears to be of the same order as that which makes up the objects of his study. If these objects turn out to reflect different orders of discourse, how much more helpless (and less helpful to us) he must prove to be in exploring those inmost fastnesses of poems which resist his own systematizing.

Finally, it must be admitted by the literary theorist who would remain a sensitive responder to poetry that the impositions of system are especially inhibiting for the reader as the subject of aesthetic experience. The immediacy and subjectivity of the experience of one engaged in the intimate encounter with the arts hardly require—indeed rather reject—the intruding presence of a mediating theory that would predict what the object is that is being confronted or what the response is that is being or should be experienced. The aesthetic impulse that moves us toward the poem seeks to preserve the sanctity of the private moment it celebrates, to keep it inviolate. To this extent it is an antitheoretical impulse, a rage for pure, unimpeded experience that resists the intervention of cool rationality. The "high priori road" of philosophical abstractions is seen to be wrongly substituted for the low, sinewy bypaths that wind about us as we struggle along the mysterious directions toward which individual works point us. The theorist is seen as thrusting himself between reader and poem with a priori principles that preclude the open innocence of a free empiricism, imposing his discursive continuities and overrunning incoherence.

Despite all these incapacities, however, I have suggested that a defense of the theorizing about literature, though a modest one indeed, can be made and—for the sake of effective literary study—must be made. The primary reason is that literary theory, like it or not, must be faced: at whatever level of self-consciousness or sophistication, it is there for all readers of poetry; it is there, and ignoring it will not make it go away. Its inevitable presence derives from the fact that each of us carries with him, as he turns to experience a poem, some distillate of his earlier experiences of poems that acts as an a priori guide to his expectations, his interpretations, and his judgments. Conscious or unconscious, informed or uninformed, systematically worked out or ad hoc and piecemeal, this distillate still serves him, in effect, as his literary theory —even if it leads him to a disdain of the very notion of theory. Once one has read his first poem, he turns to his second and to the others that will follow thereafter with an increasing series of preconceptions about the sort of activity in which he is indulging. In matters of literary experience, as in other experiences, one is a virgin but once. Thus to talk about ignoring literary theory as if the total immediacy, the unimpeded empiricism, of subject-object confrontation were a continuing possibility, even for the mature reader, is simply to encourage irresponsibility. If one cannot escape the mediating companionship of theory, he had better know the intercessor as well as he can, and he might even try, rationally, to control it, to make it serve him and his experiences instead of allowing it to bully him and distort them.

When we examine the consecutive essays of a critic who prefers to be theoretically naïve, who prefers to engage literature directly—without mediator—on what he thinks of as "its own terms," even then we find enough similarity among his assumptions for us to reconstruct his theory for him. Now it may be only a minimal theory, in that it reveals gross inconsistencies and shifting variables among its several tenets, but it helps constitute those expectations which condition—if they do not actually create—what he is even able to see. Further, all things being equal, its inconsistencies are a source of his weakness rather than strength, since they render his discourse that much less coherent by forcing him to violate the language game he is playing. And so it is with us all, the more so as we take the problem of theory more seriously, recognizing that if, as critics, we are playing (or must play) the game of systematic discourse, we should play it well: we may as well try to be in control of those presuppositions that are there to show themselves, however strong our empirical mood. The only alternative would be for the critic to release himself to the purely subjective indulgence in his own poetry that is in competition with the poem that was to have been his object, in which case he will have to earn his readers totally on his own merits, borrowing nothing from the sponsoring author. And then he will learn that even poets come trailing theoretical assumptions that condition the intentions behind their performance.

If even the naïve critic betrays a theoretical bias, how much more so does the noncritic, the historical "scholar" whose search after nonliterary sources or effects can keep him (or so he thinks) out of the critical arena and thus securely beyond the reach of theoretical issues.

But when he applies his biographical or social facts to their reflections in the work, or when he traces the reflections of the work in lives or societies outside, he is making assumptions (warranted or unwarranted) about the relations between a historical happening or a psychological datum and a component part of the literary work. The naïve biographer or historian who can assume the clear one-to-oneness of this relationship has indeed assumed a great deal—assumptions that a more sophisticated theorist might want to blast. But, however blast-worthy such assumptions may be, they make it evident that he has his theory in his portfolio along with his facts—indeed uses it to inflate the relevance of those facts for the resolving of literary issues. Whether that theory weighs him down or enables him to take off on his flights is a question for serious disputation at the theoretical level. But surely the historian or biographer is the sounder scholar to the extent that he responds with theoretical sophistication to the need to establish—and not merely to assume—the relevance of his facts to the literary meanings they are to enlighten or extend.

So I urge again that our choice is not between having a theory or not having one; for have one (or two or three or more incompatible ones) we must. Our choice is rather between having an awareness of those theoretical issues which our criticism inevitably raises or going along without such an awareness. And with such an awareness must come a concern, the concern that accompanies the careful study of difficult and complex problems. Of course, if we are concerned also about our faithfulness to the literature we superintend, we must worry also about limiting the power that our theoretical self-consciousness will try to have over our individual critical performances. The literary man in each of us is aware and even wary of the potential tyranny of theory, which would limit in advance what literary experiences we can be open for receiving or understanding. It is once again the conflict we have seen between coherence and correspondence, between the theoretical drive for narrow consistency of system and the empirical demand for adequacy to ever-enlarging experience.

Each new work challenges our theory and our theory challenges each new work. How shall our obligations to both of these be balanced? A theory must be flexible enough to accommodate the assault of the next poetic experience, and yet it must be tight enough to provide the norms by means of which that new experience can be perceived and sustained. It must provide grounds for judgment while avoiding the narrowing dogmas that prejudge and preclude. We cannot be endlessly open to indiscriminate experience, and yet we must not close ourselves to radically new and valuable experiences that beckon from outside the

7

terms of our theoretical constructs. How can we discover the constitutive forms that such new objects require for us to perceive them without reducing them to our obsolete forms, those forms without which we cannot perceive at all?

These dilemmas form the cluster of problems created by the paradoxical role of theory: though theory limits our power to perceive, we are never without one or more; we can never do with one or without one. So we can neither rest in theory nor abandon it. And this cul-de-sac only reinforces our need to subject theory to our most searching examination in order, at least, to reduce the level of our futility, though futile we shall be. But we shall be no more futile than is the practice of criticism generally. For how shall we interpret and judge the next work that comes along: according to the norms we have had until now, which will inhibit how we respond to what will be before us, or solely in its own unique terms (were this responsive ideal possible), in which case we must be indiscriminately receptive to all comers? If any part of the function of criticism is to improve taste, to reduce the gap between what is valued and what is valuable (provided such a distinction exists), then we must not be altogether inhospitable to our a priori expectations and principles, lest we be too hospitable to every new work. But if, as guardians and aggressive defenders of culture, we are to shepherd its newest forms, then we cannot be hidebound. Once more it is the problem of being at once open and closed, in control of (and at war with?) our principles to keep them from strangling us. He who would defend the study of literary theory, then, need demand no more than the acknowledgment (1) that our habits of perception make some sort of theory a necessary evil and (2) that one theory can be better than another. So long as he has self-criticism and candor, the defender will be in no danger of exaggerating the benefits of theory, of becoming a utopist of theory.[3]

[3] It should be clear by now that the phrase "theory of criticism" is a more candid substitute for "theory of literature." Usually, when we are probing for a theoretical structure for literature (that of someone else, or our own), we are really searching out a theory to account for conceptions (another's or ours) about literary works. So to talk literary theory is, perhaps more accurately, to talk critical theory. It is this observation which accounts for the title of this book.

II

Preliminary Questions and Suggested Answers

The quest for literary theory begins as soon as we first ask what is special about our response to a particular poem; and we are well in pursuit when we begin to wonder what this response has in common with our responses to other things we have thought of as "poems" (see note 1 to Chapter 1). We begin to make judgments and distinctions within our theory as we wonder about the differences among these responses, as well as the similarities. And we are setting the boundaries to our theory as we try to relate this class of responses, with all their differences, to the far more different responses we have had to other objects, those that make up the enormous class of nonpoems. It then becomes an obvious corollary for us to try to read backward from our response to define what we take to be the stimulating object. Then, comparing our response to responses of others, and taking into account that object which we have extrapolated from our response, we move toward a distinction between actual responses to the object and what responses the object *ought* to provoke.

By now we have, if only in a primitive way, started to define the nature of the poetic experience and the nature of the poetic object (which a normative experience would require us to postulate), as well as the differences between these and other varieties of experiences, together with the objects that give rise to them. We can project backward in the process yet another step to ask about the creative activity that produces such an object, one that turns out to be productive of such an experience. And all the time, in the background, we should be questioning the value of this entire process (from the making to the experiencing of the poem) in the totality of the human economy for each of us singly and for all of us in our society and its history.[1]

---

[1] The "problems of aesthetics" mentioned in this paragraph and developed in those that follow—the aesthetic experience, the aesthetic object, the possibility of

But let us isolate these several matters by looking at each of them more closely. I would like to establish in a preliminary way the separate, though thoroughly interrelated, problems, along with one set of proposed solutions that seems to promise considerable theoretical illumination of the total aesthetic process behind a single poem, from its production to its appreciation and then beyond, to its possible role in history after it has performed for its reader. At times I may appear to be suggesting that these are the problems to which any theory must provide solutions, at times merely that they are the ones for which my proposed solutions are designed. It must be conceded that, while I may claim that these problems are there for any theory to test itself upon, my putting certain questions as I have predisposes them for the sort of answers I am providing. To what extent, then, these problems are generic to literary theory or are predetermined by my theory I leave to the reader.

1

Surely it is with the questions about the distinctness of the poetic response that the very possibility of literary theory begins. At the theoretical level we can ask what would be distinctively poetic about a response that would justify its being so characterized. That is, we can ask this theoretically even if we are convinced that all our actual responses to experience are hopelessly mixed and confounded, too much so for us to make a claim about pure "types" of response, whether cognitive, moral, or aesthetic (to use the Kantian triad).[2] There are heuristic purposes—to be examined at length in Chapter 3—that require us to define what a purely poetic response would be, apart from the muddy psychological facts that surround and invest the embarrassing, blurred realities of our poetic experiences. I grant that, in the actual flow of our experiencing, what we single out as "experiences" differ from one another only in degree; but I am proposing that we

---

value judgment, the creative act, and the function of art in society—are those analyzed by Eliseo Vivas in his introductory essay to our text, *The Problems of Aesthetics* (New York, 1953), and further discussed in my prefaces to the several sections of that book. See especially his diagram (p. 12) and the discussion that follows it.

[2] I do not mean to use the terms "poetic" and "aesthetic" quite interchangeably. The generic term, covering responses to all the fine arts, is of course "aesthetic." Thus aesthetics is the branch of philosophy that treats the philosophy of the arts (or of beauty, since I do not wish to preclude the issue of natural beauty, even though it is not to my purpose to pursue the subject here). "Poetics" is the narrower term, as species is to genus, covering the aesthetics of the single fine art of poetry. And to speak of the "poetic response" is to speak of the "aesthetic response" as it functions in the experience of poems.

consider defining an experience that would differ from others in kind. And since it is an experience of language, I shall go on to define a use of language—the poetic—that would differ from other uses of language in kind, not merely in degree, even if we actually experience only different degrees of language usage. I am interested, then, not in whether experiences can occur in accordance with such defined "types" as the poetic or in whether, if they did, that would be a good thing; only in what they would be like if they did so occur, and this so that we can characterize what the verbal objects would be like that were constructed in order to lead us toward one or another of them.[3]

What, then, would constitute a sensible definition of a normative poetic experience?[4] Whatever the differences between them, we must think of cognitive and moral experiences as having in common the tendency to lead us beyond their objects to extramural interests. Looking upon an object—say, a configuration of clouds in the sky—would lead us, as cognitive creatures, to consequences beyond this experience that various hypotheses about the interrelations among elements within the object would enable us to postulate (even if we were no fancier a cognitive creature than a weather forecaster). Looking at the same object morally, we can infer certain practical consequences for human weal or woe that the elements within the object suggest (as, for example, the need to warn people in the valley below of imminent danger). By contrast to both of these, looking at the object aesthetically would require that we be locked into the rapturous exploration of its discernible elements as they relate to each other. What would characterize the experience as aesthetic rather than either cognitive or moral would be its self-sufficiency, its capacity to trap us within itself, to keep us from moving beyond it to further knowledge or to practical effects. It would thus insist, to the extent that it was aesthetic, that we stop and behold it for that interplay of elements that satisfies us, so that we do not see those elements as signs leading to consequences outside and beyond. To "use" the object would be, aesthetically, to abuse it: instead of using it, we must love it, and loving it is enough—provided, of course, it is a disinterested love. If, instead of the skies, we imagine a beautiful face,

---

[3] See my essay, "Contextualism Was Ambitious," in *The Play and Place of Criticism* (Baltimore, 1967), especially pp. 156–59, where I use this distinction between our actual mixed experiences and a theoretically pure one to answer what I saw as Walter Sutton's unjust attack upon "contextualist" critics.

[4] The discussion that follows, with its distinctions among the modes of experience and the distinction of the aesthetic as "rapt, intransitive attention," is obviously indebted to Eliseo Vivas. See especially his "The Artistic Transaction," in *The Artistic Transaction and Essays on Theory of Literature* (Columbus, Ohio, 1963), pp. 3–77.

we can imagine one doctor examining its pores and moles as pure scientist in the cognitive mode, or another examining them as a human healer in the moral mode; or we can imagine the painter or poet gazing endlessly upon it in the aesthetic mode. Of course, if our artist should have a more "interested" activity for himself in mind, an activity to which the face would merely serve as a seductive sign, then his no longer disinterested experience would fall back into the moral mode (though negatively, of course, since his thoughts may be immoral).

I have tried to establish, then, that to the degree that an experience is functioning in the aesthetic mode, we find ourselves locked within it, freely and yet in a controlled way playing among its surfaces and its depths. Instead of being led through it to consequences beyond, we respond as if the object calls to us to look at it for itself, to behold its face, content to study *it*, not to use it or go through it, beyond it. Our god does not transcend the object but lies within. If there are moments when the scientist or mathematician or even the moralist responds to his experience this way, this is only to testify that there are aesthetic aspects or moments within cognitive or practical experience. And this is, in turn, to acknowledge—as I have—that our actual experience comes to us mixed, that aesthetic or cognitive or practical components appear in each in varying degrees. But we still can describe what these various kinds of components would be, and thus, by extension, what an experience would be like that would intensify certain components to the exclusion of others.

The major advantage to the literary theorist of defining experiences as if they came in pure, distinct types is that such a definition enables him, by projection, to read back to a description of the aesthetic quality of objects, which—in a circular way—he defines by those characteristics which induce us toward (or seduce us into) the kind of experience dominated by its aesthetic components. Could he not predict what sort of linguistic entity it would be that seemed to be constructed expressly to lead us toward such a self-sufficient experience? Would not such an object have, as a major objective, the need to keep us locked within it—to keep us, that is, from escaping into the world of cognitive or practical concerns? In such an object its signs—in subversion of their normal function as signs leading outward from discourse—would struggle to create an intramural completeness for us, lest we escape to extramural concerns that would transform the way in which the object functions for us, converting it into a moral or cognitive (even a cheaply useful) object. Of course, our customary tendencies toward moral and cognitive responses can lead us to misuse *any* object, whatever its apparent structure and intention: however self-enclosing its powers may be potentially, we can persist in treating it as means rather than end. But, armed with this theory of the aesthetic experience, we can predicate those characteristics in an object that *ought* to lead the submissive and knowing reader into an aesthetic response—the response it solicits— however unaesthetic his actual response may be (that is, whatever the mixture in it of moral and cognitive with aesthetic elements). We can thus talk about the aesthetic character of a literary work, a work whose language and observable parts seem expressly manipulated to induce such a response—and to inhibit others (though in our prosaic stubbornness we may force such others). Such a character would in this way be seen as normative: we ought to apprehend *that* character in the work rather than some other.

We can now move a step further in distinguishing aesthetic from nonaesthetic objects. If we have an experience that we describe as aesthetic, we are likely to seek to find its cause in the stimulating object, to which we then attribute aesthetic value. But the issue for us as critics is whether the cause is in us or in the object. In a literal sense, of course, the source of the response must be in us, since there are other people who do not feel it when confronted by the same object and since without us there is no such response, however powerful the object and its stimulating propensities. This would appear to be especially so with words, mere marks on paper awaiting the mind that brings them to meaning, thereby realizing as phenomenal the potential that is phenomenologically in them. But I have raised the normative issue that transcends such literalistic reductions: does the object have an aesthetic character that we apprehend (and that we *ought* to apprehend) or do some of us read such aesthetic character into it, projecting it out of ourselves? If we have discovered that character, so that our experience— to the extent that it is aesthetic—is an appropriate response to that character, then we ought to be able to describe it and expect it to sponsor a similar experience with other readers. We thus can say, if they fail to apprehend the aesthetic character of the object, that the failure is in them rather than in the object. On the other hand, if we have created for ourselves the aesthetic character of the object, to which we then respond, the experience is idiosyncratic, indeed arbitrary, in that we cannot expect others to share it when responding to the same object.

The central question, then, becomes, Who is the artist? That is, who is the creator of the object that, in its totality, appears to be the cause or the pretext of our aesthetic experience? To oversimplify the epistemological issue, we can ask, has the poet put into the poem the aesthetic quality to which the reader responds or has the reader projected it there for himself? Once we ask such a question normatively, we cannot say it is the reader, unless we are speaking of an arbitrary aesthetic experience that we need not expect to be repeated with any other reader of the same poem. It should, then, be the object rather than the reader who is responsible for the aesthetic character of the experience so long as we wish to attribute aesthetic quality to it.[5]

There is, we must remember, no quarreling with any reader about the justness of his claim that he has had an experience with a high degree of aesthetic quality in it, though we *can* quarrel with him about what he claims to find in the object. Once we have defined such an experience by its self-sufficiency, by an attentiveness that keeps us within the experience rather than leading us outward from it, we cannot command or foresee when it will occur. As a psychological fact, it will occur when it occurs, and the control of it by any stimulating object cannot be predicted. So we cannot say that the experience is better when it can be referred to and anchored in an object; but we can say that an *object* is better—that is, aesthetically better, more rather than less conducive to this sort of experience—when the experience seems authorized by it, seems appropriate to it, so that we can expect it to be repeated with different readers. We would then be enabled to tell such readers that they *ought* to have an aesthetic response, that they *ought* to apprehend the aesthetic character of the object, that whether they do or not, we can point out to them what there is in the object that makes up that character. It is, then, not the experience that is at issue, but the appropriateness of the experience to the object, the anchoring of it in characters observable and operating in the object, indeed the control of it by the object.

In a post-Kantian epistemological mood we must be candid enough to admit that we are responsible for creating all our experiences, and thus for constituting the objects on our horizon in a way that helps us create those experiences as we will. If we find a continuous self-enclosure in the object, we must credit our own powers to make patterns and to fill in gaps. In such a mood, the distinction I have been arguing between creating aesthetic objects and discovering aesthetic components in objects is one that smacks of naïve philosophical realism. No poem seems so universally compelling for us to forget what a dull or unresponsive reading can do to it. We all know of horses who resist drinking at the most refreshing and flavorful of fountains—even Aganippe itself. Which of us has not seen the dogged (we'd impatiently

5 My argument here, in its concern with the "object," assumes the language of a realistic epistemology. Before the reader complains about it in its present overstated and simple form, I ask him to await my attempt to modify it in the opening pages of Chapter 3.

say "doltish") refusal to respond to our most precious aesthetic object? But, as readers and critics, we must operate as if there were a difference between an object that we are convinced has not within itself the capacity to authorize the aesthetic experience someone claims to find in it (but which we are convinced he has arbitrarily created for himself and wished on the object) and an object that can exhibit those characteristics which will persuade others to respond aesthetically, as we have. This difference is all the difference in the world to the critic. It is what keeps him in business, since to elucidate this difference, in the case of every poem, is precisely his business.

The critic, then, operates on very thin theoretical foundations. He must be pragmatist enough to assume on faith what he cannot prove or know: that there must be for him a difference between an object-in-experience and his experience of an object, even though a "critical" epistemology seeks to reduce the first to the second. For we are not about to return to things-in-themselves. Let us grant that there is no object except as he knows it in experience; he still must extrapolate from his (and all our) experiences an object to be talked about as if it had objective properties, even though he can know it and its properties only in experience. Naturally we all have only all our experiences of the object, for we have never left that Humean strand. Yet, as critics, we must have an object out there for us to talk about, independently of this single experience of it, even if all we can actually do is add other discrete experiences of it to this one. So, out of his experiences of the object, the critic must postulate an object-in-experience. Indeed, he constitutes it as an object-*for*-experience; that is, he constitutes an object made to produce the experience whose ground he can claim to find in *it*. He sees it as existing *for* his experience of it, as existing to make it possible (and necessary) for him to postulate it as an object created solely for the purpose of inducing him to postulate it this way. All this circularity should persuade the critic to have humility enough to fear that he is talking, not about the object, but about his own construct, which is to say about himself, though neither can he know it is never the naked object, stripped of his own consciousness, that he apprehends.

It is this fear which leads him to his self-conscious, if sophisticated, concern with the "hermeneutic circle."[6] This circle is emblem of the self-confirming and thus tautological hypotheses that the critic advances and parades as an empirical appeal to the evidentiary literary

[6] Although Heidegger is responsible for the wide currency given the term, credit must be given to E. D. Hirsch for reviving the concern with hermeneutics in American criticism. See *Validity in Interpretation* (New Haven, 1967), and especially its Appendix I, "Objective Interpretation," published seven years earlier.

"facts" of his text. The critic can account for the meaning and function of the separate elements of the work he experiences only as they make up a whole; but his construction of that whole is needed before he can read the elements in this way. He sees only what his categories of vision permit him to see; and, having seen this way, his prior vision is reinforced by every detail he submits as evidence, since each seems to support the theory of the whole that was required from the first for him to grasp the details as he has. In this manner, his every hypothesis about the total and partial features of the work is circularly self-enclosed, and his appeal to the "text," as if it could furnish empirical evidence to support his claims, is specious insofar as it is only self-confirming. Thus insulated, the hypothesis may seem utterly persuasive—at least to its creator, who is sturdily supporting it with its own bootstraps.

All of this is theoretically discouraging, but it hardly slows down the critic who has a dogged resilience springing from a devotion to his literary works, which stand out there so nobly as objects to be admired and—most important—shared. It is this sharing which persuades him of the practical benefits of disregarding the theoretical threat of solipsism. Not that he ought not fear the insinuation of himself into what he claims to be the domain of the work. But his colleague-competitors will quickly enough remind him of his less faithful moments, and together they will work to distinguish the idiosyncratic from the normative claim, however disabling the circularity of their procedure threatens to make their labors. The history of criticism is the history of circles touching and overlapping as well as being mutually exclusive. So there is space for the work of critics who dare claim that others *ought* to respond to a given work in a specified way, and space to convince us that the claim need not always be a self-deluding one. This is space enough for the compromising pragmatism of the critic to enable him to do his work.

In order to keep open the prospects for normative poetic experience, the critic must preserve the common-sense possibility of distinguishing between the contexts he brings to the work, the contexts the poet probably brought to the work (which scholarship can help him determine), and the context developed within the intramural system of the work itself. The reader brings to his reading his own context of meanings for the words, of psychological, social, and moral structures, and of conventional literary forms. He brings, in other words, his received collection of commonplaces that make up his language, his understanding, his attitudes, and the range of his responses. These pretty much represent everything he is until he comes upon this poem. And to this collection he must, at least initially, refer everything he meets within the poem, a tendency that leads to the danger that he will reduce the poem to the dimensions of this prior personality. In much the same way, we may assume, the poet brought to the writing of the poem his own set of contexts, which governs his intended meaning.

But theory must move beyond the sensible doctrine—enunciated, among others, by the early I. A. Richards—that the reading of the poem can be no more than the interaction of these two subjective contexts, the reader's and the poet's. If there is to be an authentically poetic experience at the hands of the poem, then its meanings cannot be reduced either to the reader's contexts or to the poet's, since either reduction—leading at once outward to the world of prior experience—would mean that the poem itself could not sustain one's lingering attention upon its internal relations as self-sufficient. Instead, the reader must be seen as coming to discover in the features of the work those transformations of apparently recognizable elements which create a new and sovereign context—out there. He discovers it and is overcome by it, surrendering his own contexts to it. (We shall see shortly that the poet did much the same with *his* contexts while writing the poem.) In this way the context in the poem comes to be the controlling one, working to enclose the reader within his experience of the enrapturing aesthetic object. It must end by changing and enlarging his contexts by imposing its own upon them, thus making possible his education (leading him out of himself by leading him into the fuller world of the poem). The tighter the context, the less free, the more compelled, the reader. The claim that the poem is a tight, compelling, finally closed context—not reducible to any prior context—leads this theoretical approach to be properly termed "contextualism." It must entertain as its phenomenological postulate (in spite of the subjective limitations of our experience) the independent existence of this soliciting structure, however troubled the critic may be as he tries to persuade himself and others that it is not his own projection. The critic must have *his* fictions if he is to gain access to the poet's.

2

What are the kinds of features the critic seeks to see himself as finding in the work as he seeks to establish its aesthetic character, its power that he claims can lead one reader after another toward aesthetic experience, if each will but submit to the control of its context? Clearly it is just such elements of control that he must try to establish. For if he cannot confirm the illusion that the controls are in the object, then he cannot argue for the repeatability of the experience with different readers that he claims *ought* to be occurring if their response to the object is an appropriate one, one that answers to those controls, to the solicitations that can be marked within its observable features. So he must claim to uncover and open to our inspection those features in the object which seek to enclose the reader within its symbolic world, preventing his escape to the world of ordinary reference and action that lies outside (before and after this experience); for this "important" outside world of doing and knowing precludes the merely contemplative paralysis of the aesthetic.

Clearly, the primary requirement of "unity," traditionally insisted upon since Aristotle, can be appreciated anew when the object is being justified by its capacity to function in aesthetic experience. For it is the unity within the object and among its elements, as the prime factor of control, that keeps the reader sufficiently attentive to it, so that he rests rather than departs. Within this approach to the aesthetic object it is no wonder that criteria like irony, ambiguity, and paradox have been seen as valuable means to prevent such an escape to extra-aesthetic reality. If one seeks in the object a unifying enclosure of internal relations, at once mutually inhibiting and mutually satisfying, then those devices which block our departure from a world of internal relations among signs to a world of external relations between signs and realities are valuable in that they increase the work's efficacy as an *aesthetic* object (which, according to our circular definition, is one whose nature and purpose seem calculated to lead us toward the experience we have denominated aesthetic). The trick is for the work to counter each thrust outward with a return movement inward. So if the reader should believe he has found the key proposition that sums up the work's meaning—the universal that absorbs its particulars—he may hug it to his bosom and want to return to his world with it, where he can display it and apply it. But the object must also furnish materials for that counter-proposition which will confront him and block his passage outside the object by bouncing him back into his propositionally confused muddle. Indeed, the work must be *organized* on such principles of opposition, so that it be more than just a muddle itself.

The reader, on the other hand, may be stubborn and may rush out, armed with his moral proposition, despite all that the work may do to confound him; but the critic must point out what he has missed and show him wrong, or at least seriously incomplete. He must show that what was thought to be a door outside is just part of a resilient wall. Thus, for example, no one would argue against the reader who sees *Heart of Darkness* as a profoundly anti-imperialistic novel. If we probe to the edge of that profundity, however, we find so much more that it is, as well, carrying rebuffs, in the name of civilization, to the anti-imperialist as well. Nor is it that the literary work engages in contradictions; instead, it engages its subject with the dramatic fullness (the dispassionate noncommitment or, rather, disinterested multiplicity of commitment) that keeps the arguments open and the poetic object closed. The contradictions are the critic's as he grapples with the conflicting propositions *his* language has imposed upon the work.

Similarly, in dealing with works whose meaning is more intensely related to their language (lyric poems primarily), the critic must descend to those minute details of philological and phonetic accident or planning (or rather accident *as* planning) by which the poet enables words to transform one another in ways that turn dictionary meanings, merely inadequate beginnings, into the unique glossary that the poetic system both provides and becomes. Looked at close up, this sort of poem is more easily seen to become discourse of a unique kind, born out of a subversion of discourse's normal ways of functioning. The critic must try to account for characteristics in the poem that remake its language, converting its signs into weighty, substantive, corporeal symbols, indeed into a system of such symbols, which can sustain the reader and then contain him within the self-sufficiencies of aesthetic experience.[7] It may seem perverse for a theory to take root in claims that poetic language must violate its normal referentiality, when this would appear to be language's essential nature and reason for being. But this theory must allow poems to remake the way words function, allowing words to violate—as they transcend—their nature by becoming things themselves, so that poems can be made to serve the self-sufficiency of aesthetic experience. We shall pursue the intricacies of this quixotic insistence later in this chapter and in later chapters. Here I mean rather to pursue its consequences for the evaluation of the poem, both in the narrow sense of the term and in the broader sense that defines it as any fiction in verse or prose.[8]

Such attempts to discover in the poem (broadly conceived as fictional literary work) features that make it an object peculiarly solicitous of aesthetic experience carry a theory of aesthetic value as their inevitable companion. For the very definition of literary work as the controlling factor in aesthetic experience is a normative, and hence an honorific, one. *If* we consider the object *only* as it functions aesthetically (though, from other perspectives, it may function in other and pre-

---

[7] Such manipulation of words and sounds abounds in poetry. See my essay, "The Innocent Insinuations of Wit: The Strategy of Language in Shakespeare's Sonnets," in *The Play and Place of Criticism*, pp. 19–36, for just a small sample.

[8] See note 1 to Chapter One. Since this is a theory for literary works treated generically as poems, I must claim that those self-enclosing characteristics, which are more obviously displayed in certain lyrics, exist in more subtle form in all works as poetic objects. It is the critic's task to point out those internal relations in a work which convert the outward thrust of its signs and forms to the mutual illumination that makes them self-sustaining. Assuming that this intramural self-sufficiency of system can characterize all varieties of Aristotelian *poesis*, from the technical verbal intensity of the lyric to the looseness of the Russian novel, I am using the terms "poem" and "literary work" interchangeably.

ferred ways), *if*, that is, we wish to have a work perform what literary discourse (defined as discourse soliciting an aesthetic response) is uniquely able to perform, then it increasingly achieves its definition as literary work as we discover in it those characteristics requisite to that function. Its potential success as literary object, which is to say its aesthetic value, is intrinsic to its very literariness. Such are the virtues of our obvious theoretical circularity. It must be conceded that what we are really talking about is its aesthetic efficiency, or what Albert Hofstadter has termed its aesthetic "validity,"[9] rather than an exiological quality, its "value." This is why I have been underlining the *if*s, to accentuate the hypothetical nature of the propositions I have been suggesting. *If* we isolate the *literary* function of an object and relate it to certain observable characteristics within it, then we can judge the efficacy of that object in performing that function by virtue of those characteristics we have found it to possess. And it may be seen as possessing value as well: *if* we find aesthetic experiences worth having, *if* we find certain objects so disposed as to make such experiences more likely, then those objects may be seen as valuable to the extent that their properties facilitate such experiences. But this value is limited to the aesthetic conditions of these circular assumptions: if the poem qua poem has a unique and indispensable function, then I, as a *literary* critic judging its *literary* (and thus aesthetic) quality, must make claims about its literary value (its potential success or unsuccess as producer of aesthetic experiences as seen in its features) and claim that such value is grounded in the object. My descriptive analysis itself, by virtue of the theoretical ground on which it proceeds, has value assumptions built into it. For "poem" is a normative rather than a descriptive category, so that the term is bestowed honorifically.

It is such assumptions as these that have permitted the contemporary, so-called contextualist critic to proceed, and to see himself as heir to the Western theoretical tradition from Aristotle to Coleridge and beyond.[10] The insistence on closed form, to which his version of unity leads him, dictates that all "literary openness" be automatically excluded from the realm of the literarily valuable (or valid), provided he cannot manage to encompass it within a broadened hypothesis that would still close it. Wherever the critic, after vain efforts at formal synthesis, finds duality between the word and its reference, he charges

[9] In "Validity versus Value: an Essay in Philosophical Aesthetics," *Journal of Philosophy* 69 (1962); 607–17. See Monroe C. Beardsley's response, "Beauty and Aesthetic Value," pp. 617–28.

[10] Chapters 4, 5, and 6, below, should reveal how thoroughly he can conceive of this as *a* tradition.

the work with allegory, a failing that relegates it to crypto-rhetoric, another kind of discourse dedicated to another mode of experience, but excluded from the honorific realm of *poesis*. Whenever unformed experience finds its way into the poem in its original, untransformed state, he again sees a violation of the enclosure he requires. For such a particle, its nature and meaning still determined from without, has not been made an organic part of the unique system being generated within the literary work as poem. Since such intrusions of extrasystematic reference lead away from the enclosing response that poems alone are to arouse, their literary value is negative. The critic may hasten to urge that this judgment not be seen as a detraction from their value within other perspectives; but within the qualifications of those "ifs" with which we saw him begin (*if* we want such an experience and, consequently, *if* we want such an object) the unenclosed work, or the intrusion that breaks the work's enclosure, is seen as detrimental. Thus a work's intrinsic and complex interpretability is itself the feature that governs its aesthetic value. Interpretation is thus a form of flattery, implicitly bestowing value as it proceeds.

We can, of course, deny the possibility and/or the desirability of aesthetic or poetic experience as I have defined it, and, consequently, we can deny the self-enclosure of literary objects (either that there are objects we can view as exclusively literary, or that there are objects out there with characteristics to be "objectively discovered," or both). We can simply reject as absurd the notion that normal discourse can be subverted so that within poems there can arise systems that generate a glossary of unique meanings. For all these denials there are good grounds. And if we deny the existence of special kinds of experiences or objects of discourse, then clearly we can no more attribute value to the poem than we can attribute discoverable and controlling characteristics to it. In the face of such denials, the critic can cling to his "if," since only such a hypothetical, if limiting, perspective as he proposes can lead him to make sense of the unique and indispensable function that poetry can perform within the complex of experiences that constitute the human economy. And so he presses on with his circular procedure, aware that the alternative would do less than justice to the literary works which, after all, are the sources and the ends of his dedication and his labors.

3

The theoretical circularity I have been tracing can be projected backward within the aesthetic process to enclose the creative act of the poet as well, as I have already suggested. The kind of object that would lead us toward the experience we have called "aesthetic" would appear to be the product of a creative activity commensurate with what issues out of it. To explain the nature of this activity we must account, first, for the relation between the finished product and both the experiences and intentions of the life and consciousness that feed it, and, second, for the relation between the ongoing process that creates the object and the linguistic medium in which it takes place. In other words, we must compare the totality of what goes into the process with the shaped whole that comes out (or ought to come out if it is a proper poem), and we must determine the extent to which that shape is indebted to its "material cause," the working of its medium. If we determine these relationships, we may begin to unlock the mysteries at the heart of the poet's creativity.

The most obvious question we must ask is the first: whether the process is essentially reproductive or is in a radical sense originally productive. What we are asking is whether we literally mean to use the word "creative" in speaking of the creative act. Is what comes out no more than a transposition or is it an utter transformation of what has gone in? And we must take the root notion of *form* literally in that word "trans*form*ation" as an alternative to transposition, seen as the mere changing of the place of a given and essentially constant entity. For if a true transformation has taken place, then the entity that emerges is in a significant sense new in that it cannot be reduced back into its genetic elements. The process would not operate like the meat-grinder, which emits only a combination of what has been fed into its receiving end, unless it was a machine that generated its own secret ingredient (not merely the residue of earlier operations), which not only was added to the rest but changed the product into a wholly new blend in which the original elements could no longer be separated out. What is at stake, then, is whether the antique theory of imitation, if it is taken at all literally, can account adequately for the literary work or whether some version of the theory of expression is a more satisfactory alternative.

Now one may prefer simply to brush aside these questions by maintaining, in a common-sense way, that the creative aspect of the creative act can never be in any doubt. For surely at the far end of the creative process there issues an object that did not exist prior to this process, an object that is totally new in that no other until now is quite like it (just ask the poet). In this minimal sense even the most conven-tion-ridden poem is a new, newly created object. This, however, is a trivial use of the notion of the "creative."

Though we may superficially grant creativity to the created object, what we must determine for a theory of the creative process is whether that object merely reflects and combines the elements that preexisted it or whether it remakes them into an indissoluble organic whole that has its own irreducible integrity. Do the chunks of prior experience that has been lived or thought, or do the borrowings from prior literature that has been written (whether conventional, technical, topological, or tropological borrowings) exist in the work as elements still intact and thus separable? Or have they been too distorted in the poet's struggle to make his object one object for them to have a recognizable, removable identity? Is there a one-to-one relationship between the parts of the work and its genetic sources, whether experiential or literary? Or are its sources a mere starting point, a generic locus, from which we can explore the changes the poet has wrought upon his materials to make them his own, for his object in its oneness? I am referring to the same difference that Coleridge belabored in his distinction between fancy and imagination.

It is obvious (even as it is circular) to maintain that the process of making the poem can be seriously creative only if that process contributes something to what that poem finally emerges from it as being. Only if what comes out is a radical transformation of what originally went in can the making process claim to be contributing (and thus helping to create) the poem. So long as the poem is in no significant way different from the already formed, prepoetic entity (that is, an entity that existed, that had its form, prior to the creations of his poem), the process by which the poem came to be made is not properly claimed to be creative. Whether such an entity comes from life, from other poems, or from the mind of the poet, the shaping took place prior to the making itself, so that the task of the process was merely to translate the preexisting shape, not to supervise its transformation into a new one. This alternative to a truly creative act is clearly consonant with what the theory of imitation always should have maintained in those moments when it took the term "imitation" literally: that the form of the poem imitated (that is, was taken from and remains dependent upon) a form that existed prior to and outside the poem.

It should be equally clear that the more creative alternative is consonant with the theory of aesthetic experience and of the aesthetic object that I have been presenting here. Any theory of making that sees the product as no more than a new combination that does not essentially disturb the form of the prepoetic entity necessarily looks toward an object characterized by a duality between its form and content. Such a duality allows us to be pointed away from the object and outward into the external meanings to which it refers. For if the elements of the poem retain their separate identities, their capacity to contain us within a unified, self-enclosing experience has been compromised. So the sort of experience I have been exclusively terming "aesthetic," which has led back to the sort of object best able to produce it in us, now joins with that object to predispose us toward a single notion of what *ought* to have happened in the creative act between the poet and his prior experience in life and letters. We should have to insist on the sort of creative interaction that has at its end the very sort of object that aesthetic experience has required.

If the act of making, considered dynamically, is to contribute to the final form that its product assumes, then the medium in which that act takes place must itself be made into a shaping force, the force that prevents the act from being a static transfer. This is the second of the problems I posed earlier, although it is an inevitable outgrowth of the first, since true creativity in the making process must have a material by means of which it occurs. When the poet sets out to write his poem, he brings with him all he has been and is, the sum of his experiences and his consciousness of himself as experiencing them; so he brings with him also whatever his society and its history have made of him, including his language and the peculiar literary heritage that his culture has provided to shape his writing habits. I have earlier referred to these varied influences as the poet's contexts (that preexist this poem); these are the areas that the biographical and historical and philological scholar is to illuminate for us. Together with these influences from life and art, the poet brings to the creative act his basic purpose in performing it: what it is he "intends" to write,[11] what he "wants to say," whether it is clearly formulated or little more than a vague, unnamed impulse to write. All that he brings of influence and intention combines to make up what is fed into the creative act.

We now have to suggest what happens to make what comes out essentially different, a sovereign object independent of its genesis. But it must be understood that what I propose happens would happen only if the poet were satisfying the definition of poet required by what I have claimed for aesthetic experience and its object. In this sense this becomes an ideal rather than an actual description of what poets do, since, obviously, they do an endless variety of things on the way to the endless variety of poems they write. But, if the poem is to be what aesthetic experience, as here defined, requires of it, then the creative process would act, through its medium and other factors still to be

---

[11] And, despite the persuasive claims of E. D. Hirsch (throughout *Validity in Interpretation*), I believe that we can freely use "intends" here whether we mean the word in its biographical *or* its phenomenological sense. For the theoretical consequences are the same in either case.

determined, in certain ways upon what was fed into it. There are other poems, as there are other ways to create them, although my normative definitions must exclude them. To this extent my circularity holds, as I press toward a definition of the creative act determined by what the critic must have it be if he is to make the poem into the "totalized" object he would have *it* be.

So the mythic creative act proceeds. As the poet attempts to transcribe his intended poem (that is, his grasp of the prepoetic entity insofar as it is an entity), he encounters the recalcitrance of his medium together with the resistance of his developing work itself as it seeks to maintain its own integrity, often against his initial intentions. These obstacles create the conditions that force these intentions to undergo changes as the poem develops. The poet may feel extremely creative and new about his initial idea (although "idea" may be too firm a word for something as vague and unformed as this often is in its prepoetic state), and he may feel irritated by what he finds to be the inhibiting requirements of an unyielding language. He may feel that his "idea" is his alone, while the words—their meanings as these interrelate with their sounds and their syntax—are inflexibly there as common givens bequeathed him by his culture. The total resources of language available to him constitute a finite collection of available items that have never before been made to serve the present individual and therefore unique purpose. How is he to make the language his own when it is the common property of us all? It has been there all along, while his vision or idea is radically new. No wonder he may come to feel that the writing of the poem demands unfortunate compromises with the uniqueness of his subjectivity, only because he condescends to "communicate" his vision.

So, anxious to be faithful to himself, he begins his struggle with the communicating medium, perhaps promising himself to be stubborn in what he gives up. (He may not be ready to admit that, until it finds its symbolic form of expression, he does not really know what, precisely, his idea or vision is.) How difficult a struggle it becomes almost from the outset. If he has not much foresight, he may feel free in the first line (if it is verse he is writing) to let the thought take its most immediate and unabridged sequence in words. But how much he is committed to already! If it is a poem in meter and rhyme, even the first line begins to narrow the possibilities of what can follow: there is a metrical pattern established, and there is a final syllable to be picked up for a rhyme shortly. He has already undertaken other commitments, too, that he will have to hold to, whether he is writing in verse or not: there may be an action initiated that sends forth lines of probability that he must fulfill, characters who must in some sense be consistent, feelings aroused that establish a controlling tone, perhaps metaphors that later words will have to carry forward. How many restraints have already been created for the words and lines to come, and how many more exert their narrowing pressures with each succeeding line? The poet can hardly expect the limited resources of the language he picks up from his culture —that well-worn collection of verbal possibilities—to respond to those special and varied functions he will come to require of each word as it serves his unique context. For however alive language may be as a creative instrument, ever waiting to be renewed, the used elements of language lying and waiting to be picked up by its user may seem stale and lifeless to him, stereotypes all in that they have served other contexts than the new one he is struggling to create.

When the rhyme scheme is established after the poet moves beyond the first line, and as action, character, tone, and metaphors develop, as the possibilities of other phonetic interrelationships open up, the choices diminish as the requirements multiply. By the time he is well into the work, the nature of these aspects has become so formed that each of them insists on its fulfillment and dictates what is needed to bring that fulfillment about. Each thus is more concerned with its own coherence than it is with carrying out the poet's initial intention. Its own nature may very well, in each case, tend away from that intention. For that nature is obedient to rules that are independent of the rules according to which the poet's initial idea took its shape.

John Crowe Ransom has put the poet's dilemma in an admirably simple reductive analogy.[12] Someone who has no problem choosing the biggest apples or the reddest apples from a collection of unsorted apples is in great difficulty when asked to pick the biggest reddest apples (assuming of course that there are very big ones not particularly red and very red ones not particularly big). In the analogy, redness and bigness are independent characteristics, so that he must decide how much bigness to sacrifice for redness and how much redness for bigness. Similarly, Ransom claims, the poet's prepoetic argument, insofar as it existed prior to his writing the poem, was determined without reference to the poetic medium, just as the technical and often arbitrary features of the medium, as the poet either chooses them or comes upon them by working through the resources of the language available to him, are indifferent to that argument. Consequently, the writing of the poem witnesses the constant need to yield one way or the other, either forcing the initial idea to give way in order to hold to technical pattern or forc-

---

[12] In the final chapter ("Wanted: An Ontological Critic") of *The New Criticism* (Norfolk, Conn., 1941), pp. 295–97.

ing the pattern to give way in order to develop the idea. And by now we should have learned to distrust the poet who hangs onto the something he insists on saying despite all that tempts him in other directions.

Further, as we have seen, the poet is faced by that developing monster which, by seeming to determine its own development (increasingly as the complexity of its internal relations increases), challenges the poet's hegemony over it. This is the most obviously mythological construct of all, and yet it is required once we project backward toward the creative process from an object we insist on viewing as an organic whole. Yet the construct is responsive to problematic moments that mark the poet's struggle. Let us take a single occurrence while he wrestles, as bearer of his argument, with his growing poem and the medium available for further growth. The needs of a critical moment in the poem, determined by everything the poem has been until then, require a word or phrase to satisfy it, a word or phrase that—by the time the occasion for it arrives—may have to do half a dozen things at once (relating to action, character, tone, images, and perhaps to meter and rhyme, as well as the original argument), and may have to unite in itself several layers of meaning. How to find just the word or phrase that this critical moment, with its multiple demands, seeks out? Or, rather, how to accept the best that comes along? And what will have to give way in order to fulfill something else? For very likely there is no verbal phrase that quite fills the prescription, and, to the eye and ear of the poet, language contains no synonyms.

But the good poet will look more hopefully at the prospects of the choice he settles upon: what will the chosen word or phrase contain that is a diversion with respect to what was thought to be needed and what was looked for in the word or phrase that he could not find, whether or not it existed? Perhaps it is an unlooked-for ironic suggestion, perhaps only a metaphorical implication of a secondary meaning or a phonetic coincidence that yokes meanings. But what can the poet make of this unexpected potential locked in the word that originally appeared to be only *almost* what he wanted and perhaps seriously less or other than he wanted? What new possibilities are opened up for his exploitation? How, in other words, is the compromise converted, first to opportunity and then to the conquest that comes with mastery? Only by making the one word or phrase that seemed to be available into precisely the inevitable word or phrase. But it is inevitable only by virtue of criteria that were not known or understood until the word or phrase, thanks to the poet's response to it, brought these unforeseen criteria into being. The word or phrase is perhaps first seen by the poet as an imperfect compromise with his initial idea and the developing poem, partly fulfilling the need which the poem and the idea seemed to demand, and partly irrelevant to or in conflict with that need. But every potential of meaning in it must be made relevant, though to do so the context that allows us to measure its relevance must be enlarged or transformed. Thus the word or phrase must be converted from a dead superimposition on the contextual moment into a living outgrowth of it. Here is the basis for the unpredictable, dynamic nature of the making process, diverting the poem from what, perhaps, it was originally meant to have been; and the test of the poem lies in the capacity of the diversion to create a new center out of which the renewed vitality of a language system can radiate.

Because it is the most evident and thus the easiest example to cite, I have dealt (and in this discussion will continue dealing) with conventional verse, in which the medium itself has norms, or generic elements, that can be manipulated in ways that are immediately apparent. The line and the stanza have metrical and rhyme forms that are predetermined, and are thus indifferent to the needs of this unique poetic occasion. The meanings demanded by any particular moment in the poem similarly have minimal requirements. With Ransom's help, I have tried to describe the process by which the poet converts the generic forms and meanings to the unique complex he requires, converting the minimal requirements to maximal satisfactions as he goes. Any one of several words may do, minimally, for sound or for meaning, but the successful poet is not merely one who settles for the overlapping group of words that may do, coincidentally, for both without any great distortion of what was intended. He is, instead, the poet who welcomes the unsettling deviation from the norm that forces him to press beyond words that satisfy minimal requirements toward those which establish unlooked-for maximal possibilities that they, to his and our surprise, satisfy. It is on such grounds as these that we can distinguish the merely conventional from the remarkable among a large group of superficially similar poems with many, easily satisfied minimal or generic elements— Petrarchan sonnets, for example.

Ransom finds conventional verse useful because in it the element of sound is a physical element, providing a sensory surface that brings language closer than it usually is toward being a true medium, with a plasticity properly belonging to a medium.[13] Language in its sign function lacks this character: it points to entities without being one itself.

---

[13] I am thinking of an analysis like D. W. Prall's of "sound and shapes and color and line" as "materials" capable of manipulation because each is possessed of an "intrinsic order" ("The Elements of Aesthetic Surface in General," *Aesthetic Judgment* [New York, 1929]). Prall would not think of attributing such a "surface" to a medium as immaterial and transparent as language. By contrast, Ransom in

As Sigurd Burckhardt later forcefully maintains, words, as we normally use them and think of them, are not a proper medium both because of what they have and because of what they haven't: they already have meaning before the poet picks them up, while a medium should be inert matter that achieves meaning only as the artist works upon it; and they do not have the "body" or "corporeality" a medium ought to have for the artist to work upon.[14] Words come to the poet apparently stuffed with the meanings their histories have burdened them with, as if this is all they could be. Thus Burckhardt's poet, in order to remake them, must strip them down to raw physical matter, using their sounds to reduce them to *being* things rather than meanings that—though empty themselves—*refer* to things.[15] Having so stripped them, forcing us to

---

several places records his sense of the arbitrary (that is, as unrelated to meaning), sensuous nature of the sound element of poetry, matter almost—it would seem—for its own sake. For example, in "Poetry: A Note in Ontology": "A formal meter impresses us as a way of regulating very drastically the material, and we do not stop to remark (that is, as readers) that it has no particular aim except some nominal sort of regimentation. It symbolizes the predatory method, like a sawmill which intends to reduce all the trees to fixed unit timbers, and as businessmen we require some sign of our business" (in *Critical Theory Since Plato*, ed. Hazard Adams (New York, 1971), p. 877). If we overlook Ransom's usual coy modesty as he speaks of the tasks of the poet, the passage may in some ways appear to be an extension of Wordsworth's view (in his 1800 preface to *Lyrical Ballads*) that meter is "superadded" to an emotionalized version of the language of prose in order to impose "similitude" upon "dissimilitude," thus holding the overflowing emotions in check. Coleridge agrees that meter is "a stimulant of the attention" and a "check" on "the workings of passion," except that his organicism requires the poet to use a language that earns "such a studied selection and artificial arrangement" as meter by having in itself "the property of exciting a more continuous and equal attention than the language of prose aims at. . . ." I discuss Coleridge's position at greater length in Chapter 5, below. Here I am only trying to establish the lineage behind the more recent position I am describing.

[14] See those remarkable early pages of "The Poet as Fool and Priest: A Discourse on Method," in *Shakespearean Meanings* (Princeton, N.J., 1968), pp. 22–46. It was Leo Spitzer who, working out of the tradition of European Stylistics, made the notion of deviations from the norm available to recent organic theory. (Spitzer originally used the notion to characterize the psychological character of the author, before his interest shifted to studies of autonomous works.) In Burckhardt the notion shows up in his key phrase, the "disturbing element." See the "appendix" (on "intrinsic interpretation") to *Shakespearean Meanings*, especially pp. 301–313.

[15] "The Poet as Fool and Priest," p. 24: "I propose that the nature and primary function of the most important poetic devices—especially rhyme, meter, and metaphor—is to release words in some measure from their bondage to meaning, their purely referential role, and to give or restore to them the corporeality which a true medium needs. To attain the position of creative sovereignty over matter, the poet must first of all reduce language to something resembling a material. He can never do so completely, only proximately. But he can—and this is his first task—drive a wedge between words and their meanings, lessen as much as possible their designatory force and thereby inhibit our all too ready flight from them to the things they point to."

see them as if for the first time, he can begin to remake them into materials for his art, like any plastic artist. Unsatisfied by the generic and the minimal, he uses their physical characteristics to make them serve, as they create, their own unique context, forged by their arbitrary sounds and their newly emerging possibilities of meaning. Such notions represent a development out of Ransom's earlier claim that the poet used the phonetic character of words to turn them into physical entities, thereby reminding the reader that they *were* entities and not just counters; that they had sensory elements, capable of being manipulated, just like the elements of which the other arts were composed.[16]

These doctrines of the potential sensuousness of the language surface seem necessarily limited in their applicability to verse itself, and principally conventional verse. Though I intend to use this as the most easily demonstrated example of how a poet's creativity can transform the generic to the unique, the minimal to the maximal, I intend also to claim that this is the paradigm for the way in which creativity can operate in poems generally—in the broad Aristotelian sense of *poesis*. Though we may not have the immediate sensory stimuli to hang onto, there are generic elements—norms—to be deviated from and pressed into new and unrepeatable configurations created *pour l'occasion,* also to be seen as new centers, open to our intense explorations and our wonder. The poet (as the creator of "fiction") who does not have the devices of verse to exploit must, often with a greater challenge to his ingenuity, create ad hoc devices to create his opportunities for deviations and reconstructions, reconstructions into new centers. What come to him as others' children, fully formed though tamed by being members of a large and traditional family, he must turn into his own encapsulated and yet fully living child.

It is because of the autonomous center of a sovereign, living object that the poet's experience before the work (though it is this experience that is fed into the work) emerges in the work as a different experience. Each element behind and before the work—a biographical character or

---

[16] "In this poem I think the critic ought to make good capital of the contrast between the amateurishness of the pleasant discourse as meaning and the hard determinate form of it phonetically. The meter on the whole is out of relation to the meaning of the poem, or to anything else specifically; it is a musical material of low grade, but plastic and only slightly resistant material, and its presence in every poem is that of an abstractionist element that belongs to the art" ("Criticism as Pure Speculation," in *Critical Theory Since Plato*, ed. Adams, p. 890). I must once again acknowledge that the organic critic (Coleridge before him or Burckhardt after him) would want this material element returned to a suddenly more complex unity, but Ransom's stubborn clinging to the material (and *arbitrarily* material) nature of poetry as sound provided an important directional signal for recent versions of this theoretical tradition.

incident, a neurotic obsession, a self-conscious urge, a literary source, a philosophical idea or social-political position—is an inadequate measure of its transformed appearance in the work, even where it may be recognizable.[17] To the extent that the reader is reading as the poem leads him to read, he will not reduce the element's appearance in the poem to its prepoetic reality, but will allow what becomes of it in the poem, in the context of its relations with the other elements, equally transformed, to work fully upon him. This is often difficult for learned readers, whose research has turned up the several kinds of sources for what is going on in the poem. But if they are critics as well as scholars, they will overcome that difficulty. Indeed, their knowledge will deepen their criticism and render it responsible: in knowing where each prepoetic element leaves off and where the aesthetic entity begins, and in being able to mark the difference between the two, they are well positioned to move in on the aesthetic center of the work. For the poem's mysterious power to function for us as poem must lie in the common area of the differences between the prepoetic sources and their transformed realities that work upon one another and upon us. (In this sense the poem is properly characterized as a "work.")

It is the location of the aesthetic center that becomes the issue of most critical debates. Further, where knowledge of sources leads scholar-critics to see little difference between the element behind the work and its mere transposition into the work (remaining an independent, unabsorbed atom within it), it may be—unless their critical perception has failed them—that they have come upon an aesthetic failing in the work, a place where it has failed to remake its materials into organic members of its self-sustaining presence. Other critical debates are properly fought over such issues. If I seem now to be talking about the object and our experience of it rather than about the creative act, it is only because one set of theoretical problems so easily slides into another, so mutually dependent are they, especially when they all issue out of the critic's need to predicate an irreducible wholeness of the

---

[17] I do not mean to suggest that the poem develops either by mere chance or by some mystic teleological power operating within language; nor would I deny that its development is most immediately traceable to the person of its maker. In the course of the poet's struggle to develop the poem across the grain of his medium and its traditions, when unforeseen meanings surface, it would be surprising if these meanings—never altogether accidental, of course—could not be traced to wellsprings of the poet's unconscious. Thus I do not mean to reject the probings of psychoanalysis as being irrelevant to such unforeseen meanings. Such probings can turn up useful keys to "unintended" directions taken in the unpredictable course of creativity, but only so long as they provide for the role of those alien and recalcitrant elements (in his medium and in the emerging inevitabilities of the poem) that counteract his unconscious as well as his conscious prepoetic intentions.

poem as his object. This indication of how to approach problems of practical criticism follows from my claim that the creative process thoroughly transforms the elements given it to work upon, so that the product that emerges from it is a radically new one.

This concept of the dynamically creative process rests wholly on an assumption as old as criticism in the West, although it is seriously questioned today: the assumption that the object whose creation the poet supervises wants above all to be one, a unified and complete whole. It is this drive toward oneness—what some disparagingly term "totalization"—felt by the form-making writer in the throes of his give-and-take struggle, that gives him his awareness of the growing monster whose demands to satisfy its own needs he must respect, even at the expense of his own original intentions. What he feels out there, restricting the unlimited freedom he might like to say what he will, is an evolving *telos*, for whose fulfillment he must be willing to compromise. It is this *telos* which makes him recognize an urgency in the object that exceeds his own original urgency and so leads him to sacrifice the latter.

But if we simply reject this assumption—if, that is, we reject the central requirement that the poem be wrought into an all-pervading unity—if we reject such "formalism" as trivial artifice at odds with life's welter of disorder, then there is no ground for viewing the creative process as operating as I have suggested. If the humanistic belief in art as the masterful imposition of human form on the chaos of nature is denied, then the messy fleshiness of life can replace the word of art, since that word no longer can give its own life by taking on flesh. The notion of random variety would take away the requiredness of the teleological *ought* in the poem, which, in accord with the tradition that calls for formal unity, I have seen as dominating the creative process. Without the call for unity, the poet would be free to do as he pleased, uninhibited, even to the point of automatic writing, if he liked.

But my position has been that, if he disdains doing battle with his medium and his developing object (though a battle he may occasionally lose), he forfeits the chance to achieve surprising victories. As we have seen, this critical tradition has valued the use of even arbitrary and superficial formal devices in poems (for an obvious example, meter and rhyme), if only because such devices give the poet a chance to be frustrated and thus forced to come upon unexpected opportunities that he can proceed to exploit. These formal devices become norms by means of which all his variations can be measured and found to become significant, helping to create the new realms he has been forced to discover. Without such norms, variations cannot be seen to occur and unity cannot have its character changed from mechanical regularity to organic plasticity. Yvor Winters may go too far when, on this principle, he declares the heroic couplet to be the most flexible of all verse forms because even the slightest variation shrieks its presence and its significance.[18] But the principle *is* a persuasive one. The aesthetic that projects it must of course find other than verbal elements to be part of the literary medium, so that it can be extended to fictional kinds that, unlike the conventional lyric, are not dependent on the tight control of their structure of words. It must come to terms with the broad variety of works that achieve their unique totality through the manipulation of whatever the elements may be that constitute its normative medium, at once resistant and plastic. And I shall have to come to terms with them too, eventually.

My version of the creative act would necessarily refer forward to the sort of experience the poem must try to make possible and from there refer back to the sort of poem that sponsors the experience and, circularly, back again to the sort of creative process needed to create that poem. For I began by distinguishing in kind the aesthetic from other modes of experience—thus art from life—in a way that set the formalist trap for myself. It follows systematically that the object be defined accordingly and that the act that created that object have a similar normative character, circumscribed by the need for a unity that casts the human form on a resistant world and its resistant materials. I see these notions as dominating the tradition in Western aesthetics from Aristotle through the modernist period. If postmodernism sees such claims as quaintly obsolete, swept aside by the deluge of three or four decades of bloody living and dying, then I write this book as a postscript to a dead past, though it still lives for many of us, lives in the art that has preeminently embodied the forms of human imagination.

4

But it is time to lay to rest any antisocial implications that many have seen in the belief in the form-giving powers of art. I turn now to the last of our preliminary problems, the relations to society of the poems we have seen produced and experienced. This is to examine the other than aesthetic function of a work whose being has been defended

---

[18] See his discussion of "The Influence of Meter on Poetic Convention," in *In Defense of Reason* (Denver, 1937), pp. 103–150. See especially p. 130: "The nearer a norm a writer hovers, the more able is he to vary his feelings in opposite or even in many directions, and the more significant will be his variations." And, on the heroic couplet, p. 141: "What, then, makes the couplet so flexible? The answer can be given briefly: its seeming inflexibility." What follows is the argument that the more predictables and invariables a form has, the more meaningful are the few unexpected variations played within them.

solely on aesthetic grounds. Much as I have emphasized the self-enclosed nature of the experience toward which the poem is to lead us, thus emphasizing also its dependence on redirecting internally any open reference to the world and the world's moral and cognitive concerns, it may seem rather late for me to try to salvage a major social function for poetry. But, as has often been claimed elsewhere by critics of my persuasion, it is precisely the role of poetry—working as it does within its own sphere—to put its meanings at the service of society in a way approached by no other discipline, however more obviously world-weighted that other discipline may be. Because what it does it does by being uniquely itself, a poem's contribution is equally peculiar to itself.

But how, if its primary function as poetry is to shut its meanings off from common meanings in order to entrap us within our exploration of the poem as object, can it make any contribution at all to meanings beyond its own? When its objectives are exclusively intramural, how can it manage to break through to the outside? Yet how can it be denied that literature has postaesthetic effects on society and its culture, that it participates in history? (By postaesthetic effects I mean, obviously, its workings upon us when we return from the poem to the world of our affairs.) Is there a way to trace such effects back to literature's unique powers as literature? Clearly there is a variety of ways, explicit or implicit, in which literary works make their impact; but we are not speaking here of an *Uncle Tom's Cabin* kind of influence, an influence of the rhetorical or propagandistic sort that is hardly consistent with aesthetic enclosure.

I am acknowledging, then, that I am interested only in those postaesthetic effects which are directly the outgrowth of the aesthetic effects that I have already treated at length. That is, I am interested in the way that a literary work leaves its mark upon us by our having gone through the aesthetic experience, as I have defined it, rather than by our using the work as a moral or cognitive instrument that leads directly to its object. For, by my definitions, the moral or cognitive effect is hardly one that it has as a poem. I prefer to ask how each of us is influenced—in the lives we conduct or in our vision of reality—after experiencing this poem, but only insofar as we are influenced through experiencing the poem (provided it satisfies our normative definition of a poem) in the special way a proper poem seeks to be experienced. How, as we return to the world, are we different as the result of experiencing this poem as the poem's aesthetic factors of control would lead us to experience it? Our postaesthetic reality should be in some way transformed if the aesthetic reality we have witnessed has done its educative work. But to find such effects we must break through the enclosed aesthetic experience even while it is preserved intact. We must uncover a form that shapes our world anew as it shapes its matter into the work of art. (My dissertation on man's constitutive powers as form maker appears in Chapter 5.)

In what way does our aesthetic experience of a poem make a difference to our postaesthetic awareness of the world, that is, make it different from what our preaesthetic awareness had been? That it does not merely reveal the extra-aesthetic world as other kinds of formal discourse do is clear from the unique ways in which we found its verbal context takes its meaning. I have claimed that poetic discourse, in establishing its own self-enclosed system, must do so by subverting the usual ways of discourse, by forcing its language to create a self-sufficient texture out of the undoing of normal reference. If this poem, then, is to contain meanings that illuminate a world beyond its own, that world must be different from the one referred to by nonpoetic systematic (or propositional) discourse. The series of claims I have been presenting here must rest, ultimately, on the claim that the objects of reference in poetry differ from those in nonpoetry as their two ways of meaning differ. For there are transcendent objects outside of, and prior to, nonpoetic discourse to which it owes allegiance, as there are not in the immanent, generative system of the poem. So nonpoetic systematic discourse, with its obligations to reference and to logical coherence, must talk about a generic world—the kind of world that is "talk-aboutable"—while poetry, in talking about itself, talks about a world so concrete and immediate that we usually think of it as beyond the mediating powers of discourse.

The approach to theory I have been advancing must have as an assumption the inefficacy of other discourse: nonpoetic discourse must be seen as deceptive in that the objects it points to as its reality would seriously mislead us about what our reality, experientially, is. At this point the theory seems to entail significant ontological claims about our reality, our language, and our delusions. It must do so if it is to leave for poetry the role of filling in what other discourse finds unavailable to itself and thus cannot make available to us. What such a notion requires is a distinction, such as an existentialist would make, between the felt immediacies of our living, breathing reality and the stale abstractions that the universalizing powers of normal discourse impose upon that reality to produce the false abridgments of it with which we live—except when we partake of the authenticity of art.

Because of the internal complications that multiply to make up the context of the proper poem, because also of the freedom it has earned from the ways in which reference and logic operate in propositional discourse, the poem can break free of the limiting blinders that language normally puts on itself to satisfy our discursive habits. But in tending to its own completeness the poem does not, in the end, turn its back on reality. Instead, it subverts our normal ways of meaning because those ways lead to the dead universals that must also be subverted if we are to break through to the throbbing existence beyond. The poem becomes almost a microcosm of the particularizations that existence offers so profusely (and these particularizations are *all* that existence offers) but that normal language, as generic, must ignore even while it absorbs them. Yet the poem is also able, because of the unified experience its form compels upon us, to unify our vision of experience. Its inward perfection provides us with a perceptive frame with which to encompass the existential awareness of the outward world our vision seeks to grasp. This hope for literature's cognitive function, and its consequent moral and social functions, will have to be pursued and developed in later chapters. But it is enough, even here, to move us beyond the simple alternatives of "intrinsic" and "extrinsic" literary functions toward a view of a social role for poetry so profound that, in holding it, we need no longer apologize to the anxious social activist within us.

After three-quarters of a century of aesthetic claims by various sorts of formalisms, the world-ridden student of literature has properly become impatient with theories that defend the autonomy of the poem as a self-sufficient world of meanings—impatient, that is, with theories that resist seeing the poem as direct reflections either of the external reality that surrounds it or of the internal life within its creator. In his impatience this student now insists that the overused charge of "irrelevance" may well apply in the case of theories based on aesthetic closure, when our world seems to require openness among discourses that speak to one another. Let me urge him not to be so impatient. Let him rather allow the poem to work as only it can, so that it can, after all, find a relevance to our living that is indispensable to us—indispensable because it shows and tells what nothing else can, and what it shows and tells is a world that cannot exist for us if this poem does not create it. And we shall be less human (I am tempted to say less than human) without it. This relation between fiction and our interior reality I shall have to explore in a later chapter.

Within the terms of that promissory note, I can suggest for now that what the poem reveals is that interior world of human response, the dynamic flowing world of subjectivity, here fixed in the verbal structures and images and characters and symbolic actions that make up a single, unchanging object—a complex of interrelations that invite and capture our contemplative imaginations. I have, until now, freely (too freely) used the term "object" to describe the poem, as if its dimensions were as discriminable and measurable as that word suggests.[19] There is always this temptation, overindulged by the New Criticism, to treat the poem in the way a scientist would, as an object of analysis, deadening it into Eliot's "patient etherized upon a table," so that we lose all sense of subject-to-subject human confrontation within the continuum of experience. So I agree that one must deal with that paradoxical "object" only as he acknowledges its temporal and dynamic character that dissolves its contours. This paradox of "object" as experiential process and as fixed form I shall return to in detail in the chapter that follows.

In this chapter I have tried to deal with another paradox, that of the self-enclosed aesthetic experience that opens the extra-aesthetic, experiential world to us. Like the paradox of the "object," this paradox will require more extensive treatment in the sequel; but I cannot promise that my struggles will dissipate either of them, or that they can be dissipated. For I must close this chapter as I began my first chapter, by confessing the inability of literary theory to account adequately for the problems posed by our actual experiences with poetry. If the justification of theory were to depend upon its capacity to render this account adequately, then it would fail to justify its existence and be seen (as many see it) as a pointless discipline. But its very inadequacies make us aware of the simultaneous and conflicting (if not altogether explicable) pulls upon us in our confrontations with poems, and that may be justification enough. If we wish to preserve literary theory as an object of study, it will have to be.

[19] For a useful history of this idea of "the object" in recent criticism and a polemical defense against attacks upon it, see W. K. Wimsatt, "Battering the Object: The Ontological Approach," *Stratford-upon-Avon Studies* 12 (1971): 60–82.

III

The Critic as Person and Persona

1

Before leaving these introductory considerations, I should return to the plight of the critic in order to examine at greater length the devices to which he resorts as he grapples with his theoretical incapacities to do what he will with his "objects." There also are more ways and more complex ways for us to see him at work and to judge that work than I could suggest in a chapter devoted to so many other issues as well. So I come back to his difficulties and will concentrate upon him and them exclusively and, I hope, candidly. If he is a humanist, the theorist, like the critic, should be obliged to accompany his analysis with acknowledgments both self-conscious and frank.

At the close of the preceding chapter I criticized my free use of the term "object" to denominate the controlling feature (as I saw it) of our process of experiencing aesthetically. I criticized it because our experience *is* a process and because what it encounters is a verbal product of a consciousness that is another process. We must admit that, as an object, the poem lives only within the dimensions of those many private imaginations which it may seek to control but which, epistemologically, are the creators of what they then call an object. Yet I myself have repeatedly referred to it as an object, out of my theoretical need to emphasize that the aesthetic experience had to take on a normative character—that it had to be controlled by an object—if we hoped for it to be a shared and repeatable experience. But it is time to recognize more explicitly than I have the obvious psychological fact that all experience, as experience, remains internal and even arbitrary, idiosyncratic. In this sense the object that functions for experience (especially one that, like a poem, functions in temporal sequence) is a fluid affair that our imaginations may fix but that—if we fully attend it—unfixes our imaginations. Indeed, I have characterized that poetic object, as it must function for us in aesthetic experience, precisely by the dynamics of its internal relations, the dynamics that unsettle normal meanings and normal reference in order to allow that subjective life to flow. Yet the verbal sequence through which it flows is fixed for good. I have suggested elsewhere the urn, that still object which encompasses endless motion, as the emblem of this twofold quality of the poem as aesthetic object.[1] It is, then, as inadequate to speak in frozen terms of a fixed object as it is to speak as if there were only the flow of our subjective consciousness, and no object at all.

Let me summarize and then move further. As the critic vainly seeks to capture in his language the object whose language has captured him, he must remain alert to its peculiar and paradoxical nature: it is an object that, as a verbal sequence, is experienced temporally; but, because it is a fixed and invariant sequence, it has formal characteristics that provoke him to claim to find spatial interrelationships within it. This is to define literary form as the imposition of spatial structures upon a temporal ground. But the critic cannot permit his own impositions of spatial structures to deceive him: the object and *its* structures are in movement and so are the structures of his consciousness, which interacts with it. The radically unique consciousness that shines through the object is a fluid one whose radical uniqueness resists the frozen state of spatial reductions. So the critic's descriptions of the object in formal and spatial terms—like his very use of the term "object" to denominate it—must be applied with a delicacy that recognizes they are *his* weak metaphors, which, if he takes them too seriously, will distort—by freezing—the object (the temporal embodiment of temporal consciousness) as less sensitive "users" of the poem would. Even at best he knows he has reduced it to the fixed structures that are the minimizing reductions that characterize his preconceptions about his own consciousness.

So there are his ineffable subjective experiences and his reducing or flattening of them to the dimensions of his preconceptions. But can there not also be a normative control that could direct the former and complicate the latter? The responsible critic is always tempted to posit "out there" an object that, formally sovereign, draws him to it, resisting his tendency to draw it to the contours of his own personality, as he has drawn those for himself. He thus tries to distinguish between what actually goes on in his struggling and abortive confrontations of the poem and the theoretical (if empirically not quite attainable) postulate, his "object"—the critic's fiction—in accordance with which he fights

[1] "The Ekphrastic Principle and the Still Movement of Poetry; or *Laokoön* Revisited," *The Play and Place of Criticism* (Baltimore, 1967), pp. 105–128.

his experiential tendencies and their reductions. There is always, in the responsible critic (which is to say that critic who is dissatisfied with the immediacies of his own subjectivity and is distrustful of them), this tension between his imperfect experience and his projected norm.

I have thus been assuming a tension between the experience he actually undergoes and the normative object he postulates, an object with a fictional (and fictitious?) integrity that solicits an experience more "aesthetic" than the one he has. This tension permits him to define that object even while he recognizes that it differs from the fluid process that is his immediate experience of it. So the sophisticated reader-critic shifts back and forth between two experiences: on the one side, the motions, false starts, unhappy interruptions, and personal intrusions or self-assertions that victimize him; and, on the other, the total organized complex of multiple dimensions that—created and discovered—beckons to free him.[2] In other words, he remains aware of diachronic elements in his experience of the poem as he seeks to impose synchronic elements upon it. This double consciousness is equally active as he attributes characteristics (diachronic as well as synchronic) to the poem as the cause of that experience. In his encounter with it, the object may dissolve into the contours of his personality and the flow of his experience, although his critical self-consciousness tries to keep it out there, apart and resistant to all terms but its own. In the first instance his experience is never complete; in the second it tries to limit itself to the controlled experience of what some would skeptically term his "totalized" object. Probably his considered experience itself becomes a tensional and still uncertain amalgam of the psychological actuality and the unlikely but unabandoned possibility. Of course, he also tries to close the gap between the two if he can, though he knows his power to do so is always limited.

All any of us has, then, is our subjective experience of the object, an experience that is *never* as good as we would like it and would want to demand it to be, so that we atone for our lapses by acknowledging the object to be potentially better than we find it to be. This experience

[2] Unlike Jacques Derrida, I see freedom in one's discovery (or, less naïvely, one's construction) of a total (and thus internally determined) object that resists being reduced to the determinacies of the perceiving self. Derrida rather sees freedom in the "free play" of the self as it retains its own determinacies and indeterminacies by resisting the determinacies of the object, or, preferably, through "deconstruction," by not seeing any there. (See his "Structure, Sign, and Play in the Discourse of the Human Sciences," in *The Languages of Criticism and the Sciences of Man: The Structuralist Controversy*, ed. Richard Macksey and Eugenio Donato [Baltimore, 1970], pp. 247–65.) Where I see a freeing *from* self by a superior and normative created order, he sees a freeing *for* a wayward self by a resistance to all "totalization."

of the object (if we may so term the flow of our movements and counter-movements) is in all ways *continuous* with all our other experiences. Yet there is our need, on the other side, to postulate that object—in its generic nature as *aesthetic* object—as potentially *dis*continuous, the potential cause of an experience that would be discontinuous with our other experiences. We would thus view it as different in kind from other verbal objects, even if our less satisfactory experience of it yielded a difference only in degree. So this discontinuous experience may be an experience we never actually have, although our need to have it (and to postulate an object that can authorize it) must be warranted by the experience we do have, since that is *all* we have. This raises again the problem of the tension between our theory of the ideal aesthetic object, with its powers of discontinuity, and the continuity of our actual and incomplete experiences, which militate against a unique (or discontinuous) mode of discourse.

But it is not only the imperfections of our experience in time that we seek to overcome; it is also the imperfections of the poem itself. As we try to compensate for the inadequacies in our actual response by an act of "objective" criticism, we may tend also to make the object better than it is as we seek to put it in control of the experience we wish we had. In creating a wholly satisfactory hypothesis for the form of the poem, we attribute a total pattern to it, overriding contrary details here and there as we go. We work to complete a configuration, eliding any hiatus or filling it in. Since it is unlikely that there are any perfect works or perfectly closed forms, in postulating our poem as aesthetic object we necessarily close what is partly open. To conceive the work as the ground for our potential aesthetic experience, we create it as a fictional whole, but only by creating *for* it a fictional self, with the integrity of a sacred object—except that we must see this construct as *our* fiction. As self-conscious critics, we must, consequently, try to discover and reveal the extent to which the elements in the poem, as they exist for us to perceive them, cooperate with our perceptions of them to lead us toward filling in the blanks as we do on our way to the hypothesis of the fictional self we create for the work. We must try to know when the filling-in follows the lead of indications plotted in the poem and when it is only our own arbitrary act serving our willful adherence to the myth of wholeness, as we reject the reality of insufficiency (whether of object or of our experience). We must try to know this, but theoretically, of course, we cannot. Despite this fact, in practice we can sometimes learn a small something about what we can know as we open ourselves to other reader-critics. Nevertheless, we must submit to the need of constructing a hypothesis for a poem perhaps more perfect than the one before us, not altogether unlike the hypothesis of an experience more complete in its enclosure than any we can have. It is not that we improve upon the poem by writing a better one (how arrogant a suggestion!). On the contrary, we treat the one already written idolatrously, finding patterns among its parts more mutually fulfilling than may be warranted.

I might say much the same thing another way if, borrowing for literature the methods and assumptions that E. H. Gombrich uses for the visual arts, I acknowledge "the beholder's share" in interpreting—by way of his learned schemata—the verbal stimuli furnished by the poem.[3] As a result of his reading habits and living habits—his habits of verbal perception and genre recognition (whether genres of art or of life)—he is thus seen to construct out of the poem's pointed "clues" the formal configurations that become his "object." In the manner of *Gestalt* perception, he completes patterns that were there to be completed that way, making sense of words and among the words. The poem uses generic signs in order to furnish clues that can be "read" into being an object, though it also, as we have seen, violates such norms so that it can persuade the "beholder" to construct forms beyond the stereotypes of his experience, patterns he recognizes as such though he has not seen them before. It must persuade the beholder to apprehend what he has not known, without reducing it to the generic dimensions of what he *has* known. Though the beholder is thus required, by his response, to provide the reading power that shares in the "illusion" that is the "object" for him, he can acknowledge an ought-ness in the poem, that which is phenomenologically present to be seen by him and which, consequently, should act normatively upon that which is phenomenally sensed. Thus the phenomenologist among us might put it that, in the face of the open and less complete experiences we have, our sophisticated expectations for poems can lead us to "intend" a complete experience, which creates the opportunity for us to "discover," and open to our analysis, an "intentional object" that can be "totalized." I need claim no more than this to defend our need to postulate the object as ideal or complete, as utterly interpretable and even "infallible,"[4] if we are to judge the stimuli of the experience we have and thereby to improve what that experience can be.

<hr />

[3] See *Art and Illusion: A Study in the Psychology of Pictorial Representation* (London, 1960), pt. 3.

[4] Sigurd Burckhardt describes a brilliant hermeneutic procedure based on just such a postulation. (See "Notes on the Theory of Intrinsic Interpretation," posthumously translated as the appendix to his *Shakespearean Meanings* [Princeton, N.J., 1968], pp. 285–313.) I find his to be preferable to other theories of interpretation we have

In spite of this need, all of our skeptical (and self-serving) instincts summon us to remind the critic (or the critic in ourselves) of his tendencies to solipsism, to remind him that he is trapped within the process of experience. He reifies the stimuli of that experience, and then—by favorable analysis of its properties—aesthetically worships what he has reified, the "object," but only at the risk of self-deception. Finally, what he has created is an idol that serves his needs.

In William Faulkner's *Light in August*, there is a dramatic turning point when Reverend Hightower, until now trapped in the weakness of sterile self-torture and a withdrawal from life, delivers Lena Grove's child and is thereby transformed into a newly vigorous believer in fecundity and action. The change in him is made manifest by his laying aside the Tennyson he had been reading previously for Shakespeare's *Henry IV*, which he now pronounces "food for a man," that is to say, *his* food. This reference to literature as "food" suggests clearly enough the notion that a reader uses his literary work, matches it to his prior needs, and then absorbs it into himself, forcing it to serve his own bodily functions. We choose our literature and in choosing make it ours, instead of discovering it and forcing ourselves (or rather allowing it to force us) to respond to it on *its* grounds, transforming ourselves as we go. It is there to accommodate us, and will be forced to, since we will not do what we must to ourselves in order to accommodate *it*.

But Hightower, we can argue, is not a critic; he is just a common user—or rather a common misuser—of literature. And we might like to say that the critic knows better, since his is the task of discovering the literary work on its own terms rather than remaking it to serve his. Yet there is a nagging skepticism that tugs at every honest critic, even after he has done his best. He must candidly ask himself, as a stand-in for all critics, Are the literary works we read our teachers, shapers of our visions and our persons, or are they reflections of our needs? Do they seize upon us and mold us, creating for us and in us the forms that become the forms of all our imaginations, or do we seize upon them, forcing them to be what our persons require them to be, putting them into a rude service for us? And, if the latter, do we then, worst of all, read these caterings to our needs back into the works and claim that they have been there all the time for us to discover them where they

---

recently been offered, although it does rest on a candid mythologizing of a totally interpretable work. My demythologizing acknowledgment of the "intentional" act of the critic, as well as the tension between that critic's raw experience and his self-conscious postulation, leaves me, I am aware, not altogether at odds with even continental thinkers as radically antiformalist as Derrida. But I return to this relationship in a later chapter.

lie? Are we doomed only to project our own imaginative forms outward, peopling all works with the single cast of monsters created by our own imagination, and so turning all works into essentially the same work, even though we persuade ourselves we are but responding to a variety of external features whose uniformity of pattern seems to confirm our hypothesis about them? In his hermeneutic circularity does the critic's every claim to objectivity reduce to this charade played out by his own personality in order to deceive—most of all—himself?

2

It is with such issues as these in mind that I look within the critic himself to see him as person and persona. In these days, when academic fashion increasingly prescribes that interior consciousness be regarded as the principal characteristic of the literature the critic studies, it is natural for him to dramatize his own position by discovering himself in his work, both as persona and as person—even to find a voice for himself that can speak with, or in competition with, the voice of the author under study. This may be only a perverse reaction to his inheritance from the New Criticism, with its exacting pretensions to objectivity. And it may very well be that such pretensions, insofar as they sprang from a notion of criticism as an impersonal would-be science, called for a reaction that celebrated the cult of the critic's personality in order to save criticism as an art. The increasing candor about the critic's epistemological limitations, which makes him aware of his hermeneutic circularity, leads him to the artful delicacy with which he surrounds and invades the object with himself. Further, he sees himself as doing so and recognizes that his criticism, to the extent that it will be artful and delicate, must embrace the surrounding and the invading, as well as the object itself. All this his criticism may now do, although he cannot distinguish between the object and the self which has both marked it off and filled it.

Can the critic save anything of the object once he faces the logical consequences of his candid admission of the self's role in constituting the object it needs and wants? The problem is an obvious but troublesome one, as old as criticism. To the extent that the critic owes his primary fealty to the object that calls him into existence, he must obliterate himself to explain and exalt *it*. Thus the object would seem to define him rather than he it; it justifies his role instead of his prescribing its nature. But to the extent that he must call into question the very possibility of his finding and marking the objective qualities of the thing itself, he must keep himself self-consciously in the midst of his operations—all for the sake of candor and in flight from self-deception—

since he is trapped within his version of the work and is unsure whether there can be a knowable work out there against which that version can be checked, or only other versions deriving from (and responding to) other personalities. The problem is what I elsewhere called the conflict between the play and the place of criticism: the need for the critic humbly to know his place, as subservient to the work, is challenged, embarrassed, and thoroughly undercut by his need for an arrogantly free play that inflates himself and our awareness of him.

How does the critic persuade us that he is dealing with a work, then, and not only with a reflection of his own personality? After we insist upon all his hermeneutic admissions, it will be quite a trick for the critic to skirt his way between—on the one side—the sheerly and randomly personal, the private and idiosyncratic, and—on the other side—those responses which, in spite of his personal intrusions, still are meant to refer roughly (how roughly!) to an object, the same object that arises out of those varied experiences of it within which each of us is trapped. It will be quite a trick because it courts logical, indeed epistemological, inconsistency to try to save the object we experience out of our random experiences of the object (or rather our experiences of the stimuli that we constitute as an apparent object).

The personal elements that significantly condition (at least!) what the critic chooses to criticize and how he then does so are not to be regretted—as these post-New Critical days have taught us to acknowl-edge—since they help him to function within criticism as an art, which is to say a humanistic discipline. But so long as we also think of it as a discipline, we must try to guard whatever normative and sharable element may yet be saved out of the critical procedure. It is our episte-mological fate to have only versions of objects rather than objects them-selves, and our selves are, obviously, self-protective about the versions they will permit. In our criticism, then, we should want—since we must have—the intrusion of the critic's person, as well as his persona. If we dig him out of his criticism as a self-conscious presence, we are the better able to deal with him, and perhaps (but only perhaps) to separate him (and his "version") from the work that claims his attention. So we search for the fellow behind the position-taking critic who maintains his system and his allegiance to it; for the fellow behind may, at times almost perversely, demur. And out of the holding back may arise a new awareness of all that the literary work may demand of us, a humane disaffection with universal systems and all that *they* demand of us, all that they make us give up. The only half-intended revelations of the critical persona, by thus opening up our responses, can make a virtue out of our hermeneutic necessity.

45

Let me try to summarize the distinctions I have been trying to make among the work (or rather the critic's attempt to speak normatively about his version of the work), the critic's persona, and his person. The literary work, with its beckonings, is what presumably stimulates the critic and what his discourse claims to be "about": it is to be at once the object and the objective of the discourse, both its material and its final cause. But hermeneutic candor requires him to confess that he has access to no works but only to versions of works. And what intrudes and distorts is the critic's self, his person and his persona.

The critic's persona I take to be the public personality he comes to adopt, and adopts with considerable conformity (we may flatter him by calling it consistency) as he moves from critique to critique or to a general statement of his critical principles, his claims about the nature of literature. However implicit or explicit, this is his system, the primary aesthetic assumptions and criteria he brings to every work to precondition it. He must fear, of course, that he may be reducing every work to *it*, with a severity that hammers consistency or conformity into mere uniformity. In this way all works would come to look the same (as do nature and Homer for Pope in *An Essay on Criticism*). Though in the confrontation with every superior work there is a challenge for him to open his closed system, the critical persona tends to resist, in the interest of integrity and systematic fidelity. (After all, if his system represents *the* theoretical solution to problems in poetics, then it ought to account for whatever comes along.) So arises the party critic (and which of us is altogether innocent of the charge of being one, at least on occasion?) who must maintain his allegiance to whatever his aesthetic principles may be. For he sees that the alternative possibility—that of being *un*principled—is not merely eclectic (in trying to put together several conflicting principles) but rather is utterly ad hoc, responding randomly to the errant occasion. And this alternative is as undesirable as it is—given our critical egos—unlikely, unless one is to hold out for a naïve empiricism, an experiential openness, that denies the censoring activity of the persona as he controls the critic's perceptions. It is, then, this allegiance, felt by the reader as much in the critic's tone as in his claims, that defines the critic's persona, his public personality as critic, the official and authorized—the dominant—voice, representative of his system and his perspective, that appears to be speaking to us—or rather at us—pedagogically. Indeed, more than ego, it acts as the critic's theoretical superego.

For the most part we see the individual critique as the intersection of the literary work (which we can speak of by extrapolation even if we cannot reach it as a neutral, independently beckoning entity) and the critic's system, represented by the persona. The yield for us, usually, is what that system permits to be grasped by perception in the work, what it permits to be grasped *as* the work. But in the sensitive critic there is a restiveness which leads him to struggle to let his system be shaped anew by the superior work, to try once more for objectivity and an open empirical encounter that breaks the circle. This struggle, thanks to the censoring persona, may finally turn out to be vain; but behind the struggle between the work and the critical persona, the sensitive critic can also permit us to see what I term his "person" striving to mount the doubly resistant beast compounded of work and system. If we think of the persona as the critic's superego, we may think of the person as his id. When the person succeeds in relaxing the persona more than most of us normally can, the persona's system opens itself (and us, as its readers) outward in order to embrace alien and challenging elements, which, as embraced, enlarge its (and our) capacity. This possibility of a free openness may finally be an illusion, though it is just this illusion that prompts and continues the considerable effort we put into critical debate with our fellows, debate which— just sometimes—persuades, and changes minds.

It may be, of course, that the person, as an antagonist of the persona, as the persona's critical underside, is really no more than a second, antisystematic persona. He would then be not the person himself, closer to the critic's self and an expression of his inner consciousness, but simply another more subtle, trickier public personality that the critic has created out of his self-conscious awareness of the limitations of his public role. Rather than theoretical superego and the id that would overcome it, the critic now is seen as setting up a strategy of dialogue, a public drama, between two created roles, his apparent persona and the resistant person behind. This alternative formulation does not bother me, so long as it does not disguise our sense of the critic's doubleness. For, regardless of which locution we prefer, the totality of the critic is to be seen by the shrewd reader as compounded of both persona and person or the two antithetical personae. And we witness the critical performance as a drama between them, while the work, alternatively obscured or revealed, but assaulted, hides in the wings.

3

Yet we must continue searching to see, out of these epistemological and phenomenological shambles, what is left of the work for us to try to share with one another. Enough must be saved so that the work, in the end, is more than a private psychological episode, a "happening" in the critic's autobiography that he records in confessional prose. It is probably true, after all, that such confessional and rhapsodic criticism as we are often now given as a recital of self-consciousness is not essentially different from that old impressionistic criticism which Anatole France termed "the adventure of [the] soul among masterpieces" (or would more philosophical candor require us to say, "among the sensory stimuli we honorifically term masterpieces"?). As they promulgated the New Criticism, René Wellek and others often reminded us, always derogatorily, of this characterization of pre-New Critical impressionism. It is, perhaps, poetic justice that so-called critics of consciousness should have succeeded the New Criticism with their new—and philosophically more guarded—version of that subjectivism. But whether in these critics we see, with the New Critics, the dominance of external system that reduces works to itself or, with the critics of consciousness, the dominance of the private sensibility that would absorb itself into each work, we must face the need to have some common residue we can refer to as the work, even though we know how hard it is to get around ourselves to point to it.

The fact is, as I have been suggesting, that even the most systematic critic (if he is also a sensitive one) reveals some struggle with the reading self that is confronting *this* poem and—on the other side—that even the most subjective critic (if he is also a responsible one) reveals some allegiance to universals that precondition (and thus mediate) his immediate encounter. This is why we find the great critics in our tradition inevitably—if quite variously—at odds with themselves at certain key points in their work. My suggestion of the conflict between persona and person[5] was meant to give us some handles with which to grasp the sometimes wayward consequences of the drama that unfolds out of the critic's dialogue with himself. As he seeks to modify his theoretical obligations with his obligations to the new and utterly unique work at hand and seeks further to keep himself at the center of what is to remain a human and humanistic experience, the critic may be seen not only as courting inconsistency, but as married to it, though he may struggle against his fate, as do most husbands. This is why I think of the history of literary criticism in the West as deriving from

[5] It should by now be hardly necessary to repeat that this conflict may be no more than the opposition between two personae, one the apparent persona and the other the apparent person underneath. When, after all, does the sophisticated public writer let us through to see the real person, if indeed there is one beneath the succession of antithetical roles he plays? An inventive student of mine, Ms. Pat Finnerty, has written suggestively, in an unpublished manuscript, of these alternative possibilities of man as either the artichoke, whose layers surround a heart, or the onion, composed of successive layers only.

48

what could be termed the "consistent inconsistency" of literary theory, if I may reword a phrase from Aristotle. Consequently, even a superficial study of the work of some representative "great critics" would reveal a rich complex of major and minor modes (or moods). So I take the time now to touch in a preliminary way the dualities of critics whom I shall study more closely in later chapters.

Even in the austere Plato himself, we find a grudging admiration—though accompanied by awe—for the poet's powers of vision and of profoundly moving his audience, an admiration that Plato occasionally permits to intrude upon his dominantly puritanical denials and prohibitions. It is as if the poet in Plato, responding as writer to the writings of others, is forcing the ascetic philosopher now and then to make his moral and metaphysical system give way to more weakly and warmly human requirements. We may thus see the damning judgment he passes upon the arts as the other side of his fears that acknowledge the full range of its powers. It is in accord with this tradition that the Platonic Augustine unhappily recalls how he "wept for Dido slain," in what is a tribute to the poet as much as it is a condemnation of himself. And in the Platonic rejection of poetry we find a formulation that, however wavering, must allow any anxiety about poetry's effects to be accompanied by an implicit tribute to its powers.

The Renaissance Neoplatonism of Sir Philip Sidney may be seen as betraying an even more marked duality. His dominant philosophical allegiances require him to treat the poem as a reflection of moral and metaphysical universals, so that the poem must serve the "foreconceit" that is its lord. But Sidney is a poet, too, and a fine one, with a commitment to the poet's creative powers. This commitment requires him to treat the poetic imagination as sovereign, creator and lord of its own domain and servant to no other. Yet his fidelity is a wavering one, so that the particular creatures of this imagination, far from arbitrary, end (in typical Renaissance Neoplatonic fashion) by finding their home in the heaven of Platonic universals. His affiliations to the conservative Italian tradition require that Sidney's native liberal tendency to exalt the poet as a free agent be directed into the safe channels of imitation, imitation metaphysically sanctified.

Even as doctrinal a critic as Alexander Pope betrays a wavering that was common among the best of the neoclassicists. In one passage he can make the most dogmatic equation among the rules, the ancients, and nature as proper (and identical) objects of imitation; but he follows this passage immediately with the call to the poet to be a liberated Pegasus, deviating from "the common track" in order to "snatch a grace beyond the reach of art." And he can defend Shakespeare while he chides him, giving him the right to ignore the rules of one kind of art since—with an immediate access to nature—he was practicing another. Thus does the Longinian concern with original genius intrude itself upon the Horatian strictures, with an unrestrained openness that threatens to break in upon the closet of the neoclassical system. Despite such momentary lapses, the dominant fidelity to the system holds.

Of course, in all these cases but most obviously in Pope's, the duality of attitude could spring from conflicting theoretical and philosophical traditions rather than from a conflict between the person and his theoretical tradition. The very tightness of the neoclassical system, its total inhibition of creativity, required its defender—if he were at all sensitive to what the poet's mind is capable of—to provide an anti-systematic annex to accommodate some exceptions that the system would normally have to reject: any system that wanted to stay in business could not afford summarily to reject these. In this way, what was potentially subversive was made to serve the system by providing —at the cost of inconsistency—for what had to be provided for. Thus the notion of original genius, of the *lusus naturae*, at once *un*natural and within nature, breaks in, as an errant particular, upon a closed doctrine of nature as a perfect artifact that permits no particular aberrations. What should threaten to destroy the system is made, through the psychological comfort it provides, to reinforce it. Pope has, then, an alternative theoretical tradition with which to counter the tradition to which he owes his primary allegiance, though it may also be his person as poet that, having sensitized him, induces him to invoke it so forcefully. Surely that person must be called upon to create a single critical personality out of such antithetical strains. It is a tribute to Pope to say that he achieves in his work a personal unity that overrides its internal theoretical conflicts.

The conflict in Dr. Johnson seems more clearly traceable to the struggle of the person to resist accepting the dogmas that his system, represented by his majestic critical persona, sought to impose. Johnson's usual insistence on the poem's need to adhere to general nature, at whatever sacrifice of particularity, is undercut at moments here and there (though at strategically important moments) by his antibookish, antiartificial interest in the chaotic way events actually (and accidentally) occur in "the real state of sublunary nature."[6] In the midst of his

---

[6] I discuss this striking ambivalence at length in "Fiction, Nature, and Literary Kinds in Johnson's Criticism of Shakespeare," *Eighteenth-Century Studies* 4 (1970–71): 184–98, and in "Samuel Johnson: The 'Extensive View' of Mankind and the Cost of Acceptance," *The Classic Vision: The Retreat from Extremity in Modern Literature* (Baltimore, 1971), pp. 125–45.

dedication to the moral notion of how things—by universal design—ought to be, he wants to dedicate the poet to the realism of how things—just happening, without design—in fact are. It is as if Johnson would claim that an orderly pattern contains the world's errant particulars, except that he at times doubts that these particulars can be so confined, doubts that the ordering universals are more than conventions imposed by men. His claim to the rational order is what characterizes the critical persona that is our monumental picture of Dr. Johnson as the high priest of neoclassicism, and his doubts are the voice of the late eighteenth-century person who can no longer be constantly appeased by the well-made moral and metaphysical schemes to which both person and persona are supposed, in the eighteenth century, to owe their fealty.

By the time of Samuel Taylor Coleridge, the theorist is free to postulate the power of imaginative vision to create its world. So the Coleridgean persona, in accordance with Kantian and post-Kantian (largely Schellingian) epistemology, can dedicate itself to the life-infusing power that the imagination (as the I AM) bestows upon every object, thereby destroying its status as mere object. But Coleridge (perhaps via his person as working poet) wants also to modify this epistemological freeing of imaginative vision with the poet's mundane struggle to convert his materials into the constructed object that is his poem. Thus Coleridge introduces the dual notion of primary and secondary imaginations, with an indecisive effort to determine which of them has the dominant responsibility for the making of the poem. These partly conflicting definitions lead to an equally confusing pair of definitions: the essentially psychological definition of "poetry" as resulting from the author's power of vision and the essentially aesthetic definition of the "poem" as resulting from its author's power to produce an organic whole. Coleridge, like so many after him, must reconcile man's generally epistemological power of life-bestowing vision, granted him by transcendental idealism, with the poet's special power of making, granted him by aestheticians concerned with what forms and language can create and embody. The first of these he shares with his philosophic contemporaries; the second undercuts their epistemological foundations by introducing questions about the formative function of the literary medium, questions that become central issues in poetics for the century and a half that follow. Although Coleridge could not reconcile the divergent elements in this self-dialogue that persists through most of his work, the very doubleness of his attitudes and theoretical attachments deepened the possibilities for all Romantic theory that is influenced by him.

51

Both Shelley and Benedetto Croce, in considerably different ways, extend the Romantic idealism that runs through Coleridge, though neither can escape being troubled by Coleridge's own restraints. Shelley is of course far less inhibited than Coleridge in the claims he makes for the purely visionary power. For him the seeing is itself the guarantor of the infinite and eternal validity of what is seen. Yet even Shelley cannot consistently avoid the responsibility of the poet as maker-in-language; what poet could? So he can accompany the most universalizing concept of the poem as "the very image of life expressed in its eternal truth" with the insistence that a poem is untranslatable, its sounds and meanings creating a unique and fixed entity, hence utterly particular.[7] The poet who is the maker of the finite thing itself thus arises (if only momentarily) to challenge the Platonizing mystic who travels through all human and supernal orders to the all-absorbing unity of Godhead itself.

Croce's struggle is similar in kind. Because he is a thoroughgoing idealist, Croce must feel contempt for the material embodiment of the vision he refers to as "intuition." The intuition must be self-sufficient, so that the "externalization"—the making of the object itself—takes place only as a translation of the intuition into a sensory stimulus for the aesthetic experience of others. The externalization, then, is aesthetically unnecessary in that the form of the intuition is already complete without it. But earlier in his treatise[8] Croce, recognizing the symbolic nature of human thought, identifies intuition with expression. Here most of us would see Croce as conceding the dependence of the visionary side of poetry upon its making side, since we would assume that "expression" includes (or is essentially one with) "externalization." Because the symbolic medium is that in which and by means of which we intuit, the expression that is simultaneous with the intuition must be simultaneous also with its externalization. Who but a most driven idealist could see these (expression and externalization) as two rather than one? Such is Croce, whose idealistic persona cannot permit expression to depend upon the material fact of externalization but must make a factitious distinction between them. He must claim a difference (which he can hardly demonstrate) between internal expres-

---

[7] In *A Defense of Poetry* Shelley refers to the "peculiar order" that relates sound and thought in the words of a poem: "Hence the vanity of translation; it were as wise to cast a violet into a crucible that you might discover the formal principle of its colour and odour, as seek to transfuse from one language into another the creations of a poet. The plant must spring again from its seed, or it will bear no flower—and this is the burthen of the curse of Babel."

[8] See Chapters 1–4 in contrast to Chapters 13 and 15 of *Aesthetic*.

sion and the technical feat that permits the external physical fact that he thinks of as the aesthetic object ("the physical stimulus for reproduction"). Yet Croce, in the person of the sensitive critic, has sufficient respect for the symbolic nature of expression to persuade himself to identify intuitive vision with it, even if he must back off from acknowledging (as the nonidealist would) that the poet's manipulation of his medium is at once symbolic-expressive and technical. So the inconsistency for him remains: he cannot reconcile the part of him that grants the immediacy of the created poem with that more ideologically restrained part of him which insists on the immediacy of interior vision itself, self-sufficient and disembodied.

With several of these critics I have suggested a pattern in which a more sensitive person, sometimes a poet's person, celebrates poetry's magical powers that undo the critic-theorist's systems. In Matthew Arnold we find a striking variation upon this pattern. His important criticism is written after he turns from the primary pursuit of writing poetry, so that his person helps turn him into an apologist for criticism, although there will be another person in him who will turn again. From what Arnold the theorist tells us of the poet's plight in periods like his, when the shortage of available ideas forces the poet to be idea-maker as well as maker of poems, we may gather that he is condemning his own poetry as too flat and overly philosophical, and is encouraging himself to concentrate on writing criticism rather than poetry.[9] For at such a time, and with such limits placed upon what poetry can do, why not invent ideas directly—as criticism does—and prepare the way for future poets? With this suggestion Arnold has created the theoretical framework in which the critic turns out to have the more significant—indeed, even the more creative—role in our culture, more creative than the "creative power" of the poet, who creates objects, but not ideas, the essential ingredients of poems. Arnold thus persuades himself that he has done well in his own commitment to vocation.

But the dedication to poetry also persists in Arnold, as does the awe with which he contemplates its power to move its reader. Hence, although he may often overemphasize poetry's dependence upon the ideational content, which it is to borrow from criticism, he is able later to declaim in behalf of its almost apocalyptic nature, in the opening pages of "The Study of Poetry":

The future of poetry is immense, because in poetry, where it is

---

[9] See Arnold's arguments concerning the "creative power" versus the "critical power" and "the power of the man" versus "the power of the moment" in the early pages of his essay "The Function of Criticism at the Present Time."

*worthy of its high destinies, our race, as time goes on, will find
an ever surer and surer stay. . . . Without poetry, our science will
appear incomplete; and most of what now passes with us for
religion and philosophy will be replaced by poetry. . . . The day
will come when we shall wonder at ourselves for having trusted
to them, for having taken them seriously; and the more we perceive their hollowness, the more we shall prize "the breath and
finer spirit of knowledge" offered to us by poetry.*

Here is a magnanimous gesture to poetry's superiority to idea, to its
omnipotence, by one who, in straying from its calling, had severely
denied the extent of its power.

4

What I have presented is not intended to be a thumbnail sketch
of the history of criticism; it is rather intended to indicate the continuing need for theoretical inconsistency—for major and minor strains
sustained at considerable cost—in the work of a few obvious, though
representative, major critic-theorists in our history. And I have tried
to suggest the theoretical impatience that accompanies any major critic
as he confronts the complexity of his particular experience and its resistance to the theoretical universals that are supposed to govern it. Yet
in each case the critical persona returns persistently enough to dominate
the discourse, though the unsettling intrusion of the critic's person (or
the apparent person) gives it the special mark, the signature, that we
associate with a major critical personality: it breathes the warmth of
human relevance into the system it seeks to undo.

The persona says, "I am right about this object and about our
general experience with literary objects, of which this object is an in-
structive example. You ought to agree with me." The person (or the
apparent person) rather insists, "It is exclusively *I* who is having this
experience, which has never occurred before. I must guard its authenticity and my private investment in it, whether or not others will agree
with what I find in it and even whether or not it accords with other
experiences of my own." If what the person finds undermines the
commitments of the persona, so much the better; for it is then more
likely that an inviolate human encounter has occurred, with its subjectivity intact. But I have more than once suggested that it may only
be an apparent person—a counterpersona—who is the alternative to
the persona. I have done so because such a partial withdrawal from
theoretical commitment is often only a shrewd tactic that the critic-
theorist uses to persuade (perhaps to persuade himself as well as us!)

that he will keep his critical operation open and human, at whatever cost to its self-assuredness and its certainty, these latter hardly being humanistic virtues. In so doing he would be creating a second voice for himself that is no less fictional than his first. This device can make his criticism more persuasive, and even more just to its object, though at a high cost to his theoretical allegiance.

But the person of the critic—and here I mean the true, inward person—does have another kind of function, one that often serves to reinforce rather than to undermine the dominant theory he espouses. Indeed, the person often provides the internal, existential pressures that lead to the theoretical espousal or even invention. We could take, as an obvious case, Hegel's theory of tragedy, which clearly derives from his general system, both his metaphysic and his philosophic method. The relation of the tragic hero, as individual, to the "ethical substance," his drive to alienation and the cosmic insistence on re-absorbing him—these basic notions in Hegel's theory of tragedy clearly reflect his systematic philosophy of history and the role of universals in it. Hegel's favorite play, *Antigone,* is the work by means of which his theory of tragedy develops. It becomes an almost inevitable choice for him—especially given his interpretation of it, which is equally inevitable. Despite his concentration on this play, we can hardly charge him with being inadequately empirical, pinning too much on a single case, since his procedure is so openly the opposite of empirical, with the system dictating the theory and the theory dictating the work and his reading of it. Using the terms I have introduced here, we could argue that the person, having created the system-defending persona, creates those structures of literary theory and those works and critical readings which are needed to reinforce and justify that persona.

We are talking about what has been termed the "metaphysical pathos" behind the literary theory, the criticism that flows from it, and the hierarchy of works that the criticism would appear to recommend. It is this metaphysical pathos[10] which predisposes the person to create the systems and personae that he creates, and these in turn determine the style of his criticism and choose the works that this criticism can most conveniently treat—or, to put it more candidly, the works it can use to establish and reinforce itself. Far from empirically grounded, one's theory is thus seen as hardly literary in its source within the person.

Is all theory, then—together with the choice and the criticism of

[10] This phrase, as used here, means no more than one's conceptual assumptions (conscious or unconscious, but probably unexamined) about the nature of reality, assumptions his primary existential stance requires him to make.

works that theory dictates—only the person's rationalization of his metaphysical pathos? Examples such as Hegel's may make it tempting to say so. But of course such a claim suggests a solipsism so complete that it leads to an utter indifference to the objects of contemplation and to the problems they pose on their own grounds. For here there are no grounds but the subject's. This is hardly very promising for criticism as a progressive discipline, as one in which any dialogue is possible. So there is good reason to resist limiting all that the theorist and critic can say to mere rationalization.

Yet the evidence we glean from searching through the history of successive and conflicting literary fashions is not reassuring to any who wish to urge an alternative to critical subjectivisim. It is also true that an examination of the work of recent theorist-critics can lead us, though in a less sweeping way, to the kind of charges we make against Hegel, who is admittedly an extreme case, since he is, primarily and almost exclusively, a philosopher, and only derivatively a literary theorist and critic. It has often been pointed out, for example, that criticism and literary theory in the wake of Eliot—the old New Criticism—was in large part guided by its attitude toward religion, man, and authority as it created a method that chose and served the Metaphysical Poets. Whether it was dealing with poems for which its method seemed to have been created, downgrading poems unsuited to it, or reinterpreting them radically in order to make them proper objects for it, the bias of this criticism and the other than literary reasons for it could be (as it has been) demonstrated.

When, as an antidote for such antiromantic and at times theological assumptions as underlie this criticism, Northrop Frye introduced to another critical generation a new set of terms and methods, they were automatically accompanied by a new set of heroes and rejects, of favored and less favored texts, and of some violently reinterpreted ones. Literature was to circulate about a new center, and its name was William Blake, Eliot's Antichrist now canonized. And behind Frye's vast structure in *Anatomy of Criticism* we sense the profound commitment, personal and professional, that propelled his faithful study of Blake, *Fearful Symmetry*. The further we go from Frye's system's center in Blake—to Shakespeare or to Milton, for example—the more we sense the imprint of Frye's vision at the expense of our previous sense of the poet himself.

The same sort of difference appears when we move from Georges Poulet on Mallarmé to Poulet on, say, Balzac.[11] Poulet and his associates,

---

[11] See Chapter 5 and Chapter 9, the concluding chapter, of *La Distance intérieure*.

the so-called critics of consciousness, provide another Romantic alternative to the New Critics. If we feel comfortable with Poulet on Mallarmé (as we did with Frye on Blake), it is because he is at home there, his person—as he tells us—becoming one with his object. So he is being faithful to this poet because he can do so by being faithful to himself. It is when he moves off to objects less congenial to him, less obviously a reflection of himself, that we feel the need to forgo our former sense of the author if we are to accept the critic who has usurped his place. Thus Balzac appears to us, via Poulet, as too much the soaring lyric poet. In such airiness what has become of the prosaic chronicler of a solid world whose heavy furnishings so impressively weigh down his work with their bulky reality? If Poulet is also one with his object here, it is because he has transformed his object to himself. His empathic desire for the critic to overcome (and overwhelm) the literary work as object, as the mediating element between him and the author's *cogito,* leads to a dissolving of separateness among these entities—usually, of course, blending into the critic's self, however much he might hope for the process to move in the other direction. Consequently, few contemporary critics seem to make freer with their authors than does Poulet, as he openly reduces them to his reading self, too often making many different works seem like only slight variations of the same work.[12] Still, this is but a stronger and candidly self-directed version of the charge I have been suggesting against critics generally.

In another essay I have tried to suggest and to probe the existentialist consciousness that lies behind that development out of the later New Criticism which I have termed "contextualism."[13] This essay traced the relationship I saw between the theoretical interest in literary complexity and the philosophical distrust of universals. The critic's search for a unique system of interrelations among the elements of a literary work turns out to reflect his conviction that existence presents a series of irreducibly particular persons engaged in problematic moral experiences. Irony, paradox, tension become effective literary devices for those who believe that existence is equally enigmatic, beyond the reach of philosophic propositions, and needs an enigmatic literature to illuminate it. Poetic discourse, accordingly, comes to be treated as a series of special and autonomous systems (one per poem); it is seen to be distinguished from normal discourse by the nonreferential particularities that multiply themselves, thanks to the poem's internal rela-

[12] In fairness to Poulet we must recall that he does not think of himself as a critic in the usual sense, but as a writer of "literature about literature."

[13] "The Existential Basis of Contextual Criticism," *The Play and Place of Criticism* (Baltimore, 1967), pp. 239–51.

tions. It may be, then, that, because the person of the critic needs to create a literature that will justify his existentialist commitment, he proclaims and propagates a contextualist aesthetic. He arranges his collection of valued works accordingly, whether convenient to his critical (and existential) needs or rendered convenient by his strenuous operations upon them.

It is true that I earlier claimed to find a traditional and theological set of prejudices behind criticism in the wake of Eliot, while I now find an antiauthoritarian, even subversively antisystematic tendency as a motivating force for this later development of it, which I call "contextualism." Aside from changes that occurred along this developing line, we must take into account the extent to which, from T. E. Hulme and Ezra Pound onward, Bergsonian dynamics and its consequent organicism accompany and modify—even if they contradict— the drive to freeze literature into serving static universals.[14] Perhaps this is a useful way to remind us that we earlier looked, at some length, at ways in which the critic's person disrupted the system of the critical persona by introducing contradictory, or at least antagonistic, elements. Then we turned this process on its head, by finding ways in which the person had originally justified his attachment to existential commitments by creating that literary system for his persona. The first process saw an existing systematic attachment for the persona that was subverted by the person; the second saw the system that was to be represented by the persona as having been created to begin with as a rationalization of the person's existential needs. We can trace elements of both processes, both operations—systematic and antisystematic—of what I have been calling the critic's "person," in the confusions of at least the older New Critical formulations.

As contextualist theory developed and more systematically emerged—at least as I have seen it and worked with it these last dozen or so years—the conservative and static elements appear to have been dropped in favor of the greater and more consistent emphasis on those dynamic elements that represented the existentialist impulse from the time of the earliest New Critics, well before they were aware of, or would care to claim, any such influence or allegiance. Thus, as a more recent contextualist, I must openly face the likelihood, strongly pressed

[14] The influence of Bergson, it should be mentioned, is shared by this group and the group I have represented by Poulet. This common influence should make the opposition between the two groups less extreme than the history of recent theory would suggest. It is this uncertainty about the exclusively anti-Romantic sources of contextualism, and about its anti-Romantic nature, that I am suggesting here. But I could hardly turn around and suggest an equal modification of the antiformalism of the Poulet group.

by W. K. Wimsatt,[15] that my theoretical claims rest on motives that are other than literary and that the works I have chosen to treat have been either too carefully selected or too persistently adapted to my vision, so that a variety of authors have been converted into unwitting fellow existentialists. And, turning my own complaints against others upon me, some readers may well feel more strain in my treatment of Alexander Pope or Dr. Johnson than in my treatment, say, of Herman Melville or Joseph Conrad.

Like the other critics discussed here, however, I must hope that I am searching for truth (a truth that will hold for more than myself), that my generic claims about literature *really* tell us something about it that is so, that the works *really* are as I say they are—and are not just my reckless and subjective manipulation of them. But my person, with his interests, stands somewhat behind my efforts, reminding me how many of my pretentious claims to normative and objective reality are only a reflection of his demands—reminding me of all this and sneering just a little. Of course, even if the critic allows the person to reveal himself behind the mask of the system—as I seem to be doing here— we must not trust him, since, once the person goes public, he becomes a persona—and another mask—himself. So, as I expose the existential pressures to which my theoretical claims either happily and coincidentally conform or just dutifully respond, I am confessing the role of the person; and I invite both trust and distrust—both of these for both the system *and* the person—while I apologize for the partial, parochial, or even sectarian nature of my theory, its foundation in other-than-literary issues. As I have tried to show, rival critical positions are subject to similar exposures. The critic's role *is* a complex one, as is his struggle for balance among his several selves that face the selves revealed in the work before him.

5

This entire discussion treats the critic as a paradoxically dramatic figure. This is to treat him and his strategies as Kenneth Burke would, or as Stanley Edgar Hyman treated his thinkers—as self-conscious makers of metaphor in competition with the poets—in *The Tangled Bank*. How and why they conceive discloses their creativity and vision more than does what they say. But such a view of criticism returns us to the extreme skepticism of my starting point, where we saw Faulkner's Hightower, in turning from Tennyson to *Henry IV*, create for literature

[15] I have included his extended criticism of my position in *The Play and Place of Criticism* ("Platonism, Manichaeism, and the Resolution of Tension: A Dialogue"), pp. 195–218.

the function of feeding his existential needs. For all their fancier literary notions of what they are doing, the persons of critics might be seen as preventing them from doing much more than he did. If our poetics is only a pragmatic structure to help us justify who we are, then the works themselves must equally be victims of that rationalization. And all we see is what the constitutive forms of neo-Kantian philosophy permit us to conceive to be our reality, so that our existential insularity is epistemologically—and then ontologically—sanctified.

If we assume that criticism as a collective endeavor has the obligation to transcend these subjective traps, that it must preserve the corrigibility of individual judgment as a hoped-for possibility, then we may be tempted to work toward neutralizing what is individual in our response in order to preserve and elevate what is common in it. In a manner like that of eighteenth-century common-sense universalism, our realistic yearning leads us to ask for the purging of the personal as eccentric and even idiosyncratic, and to expect, as a result of multiple cancellations of the private, that what is left will be meaningful to the common core of humanity. This yearning suggests that we throw the many hermeneutic circles at one another; even if, where they fall, there may be only the slightest portion of them that overlaps, we can eliminate all but that overlapping and preserve *it* as the precious residue of the meaning and the judgment that criticism must preserve. The objective work, available to us all (if we too are stripped of our idiosyncrasies), would be what was left when all that was personal (imposed on it by persons or personae) was deducted.

But such cheery empirical universalism did not work in the eighteenth century, and it will not work now. Experience, as filtered through consciousness, just does not happen that way. All our subtractions of eccentricities are only subtractions of the human from human experience, and not the sum of human experience. The common residue of such subtractions tells us how little a work can mean in its commonness, not how much it can mean in its uniqueness. Once we reject the naïve realism that posits a universal core at the center of rings of peripheral particulars, we recognize that collective criticism cannot provide more than a series of partial, unyielding, and often incompatible responses. But these responses are, each of them, the product of fully human consciousness, and hence indivisible. So we must work with the totality of the criticism, saturated as it is with persona and person, for finally there are no separable elements in the vision and the version of the work and its world that that criticism gives us. And yet, even when we accept the hermeneutic gap that separates every critique from the work, we need not deny the reality of that work, or deny our need to confront that reality along with the critical transpositions of it by others. For, as readers of literature and its criticism, we never, in our own persons, turn away from the fact that the work *is* beckoningly out there; and it's the same work that all these other fellows are talking about, some more faithfully than others, though none altogether faithfully. At some level, in spite of persuasive epistemological skepticism, all of us share Dr. Johnson's hard-headed, rock-kicking impatience with the unbridgeable private worlds of solipsism.

For most of us there has always been the tension between our vision of the world—the world as we would have it—and the unyielding contingent reality that we fear is out there on its own, indifferent to us and our visions. We may share the "dream of man" that is the product of Northrop Frye's conception of human imagination, embodied in our "order of words"; but we are also aware of that external, inhuman reality which makes up what he terms the "order of nature." Or, to put it as Wallace Stevens did, we may live within and celebrate the human construct as our necessary fiction, but not without remembering that it is, after all, a fiction, with a nagging reality beyond, that remains stubbornly unadaptable. We all remember the wondrous, if humorous, metaphorical worlds that create the eccentric realities in which the characters of *Tristram Shandy* live. They are all up on their hobby-horses, riding off in their many solipsistic directions. But there is another reality that will not be hobby-horsed away, the reality of chronological and biological facts that finally have their way, in spite of all human inventiveness. All of Tristram's metaphors are undone— Tristram the supreme hobby-horse rider—as he is pursued on horseback by Death, in a metaphor that signals the end of metaphor, that threatens to empty all metaphor into the common refuse heap of factual, time-ridden history.

But the internal forms of private imagination can take a permanently visible form in the materials of public reality, the artist's medium. So the literary object, though a product of inner reality and transformed by our experience of it into another inner reality, is yet an object; as such it is so fixed in its final form that—despite its wondrous humanity —it becomes a chunk of that (usually inhuman) external reality too. Though a human metaphor that serves our hobby-horse mythologies, it exists, finitely and measurably, in the world of time as well. Fiction may defy history's reality, but as an object it takes its place in history. And it would be a mistake for us, enamored by the subjective necessities of the critical act, to refuse to grant the literary work its special status as object, though an object freighted by all the subjectivities of consciousness that normally resist object-ness. Not even the persons of critics, whether they are creating or undoing their personae, should keep us from taking advantage of this unique doubleness in the literature they treat: its function as a metaphor that transforms reality into human hobby-horsical shape, and its function as a completed entity that becomes part of that extra-human reality, changing that reality as it takes its place in it.

I put this matter (of the resistant reality of the object despite our subjective remakings of it) perhaps more cogently in an earlier statement of it.[16]

> *Whatever our decision about the ontological status of the literary object, its existence, meaning, and value before we collide with it, we know that we can speak of it only out of the dust of that collision. We pick ourselves up, no longer quite the same selves, and try to speak with precision about what has struck us and the force of its impact. And we probably will give the usual one-sided version of what has transpired and what sort of antagonist we have encountered. Who is to correct us except others who have suffered similar encounters and whose descriptions will be as partial and as self-serving? None may deny the encounter, none deny how profoundly he has been changed by it; yet each will have his own version, each levy his own assessment. Since each is changed, the alienating quality of the force—and its forcefulness—are beyond question. . . . The force which is the work itself lives only in those singular visions and in their mutual modifications by men honestly trying to look, and to move, beyond their own limitations, though it is these limitations that define who they are. Yet it is the force that helps define who they are to become.*

For the critic, the crucial part of that stubborn reality out there, which resists being dissolved into our idealisms, consists in those approachable, but hardly knowable, aesthetic objects around which his and his fellows' arguments try to—and often seem to—revolve. And the wholly purposive form of such an object may make it a valuable model that tells him about the less purposive parts of that reality—which is why it is, for the critic, the crucial part.

It is his willingness to indulge this useful fiction, that the work hangs out there in reality as a normative object after all, which I believe gives the contextualist poetic an advantage over others. We have granted that even the most modest critic attempts to reduce the object

[16]In the concluding paragraph of "Literary Analysis and Evaluation—and the Ambidextrous Critic," in *Criticism: Speculative and Analytical Essays*, ed. L. S. Dembo (Madison, Wis., 1968), pp. 16–36.

to himself, and in so doing cannot help but impose his own language upon the language of the work. But the contextualist begins by maintaining that the work can be treated as an intramural system that can be reduced to no forms or language beyond its own. He can claim that all prior language, including the critic's, are inadequate to the peculiar set of contextual interrelations that define the full language system of the work, so that for the critic to impose any definition from the outside is for him to violate the principle of formal integrity that gives life to the work. He would thereby deaden it by adapting it to an alien set of transcendent meanings, those which existed prior to and independently of the special symbolic cluster that makes up its total meaning. All this the contextualist can claim in theory, although of course in practice he is subject to all the hermeneutic traps that beset his colleagues. But his initial theoretical stance at least prepares him for the humility that looks for an ought-ness in the object by putting the soliciting power out there in it and no more than a responsive potentiality in him. This theoretical humility can surely turn into self-assertive arrogance in practice, and in any case his response, once he tries to put it in his language, is guaranteed to be inadequate to its object, the unique poetic context. His language must be one that preexisted this poem: it is necessarily generic insofar as it is drawn from other experiences of other poems, while the language of this poem should be an original synthesis that violates and reconstitutes forms and meanings that came before.

If, then, as we have seen, the critic is doomed to the self-deception that imposes subjective structures and calls them the object, is there not an advantage to the theory that proclaims his failure as a necessary one and suggests that he *can* be corrected by the object? Whatever configuration he finds that he proclaims to be the form of the poetic context may indeed be his rather than the poem's, despite the "data" in the text that his critic's ingenuity parades as his "evidence."

We can renew our suspicion that his hope for impersonal findings is a fond and delusive one by recalling the charges I have mentioned that contextualist critics have shown excessive zeal in "discovering" irrationalist, antipropositional dramatic structures. Nevertheless it would seem that, if the critic must be dominated by the primal (and more than literary) interests of his subjectivity, his best chance to move beyond the vanity of his task lies in a criticism that has an other-directed, work-centered impulse—even if, at its strongest, this impulse is doomed to be thwarted. And if this criticism requires its practitioner to assume also that the poem is a completed language complex that resists definition by all other languages, including his own, then his delusion will at least be that much lessened. If he cannot eliminate his personality in the face of the work, at least he need not cultivate it in order to outface the work.

Contextualism may, then, be representative of that mood in us which holds onto our imagined reality, while retaining an awareness (I almost said "a wariness") of that other reality outside—and struggles with the maddening incompatibility of the two. It encourages us at once to hold and to reject the metaphor that is the literary work, that sweep of subjectivity which is also a fixed thing in the external world. We can—and do—open ourselves to the work's system in spite of our attempt to reduce it to our own. We may seek automatically to control reality by forcing it into our categories, thus hobby-horsing it away. But we also respond to that alien reality, occasionally even reshaping our categories and altering personality. And no piece of reality can grasp us and change us more profoundly than can the work of art, because—though a fixed object—it is not *only* alien, but is humanly responsive to our humanity. Like all extrahuman reality, *King Lear* will always be *King Lear*, extending and ending itself in the same way, with the same words and actions, whatever we do with it and whoever the *we* are who do it. As we accept that fact, no matter how many ways we seek to remake the work, we come also to allow it to remake us. In short, we learn from it. And it must exist independently from us for it to educate us and enlarge us.

So the critic's personality (however compounded of person and persona) is the powerful, primitive moving force behind all he can do for the rest of us, giving us his reality as the container for the literary works that make it up. But the work also has its own reality for us, outside even the most powerful critical personality and the shapings of the work that that personality gives us. It can be, in rarely splendid works, a reality that more than supports our critic's myth about it. Finally, beyond the critique, then, the work remains, unabsorbed, as unshakably there as the Peele Castle described by Wordsworth in "Elegiac Stanzas." Like Peele Castle, it is a grand reality unshaken even by the fact of death. For the world of objects, the fact-ridden world beyond man, beyond man's control by his hobby-horses, will in the end be responded to directly, or will preclude man's response: it will, alas, overwhelm both the person and persona of the critic with its reality that persists—as these do not. But if, in this outside reality which persists, there is an objective embodiment of human consciousness within a humanly created form, then it will be humanity itself that persists.

64

Part Two  The Humanistic Theoretical Tradition

IV

The Deceptive Opposition Between Mimetic and Expressive Theories

I would like to establish a basis in the history of criticism for the theory that I have been outlining. For I hope to show this theory to be a systematic outgrowth of what has been central to the tradition of literary theory in the West since Aristotle (although I freely admit that what seems central depends on which aspect of that tradition the modern theorist wishes to emphasize). Still, the theory I am pressing can be shown to be a consistent consequence of certain tendencies I mean to trace. But, as I have acknowledged, there are leads in other directions, grounds to be found for other theories, as well. My first task, then, is to reveal the major alternatives—in both imitation and expression theory—to the direction I shall be following here. This negative entrance upon my subject should open helpfully into the tradition in which I find indispensable precedents for my theorizing.

My introductory chapters should have made it clear that imitation theory is the enemy. The very term "imitation," as a description of both the epistemological and the aesthetic function of poetry, seems to announce that it deprives more than it provides. It is more a denier than a maker of claims, precluding poetic creativity rather than explaining its nature. Because of its thrust outward from the poem, "imitation" must relegate that poem to a position below that of its external object. This sense it gives us is in keeping with the orginally denigrating introduction of the term "imitation" by Plato as he carried on the war of the philosophers against the poets. Plato's use of the term, after all, derives from his metaphysics, so that his aesthetic derogation of the imitative arts was a reflection of his metaphysical contempt. Imitation for Plato is the mark of the phenomenal world's incapacity as well as of the poem's aesthetic limitation. As the phenomenal world is but a shabby imitation of the archetypal idea, so the object in the work is an inferior replica of the worldly entity to which it owes its form. Plato, then, sees imitation as imposing a double deprivation: first, even before the poem begins to come about, it is metaphysically deprived in its obligations to a worldly object itself merely imitative; second, its own merely imitative nature makes it aesthetically deprived, since there is allowed no creative power behind it that can surpass—or even quite match—its all-controlling, if metaphysically deprived object.

Despite such obvious shortcomings for any theorist who would be a partisan for poetry, imitation theory has been ubiquitous in our critical tradition. Although there are many varieties of claims about the mimetic nature of poetry, it often seems as if there has been little in our theoretical tradition except such varieties. Can I uncover senses in which the resistant term "imitation" has been taken by our older critics so as to provide myself precedents for the antimimetic directions I have suggested in Chapter 2? The present chapter is to pursue both the resistance in the term and yet its expansiveness that suggests such precedence.

Earlier I broadened "imitation" to include any theory that defined the literary work as a receptacle for transposed versions of fully formed prepoetic entities (that is, entities that were fully formed prior to the creating of this poem). So the history of the varieties of imitation theory in our criticism is the story of the different sources, external and internal, for these prepoetic entities. At times it may seem as if the history of criticism consists of little except the multiplication of such varieties. Let me put the matter another way: If imitation theory requires only a wholly formed entity that preexists the poem as its "object" (to use the Aristotelian terminology), then we can bring together many theories as mimetic, finding them to differ only by virtue of the different sources of their "objects of imitation," and we may find that between so-called mimetic theories and expressive ones the distinction often collapses.

1

The austerely simplistic use of the term "imitation" in Plato's *Republic* (Book X)[1] assumes that it is the particular experienced object in the external world that the artist is obliged to imitate—whatever the eventual grounding of these particulars in metaphysical universals. This is as literal a sense of "imitation" as we have in the history of mimetic theory. It is a literalism that is only reinforced by Plato's use of imitation in a later dialogue like the *Sophist*.

[1] In contrast to the more restricted sense of "imitation," as narrative or dramatic point of view, in Book III. I discuss this sense of the word below, shortly.

As is well known, it is the very particularity of the object of imitation that Plato's metaphysic requires him to condemn. No history of criticism can begin without citing Plato's insistence, in *The Republic*, on art's double remove from reality by virtue of its being only an imitation of an imitation, since all existent particulars are imperfect imitations of subsistent universal archetypes, which are intelligible but not sensible. What is at once apparent is that imitation is for Plato a downward movement, in each case the imitation itself being inferior to the object it imitates. A movement downward from pure intelligibility to increasing engrossment by the senses, it is also a movement downward from singleness to multiplicity, so that "lower" here must mean further from the unchanging, indivisible, all-encompassing One. As imitations multiply, particulars are increasingly proliferated. Imitation thus stands as the antagonist of universality, the agent of dynamic differentiation in the world of becoming in opposition to the stasis of being.

When Plato looks at drama, he sees the existential consequences of his general fears for art. At the heart of drama is conflict, produced by imperfect, struggling creatures in the dynamic interaction that is enemy to the stasis of the metaphysical idea. Where Aristotle will construct a poetic by formulating tactics that celebrate the dynamics of conflict, Plato cannot yield so much to the way of men and the world and must disdain all that such an art, however developed, might promise. Indeed, the more successful it is dramatically, the more dangerous, metaphysically and morally, it must be for Plato, the more subversive of the unchallengeable perfection of his static universals. To make matters worse, drama magnifies its imitative and hence fragmented nature by its very manner of presentation: the poet, instead of speaking in his own voice, impersonates the voices of his several characters. He is, in effect, a ventriloquist who reserves no part to be delivered in his own person. There is not even this much honesty in him: a single imitator may be bad enough, but how much worse when, in hiding himself, he is broken up into an illusionary spectrum of pretend-characters so that we know not where to find him. All we have is the multiplication of perspectives, and beyond all of them the single universal truth becomes more distant than ever. Thus is imitation compounded by those whom Plato scornfully calls "the imitative tribe." Impersonating the speech of characters, which is the natural way of the dramatist, becomes an additional meaning given "imitation" (Book III)—except that, in proper dialectical fashion, it turns out to be a narrower sense of the same notion of "imitation" (as the making and multiplying of false, would-be likenesses), now found at another, advanced (or rather debased) level of proliferation. And again it is the descent into a greater number of ever weaker imitations, each inferior to *its* object and increasingly distant from that aboriginal object. Instead of artistic imitation, what the moralistic Plato calls for is emulation—a metaphysical and moral imitation that moves upward and out of itself—although this can hardly be derived from the downward procedures of the lowly "imitative tribe" of poets.

The dramatic poet, an extreme version of the imitative element in all artistic creators, multiplies perspectives, but only by giving up the thing itself and, through it, the higher entity *it* imitates. He moves downward through increasingly illusionary imitations rather than upward through emulation of the One. By dwelling upon the variegated worlds of our epistemologies, he neglects or even negates the sovereign world of ontology. In celebrating illusion over reality, his work is as attractive as it is dangerous to his seducible audience. Through this emphasis on illusion over reality as the artist's focus, Plato is able (in the *Sophist*) to link the artist to the sophist, indeed to see him as a variety of sophist. He finds in the artist and his imitation a narrow version of the general deceptions perpetrated by the artful illusions of the sophists in their penchant for falsehood. This emphasis on illusion unites the dramatic poet with all artists, thus allowing Plato the blanket condemnation of all imitation with which he began.

Plato complains that mimetic art concerns itself with how things appear to us rather than with things in themselves. And, depending each moment upon who we are, when we are, and where we are, we shall continually find the same thing appearing differently to us. Of course, our involvement with such transient appearances only aggravates the moment-by-moment changeability of the world of becoming. If the mimetic artist views his task as that of giving us the illusion that we are viewing the object of imitation from his momentary vantage point, then perspective becomes all important. This accounts for the illusionary use of foreshortening or elongation in the visual arts, and Plato accordingly condemns these. For he sees these distortions as falsehoods imposed upon the object's reality, which would be that reality-beyond-appearance which the artist does not show us, since he feels obliged to imitate what he sees as he sees it, not what is there to be seen.[2] It is this distinction, in "images" or imitations, between true likeness-making and mere appearance-making, as he draws it in the

---

[2] We must admit that the existence of Greek illusionary painting and sculpture may well have exacerbated Plato's theoretical antagonism to imitation. But, as we have observed, he saw and condemned a similar illusion fostered by the impersonations or mimicry that constituted Greek drama.

Sophist, that enables Plato to define as "phantastic" the illusionary art he would outlaw.[3]

As Plato sees it, then, art adds phenomenal insults to the metaphysical injury it inflicts on reality. Not only is it obliged to imitate a particular object, which is itself metaphysically mimetic, but it is obliged to imitate the most particular aspects of that object as phenomenon. In other words, even the particular object (metaphysically debased as it is) has a universal sensible aspect: the object as it stands, ready to be viewed, prior to and independently of every particular view of it. And it is this universal aspect of the particular object, as it exists out there for us all, that Plato laments is ignored by the illusionary art that restricts itself to a single perspective (or the particular aspect of the particular).

Plato's view of the dramatist allows the latter to join the painter and sculptor as the illusionary multiplier of particularity. Plato characterizes art's very nature, we have seen, as illusionary, as that which fosters our awareness of the particularity of our angle of vision, however much this angle misrepresents the "reality" of the thing we see. It is just this particularity that the dramatist also exploits in multiplying his voice among several characters, leaving none to himself as a center that contains them.[4] Thus the "phantastic" sculptor or painter

[3] Here Plato creates the precedent for the long history of the "phantastic"—father to the later term "fancy"—in literary theory. Yet it is an odd history that sees the word's meaning inverted, even as the condemnation of it by literal-minded mimetic theorists continues. For Plato treats as "phantastic" those imitations which increase the distance from ultimate, archetypal reality by giving us, not the imitation of the thing itself, but our individual, momentary image of it as our mind then perceives it. Later theorists (for example, Mazzoni), less concerned about the nice distinction between the actual world and our empirical version of it, will still use "phantastic" to characterize the capricious aberrations of our minds, though these aberrations will yield imaginative alternatives to reality rather than the most literal empirical reproductions of it. Thus the term "icastic" will refer to literally mimetic images—that is, of real objects and actions, without further epistemological quibbles—and its opposed term "phantastic" to the arbitrary impositions of the private imagination. Ironically, Plato's "phantastic" moves from being most restrictively tied to our experienced reality to being utterly freed from it in favor of the poet's invented world, as all real objects—as out there or as experienced—are handed over to the fidelity of the "icastic." But, either way, there seem to be properly Platonic reasons to condemn the "phantastic" (see Tasso, for example), unless, like Mazzoni, one finds himself trying to justify an alternative to the faithfulness of literal mimesis.

[4] I must here record an obvious observation: Plato himself seems, ironically, to subject himself to his own strictures about drama in that his own dialogues reveal the divided voices of dramatic form. The equally obvious answer to this observation—that the reader usually is pretty clearly directed toward the voice that is the barely disguised version of Plato's—does not fully meet the charge in its methodological profundity.

shares his sophistic weakness with the "phantastic" playwright. (Both, of course, are "phantastic" not, as later theorists claim, because they depart from the worldly appearance of their immediate reality but because they reproduce it, as they see it, all too uncritically.)

2

The uncertainties concerning the term "imitation"—its particularity or its universality, its relation to the world we discover or to the world our senses create—come out of Plato to pursue Aristotle. In the case of Aristotle, they have given rise to centuries of debate. At this point I would prefer not to add to them (although I shall later). But the debates at least make clear that Aristotle must mean by the word either the inventing of a plot form or the borrowing of a plot form from either history or literary tradition; further, that we may be in trouble if we give a simple metaphysical or moral interpretation of his claim that poetry is more philosophical and universal than history. And the treatment of the second issue clearly follows from the choice we make about the first.

While I reserve for a while treating the long-debated problems in reading Aristotle, here I take for granted the conventional reading of the *Poetics* which, despite minor variations, was the principal influence through the neoclassical theorists. However un-Aristotelian, this reading transfers the object of imitation from the external particulars, which led to Plato's complaints, to the universals of the metaphysical and, hence, the moral realm. By the time a Scaliger or a Sidney finishes with his Platonized version of Aristotle, poetry is enabled to bring into its reality those very metaphysical and moral universals which Plato damned poetry for not being able to apprehend. Of course, Horace has, though unwittingly, performed a middleman's service for this version of Aristotle's object of imitation. Horace, in what is an epigrammatic series of casual suggestions rather than a theoretical statement, is concerned more with literary convention than with metaphysical necessity. He speaks of fidelity to stock character types, whose authenticity and consistency relate to the way in which they are usually treated in literary works rather than to their ontological reality as universals. So it is not really imitation at all that he is speaking of, unless we mean the imitation of earlier writers.

But later critics, who think of themselves as both Horatian and Aristotelian, transform Horace's stereotypes—in the spirit of the Platonic reading of Aristotle—so that arbitrary conventions are seen as moral and metaphysical archetypes. Their interpretation of poetry's philosophical and universal nature in Chapter 9 of the *Poetics*, and of poetry's commitment to "things as they ought to be" in Chapter 25, leads them to identify the typicality of literary characters with the archetypal reality behind human nature. The universality of poetry comes to have metaphysical consequences for them and the ought-to-be character of poetry comes to have moral consequences, regardless of whether or not they had these for Aristotle. Accordingly, they convert Horace also into being a metaphysical and moral theorist, as he most certainly was not. So Horace may advise the poet to intersperse moral *sententiae* in order to add a teaching element to the delight his work provides, thereby broadening his poetic audience to include the more sober sort; but Renaissance Horatian-Aristotelians turn this incidental emphasis on occasional teaching into a precedent for their requirement that poetry have an overall didactic function, indeed that the very structure of the poem have an allegorical justification. As Scaliger neatly puts it, poetry is to "imitate the truth by fiction."

Of course, Plato's is a major influence on these conversions of Horace and Aristotle, for the allegory that uses apparent particulars to exemplify the universal reveals a capacity for poetry that Plato condemned it for lacking. Hence the Renaissance theorist can attempt to combat Plato with Plato, to answer Plato's attack on poetry with Platonic arguments that would give poetry a Platonic function. Further, the allegorical nature of medieval drama provided the formula which the ought-ness and the universality of drama, as prescribed by Renaissance theory, were to follow. Thus the external object of imitation, seen as metaphysical and moral universals (how the world ought to be if it is a "good" world and how, behind the façade of errant particulars in a fallen world, it really is archetypally), is confirmed for the Renaissance by Platonic modifications upon Aristotle and Horace, as these are reinforced by the allegorical theory and practice of the Middle Ages. And, with minor variations and only a few holdouts, this notion persists through the work of Pope and into much of the work of Dr. Johnson.

But, though poetry's imitation was seen to change from what Plato saw and condemned as its simple dependence on immediate and particular external reality, this transcendent elevation of its object did not change poetry's mode of being, the way in which it takes its meaning. There still must be an external reality, though now universal rather than particular, that preexists the poem as its object, as that on which it relies to have a meaning, so that its meaning, as it exists within the poem, is not essentially changed from what that meaning had been before the poem. That meaning or object has changed its locus, but not its nature; from the standpoint of the poem it is a removable part, and from the standpoint of the meaning the poem is a dispensable vehicle.

In the context of such imitationism, it would be presumptuous—or even sacrilegious—for a defender of poetry to suggest that the relation between the poem and its meaning or object could be more interdependent than this.

3

The more literal—or more skeptical—among us might ask how, once the theorist made the poem's external object of imitation universal rather than particular, we can know that it is external, that it is really out there and not a projection out of ourselves. If we read a description of a single person, or of any particular, as proper imitationists we can seek to check for accuracy the poetic representation against the original; but if we read a description of generic man of one sort or another, we cannot check in the same way since we do not meet generic man or, so far as we know, encounter universals at all. Our differing judgments through the long history of philosophy and taste also argue against empirical generalizations; such disagreements suggest that what we claim to be objectively universal may not even be subjectively universal, but may rather be radically subjective, even idiosyncratic, at least so far as we can know.[5] How, then, is the reader to judge whether the universal we may suppose we see imitated in poetry really resembles what is portrayed? How, in other words, is he to judge whether the poem is (as Dr. Johnson puts it) "a just picture of a real original," or whether it is the author's arbitrary invention? Is the original out there in the world or is it up there in a transcendent universe of ideals or is it just inside here, the poet's head? To put the matter most radically, is the poet imitating or only self-expressing? Looking at his claimed universals, how can we decide? But, more significantly, if our primary concern is with the ways of poetic meaning, our answers to these questions finally will not affect our attitude toward the manner in which the poem itself functions as a verbal imitation.

Sidney furnishes an excellent example of how difficult it is to find where the object of the poem is when it has an archetypal character attributed to it. In his *Apology* we seem to find that object sometimes in the poet's mind and sometimes in the unchanging Platonic ideal world. On the one hand he seems to give the poet's imagination full rein to see in its own peculiar way, while on the other hand he seems to restrict it

---

[5] For purposes of my argument here, then, I do not see the need to distinguish between a priori universals, as in the Platonic and the rationalistic traditions, and a posteriori or empirical universals of the sort found in eighteenth-century thinkers as unlike as Hume and Reynolds. From the standpoint of mimetic method, the two sorts function similarly as objects of imitation.

to echoing the moral and metaphysical universals that are always the same and must, therefore, be seen in the same way. Unlike all other workers in the arts and sciences, the poet, "freely ranging only within the zodiac of his own wit," disdains the limitations of nature's world and refuses to curtail his own invented world to match nature's. Instead, he alone can "grow in effect, another nature, in making things either better than nature bringeth forth, or quite a new form as never were in nature."

However, we are shortly told also that the poet's supposed free range is confined after all, or at least that poets are always expected to range in the same way, or in the same place: disdaining the empirical world "of what is, hath been, or shall be," the poet is to "range only reined with learned discretion, into the divine consideration of what may be, and should be." Performing in this way, the poet teaches men—though by delighting them—what goodness is and how to act in accordance with it. The ought-to-be world is the universal world of idealized characters ("not only to make a *Cyrus*, which had been but a particular excellence, as nature might have done, but to bestow a Cyrus upon the world, to make many *Cyruses*, if they will learn aright, when, and how that Maker made him"). Such characters provide their audience with examples of "each thing to be followed," just as evil characters show "nothing that is not to be shunned." So "certainly is more doctrinable the feigned *Cyrus* of Xenophon than the true *Cyrus* in *Justine*." The poet indeed imitates the truth (the moral ought-to-be and the metaphysical universal) through fiction (the feigned appearance of particularity).

From the two sorts of ranging allowed to the poet—one "within the zodiac of his own wit" and one within the ought-to-be world of Platonic universals—it might seem that he would be in some difficulty about assessing the degree of his freedom to invent or his restriction to imitate. Sidney himself seems unconcerned about a possible contradiction, for he has a theological resolution that makes the two compatible. This resolution requires the assumption that the Fall of Man, however it affects our capacity for action, does not necessarily affect our capacity for knowledge. Thus "our erected wit, maketh us know what perfection is, and yet our infected will, keepeth us from reaching unto it." Our "wit" is not fallen (hence even now "erected") though our "will," as infected by the sickness induced by the Fall, keeps us lowly, and thus unable to reach up to the perfection that is the knowledge attainable by our erected wit. The latter can apprehend perfection but can do nothing about it, since doing is the province of will, which in fallen man is out of joint with wit. Clearly, it is the poet who can serve as the potentially reuniting force for wit and will: his wit can demonstrate the perfection for the rest of us to reach toward, as we subdue our wills to bring them into conformity with what we have been shown. Since it is this fallen world of empirical particulars which serves our debased will and is served by it, the poet's value to us lies in his special freedom from that world, in his specially erected wit that frees him from our willful world to fly above it in its own. His victory of wit over will is thus a moral one, although—in the world of wit rather than of will—he produces only mock actions rather than actions themselves; it is for us, in aping the fictional product of his wit, to bring the perfections of an ought-to-be golden reality into a brazen world of will that becomes elevated thereby.[6] Particular reality becomes less unlike universal reality, as the poet-doctor attends our infection.

It is in this way that the two sorts of ranging can be seen as one. For the poet's "own wit" is no longer a realm of arbitrary subjectivity; it is, by fiat, identical with the Platonic ideal world. So, however freely the poet is called upon to range within the zodiac of that wit, he will turn out to be ranging within that ontologically solid world of universals that gathers all our wits to its perfection. One's own wit—automatically, as it were—partakes of the golden world. Thus the poet, in growing "another nature," produces a better world than nature does insofar as nature's world, the one in which our will operates, is a brazen one. And since particularity (the individual willfully satisfying itself) is intrinsic to its brazenness, it is universal sameness that characterizes the golden world and brings the zodiacs of all our wits into uniformity. Although the poet's world is different from nature's by virtue of its being better (replacing the apparent truths of brazen reality with the golden truth), it is different also by virtue of its sovereign capacity to invent new and unnatural forms ("Heroes, Demigods, Cyclops, Chimeras, Furies, and such like"). The latter difference is not related to poetry's superior moral power, but derives from poetry's fiction-making power, though this power is always subsidiary to the moral purpose. Hence, fiction (as apparent particulars) exists for the service of truth (which reveals them to be not really particulars, but only exempla of universals). Once more we are returned to the Scaligerian formula that would have the poet "imitate the truth by fiction."

---

[6] Sidney's attack on will and his association of poetic contemplation with will-lessness is an early version—though on different grounds—of an opposition to the world of will that becomes a tradition in aesthetics in the nineteenth and twentieth centuries. Following Kant's doctrine of disinterestedness, we find this strain—with reinforcements from Eastern philosophy—in Coleridge, Schopenhauer, Nietzsche, Bergson, Hulme, Yeats, Ransom, and Tate. I trace this philosophic development in "The Existential Basis of Contextual Criticism," *The Play and Place of Criticism* (Baltimore, 1967), especially pp. 241–48.

This formula, in making clear the poet's subservience to truth, however freely his fiction-making power is asked to range, establishes the dominance of an external object of imitation. This object is allowed to be in his wit only because the theorist has defined that wit, honorifically, as deserving to be called true wit since it partakes of objective universals. Where, except in our wits (and in the poems produced by those wits), can those universals be observed? Surely not in the empirical world, since this is defined as a fallen world that, finally (which is to say metaphysically), is untrue. What Sidney is saying, then, is that the poet looks within himself for invention, but that we must take his word for it that what he seems to be inventing is metaphysically authenticated in the subsistent world of Platonic universals. "Honestly, I am imitating," Sidney's poet appears to be saying, "although my imitation comes out of my head and you cannot check it against your world since it is not your particulars but my universals that I am imitating. And, thanks to Plato, this means that they are not merely *my* universals, but all our universals." If we ask how we can know that these are all our universals and not just his idiosyncratic fictions that he would impose upon us—if, that is, we are worried about distinguishing between the subjectively arbitrary and the objectively necessary—he can give us little assurance, except to appeal to authority and convention. With no "object" out there to be examined in light of its imitation, we are hard put to tell an imitation from a wayward bit of self-expression. It is not at all surprising that such a theory would try to bolster its claim to being a just imitation by pointing to other literary works that seem to be imitating the same universal objects. Hence, in a spirit that becomes Horatian all over again, archetype can be reconverted to stereotype as all the universals in that static world of gold turn out to be the same, so that the imitations can imitate one another. We are on our way to Pope, whose Virgil, we recall, found that nature and Homer were the same.

Once the mimetic poet forsakes literal imitation (that is, imitation of external particulars), we have seen that he has considerable difficulty persuading us that there really is an external object of imitation standing behind his work. He can slavishly imitate other literary works to persuade us of the commonness of his universals, but then we can worry—despite Pope's assurances—about whether it is common universals that are being imitated or just a common literary fashion that keeps us, as Dryden said, looking at the world "through the spectacles of books." And bookishness hardly guarantees authentic otherworldliness. Our imitations may not be getting us outside the world of books at all. No, metaphysical uniformity is not a convincing euphemism for what is at best conventionality and at worst plagiarism.

I have, in effect, been claiming that the broadening of the object of imitation to include universals ends by making us doubt whether imitation is any longer the proper term for what is occurring—whether, in other words, imitation is not a self-deceived excuse for what is actually arbitrary invention. Sidney's own ambivalence of attitude toward the poet's free range within his wit leads him to blur his imitationism with his incipient expressionism. Although the Renaissance scholar can reduce the latter to the former by introducing the restraining influence of Scaliger and Renaissance Platonism to help us read Sidney, we can still understand why so rabid an expressionist as Shelley saw himself as Sidney's heir and made his major theoretical essay a namesake of his progenitor's.

Defining poetry as "the expression of the imagination," Shelley attributes to man the active power to respond creatively to the impressions thrust upon him by the external world. He acknowledges that, for the most part, the mind is a receptacle for the sensations produced upon it by external nature, in the manner of the wind harp that is sounded by what strikes it. In this admission Shelley does not dispute the claims of the British empiricist tradition; nor does this run counter to the central imitationist doctrine that sees the poet as passively reproducing (as he reshuffles) the data furnished him by the external world. But Shelley also attributes to man

> a principle . . . which acts otherwise than in the lyre, and produces not melody alone, but harmony, by an internal adjustment of the sounds or motions thus excited to the impressions which excite them. It is as if the lyre could accommodate its chords to the motions of that which strikes them, in a determined proportion of sound . . .

This principle of harmony, which is to say the power of producing an order among sensory impressions, is an original and synthetic power of mind that, after Coleridge, Shelley calls imagination. It turns out, however, that it is only the primary imagination of Coleridge that Shelley borrows, since he confines himself to man's visionary power to attain to a cosmic force (as Coleridge puts it, "a repetition in the finite mind of the eternal act of creation in the infinite I AM") rather than, as in the secondary imagination, his conscious effort to put this power into service to make a work of art.

Shelley's commitment to the imagination as the immediate agent of vision seems to be an absolute one. Indeed, his claim that poetry (in the most limited and technical of the many senses, narrow and broad, that Shelley gives this word) is the supremely revelatory art is based on the fact that it is not impeded, like the other arts, by media that have their own interrelated material orders "which limit and interpose between conception and expression." Any medium based on its own interrelations acts like "a cloud which enfeebles" the light of imagination, while the immediacy of language "reflects" it, like "a mirror," directly. For language is nothing less than "the hieroglyphic of [one's] thoughts," produced by the imagination "arbitrarily." For Shelley, it is precisely the failure of language to have the attributes of a medium—its lack of a system of internal relations—that permits it to reflect the imagination so faithfully. Happily, the poet has no orders external to himself to wrestle with. The imagination, then, says as it sees, with the saying in the seeing, without inhibition or need for mediation. So the primary imagination of Coleridge *is* enough, with the poet as maker an unnecessary intruder upon the automatic operations of the poet as seer-sayer. And it is poetry's capacity to be free of the technical attributes of the other arts that enables it to be the direct spokesman of imagination.

But when Shelley, in the passage immediately following, comes to speak of poetry as "measured language," he attributes to such language the very attributes of a sensuous medium: "Sounds as well as thought have relation both between each other and towards that which they represent . . ." Thus poetry, in its narrowest and most distinctive sense as verse, works to achieve a "uniform and harmonious recurrence of sound." Shelley even argues for the untranslatability of poems.[7] In attributing internal relations to the medium of poetry, however, he unwittingly removes its immunity from the clouding effects of those media of the other arts. Poetry is no longer an unmediated language (a medium that does not mediate), with a unique dispensation to reflect the imagination directly and without interposition. Instead, it is now in the same condition as the physical media, from whom he distinguished it in the preceding paragraph, for it too has been granted inner workings that inhibit its powers to reflect the poet immediately— though at this point Shelley is only lauding the unique wedding of sound to meaning in verse. Of course, this moving description of the "peculiar order" used in poetry seems to be only a momentary inconsistency, as we are returned almost at once to the broader sense of

---

[7] I refer the reader to my brief discussion of Shelley in Chapter 3 and especially to note 7 to that chapter, in which the quotation on the untranslatability of verse appears. It should be noted that Shelley has been treating the "orders" of sensuous media as modern aestheticians have, and his singular attempt to include the language of verse within such plasticity is echoed in critics like Ransom and Burckhardt. See Chapter 2, note 13.

poetry—as a direct projection of vision—which dominates Shelley's *Defence*.

Although Shelley's interest is in the visionary power of mind, rather than in the making power of the poet, the vision toward which he reaches and leads the rest of us is a vision of the order and harmony that suffuse the universe. The vision is a product of the poet as gnostic, not just an errant product of his own subjectivity. Thanks to Shelley's free and undifferentiating use of terms like "order" and "harmony" on all the levels—musical, political, cosmic—to which we usually, half-metaphorically, apply them, Shelley sees all that the poet creates, from metric to doctrine, as an expression of the harmonic principle that lies at the heart of metaphysical reality. He has traveled far from his mundane, but momentary, consideration of language as the poet's plastic medium. Thus the "poet participates in the eternal, the infinite, and the one. . . ." Thus also, in words that cherish universality at least as much as Sidney did, "as far as relates to his [the poet's] conceptions, time and place and number are not." So the poet's visions are not errant ravings but partake of universal truth.

If Sidney's attempt to find a home in the sky for the zodiac of man's wit leaves us unable to determine whether his claim that the poet imitates universals is finally a license to create chimeras, conversely Shelley's brief for imagination ends by identifying all that it can imagine as a single, indivisible unity, universally one, whatever its momentary particular guise. With universals it does not finally matter whether one begins at the objective or the subjective end, Sidney's way or Shelley's. Each finally must claim to absorb the other in an embrace that denies the opposition. All works are allegories still, imitations of a preexistent object, fully formed as The Form, the model for them all. This is the vision, locked in the primary imagination that frees it for display, the vision that comes before, during, and after the poem, essentially unchanged because it is unchangeable. The skeptical observer, looking at the poet as defined either by Sidney's *Defence* or by Shelley's, must confess to seeing as merely arbitrary all that has been claimed to be metaphysically sanctioned. What such a poet claims to be the imitation of objective forces this observer views as the private consequence of self-expression.

Although the quarrel may persist between those who maintain that the fully formed entity that stands behind the poem has an ontological status in external reality and those who see such an entity as a visionary emanation from the poet as man-god, one with a phenomenological bias might insist that it makes no difference. What is significant instead is that, in both cases, the entity is really conceived of as an object of imitation, wtih the poem conceived of as that imitation. The object may be externally derived (in which case the theory behind the claim is conventionally termed a mimetic one) or the object may be internally derived (in which case the theory behind the claim is conventionally termed an expressive one); but both are equally seen as mimetic if we define imitation theory more broadly (as I have) as the systematic claim that the "soul" of the poem (as Aristotle means that word) consists of a newly dressed but not essentially changed version of an object which has already existed prior to the poem and could be formulated independently of its formulation in the poem. Whether, as in literal imitation, we are speaking of particulars (people or historical events) in external reality or, as in universalistic theories of imitation, we are speaking of ideal types in an ought-to-be reality either in a Platonic onticsphere or in the visions of an enraptured poet-prophet, we are placing the essence of the poem—its central meaning—outside the poem, thereby restricting that poem to being an imitation, though with a new dressing-up, of that preexistent object. The creation of an original object, of a unique vision, within the poem, as the result of a making of the poem that is a truly creative act, is beyond any of these versions of mimetic theory. There is, of course, some creativity in the making of any poem, even one so limited in its originating powers as mimetic theory allows: even the new dress must be made, the old content given a new form. But this is a superficial notion of form— and of creativity—since it leaves the "soul" of the poem untouched.

Viewed as my argument suggests, the shift from mimetic to expressive theory (a reflection of the shift in philosophy from realism to idealism) is hardly as radical a shift as most historians of literary theory make it out to be. So revolutionary a change in attitude about the sources of poetic inspiration did not at all revolutionize how the poem was related to what it is *about*—did not, that is, revolutionize the way in which poems were seen to take their meanings. The source of imitation may shift, now coming from within the poet rather than from outside him. But its status *as* object, together with the poem's subsidiary status, is unchanged.

The poem, then, remains a handmaid, now (as with Shelley) a handmaid to mysticism as before (as with Sidney) it had been a handmaid to rational philosophy. M. H. Abrams has described the change from imitation to expression as the change from metaphors of the mirror to metaphors of the lamp.[8] That is, the theory of imitation assumes that the poem is only a reflection, without excessive distortion, of a

---

[8] *The Mirror and the Lamp: Romantic Theory and the Critical Tradition* (New York, 1953.)

reality whose light is elsewhere; while the theory of expression that replaces it assumes that the poem is illuminated from within, by the lamp of the poet's imagination, source of the poem's only reality. But more than the mirror or the lamp, the poem can be seen—in expressive theory—as the mirror *of* the lamp. For, viewed from the standpoint of how the poem comes to mean, what we have—in mimetic *and* expressive theory—is not an opposition between the poem as mirror and the poem as lamp so much as an opposition between the poem as mirror of reality and the poem as mirror of the lamp. But in both concepts the poems are equally mirrors. We could thus collapse the mimetic-expressive opposition, as we have seen it operating so far, by saying that, on the whole, the history of literary theory is the story of the many varied roads that have led to imitation.

It will take another poetic entirely, one that gives the poem the power totally to reconstitute its meaning, to make the poem itself into lamp, itself the expressive source of meaning. Such a poetic would see the poem as the product of a creative act that projects and embodies the human impulse to form. From what we have seen, however, if mimetic theory is the enemy to this poetic, expressive theory—in the common forms it has taken—is hardly its ally. For both similarly preclude any view that the poem itself is the source and the locus of its power. They prevent us, consequently, from attributing to the poem the capacity to create any special meaning it can have for us, since *their* sort of meaning, existing independently, would not need the poem in order to express itself. For neither mimetic nor expressive theory requires that a single verbal formula be created as the equivalent of that meaning.

Even someone like Edward Young, who is frequently cited as one of the heroes of that mid-eighteenth century transition to expressionism, is trapped within the confines of explicitly mimetic theory in the midst of his championing of the organic, "vegetable nature" of "original composition." His call for "original genius" often sounds bold enough, but in reality it only beckons writers to imitate nature instead of books—that is, to go to nature directly rather than by way of earlier literary works or the conventions that arise from them.[9] Indeed, the author is warned away from "the too great indulgence of genius," which would lead him pridefully to seek to go beyond nature to create what Sidney would have thought of as a second nature out of his own

[9] Young himself uses the term "imitation" only with respect to earlier literary works, so that he speaks of it as something to be avoided. But, as the following discussion should make clear, he sees as the praiseworthy alternative to "imitation" (of authors and rules derived from authors) the imitation of nature directly, although he does not use the term this way. I impose the more universal use of imitation since the notion, if not the term itself, is in accord with Young's essay.

(Platonically ordained) imagination. This warning occurs in a piously restrictive passage in "Conjectures on Original Composition," which must be seen as highly significant, whether Young pronounced its major inhibitions himself or, as we have learned, permitted Samuel Richardson to intrude them upon the essay with his endorsement. Whatever the powers of genius (or perhaps only "fancied genius," Young's equivalent for Pope's "proud man's pretending wit") in "the fairyland of fancy," genius "may range unconfined" within "the wide field of Nature" only "as far as visible Nature extends." The restriction to "visible Nature" is reinforced when we are told that the poet" can give us only what by his own or other's eyes has been seen."[10]

If we sense an echo of Sidney when Young permits genius to "range unconfined" within the "wide field of Nature," we must also sense the difference between them. The poet, let loose by Sidney to range within the zodiac of his own wit, is expressly freed from the domination of nature to grow another nature, his own second nature, coordinate—as it were—with nature's nature. Of course, this second nature will turn out to be one with a Platonic ideal nature, so that the poet who ranges within the zodiac of his own wit is also, thereby, ranging "into the divine consideration of what may be, and should be." It is this double, coincidental ranging—at once free and predetermined —that enables Sidney to absolve his imaginative poet from charges of an impious rivalry with God (the very charge suggested by Young-Richardson).[11] Clearly the "range" of Sidney's poet is considerably more metaphysical than the range of Young's. Both end by being imitative, though the objects of imitation differ, as do the empirical and the ideal worlds.

Young echoes Sidney not only in his use of "range," but also in his concern about "chimeras." We saw that Sidney's poet declared his independence of nature by producing a world at once morally superior to nature's and simply different from nature's, filled with creatures that never were ("*Heroes, Demigods, Cyclops, Chimeras, Furies,* and such like"). Young, who wants the poet bound to God's world, could not

[10] This confinement within what would appear to be the empiricist's closed world of sensory experience is not significantly modified by the concessive phrase that allows the seen world to be "infinitely compounded, raised, burlesqued, dishonoured, or adorned." Within the empiricist tradition we can hardly take the adverb "infinitely" as literally meant, since the entire intention of the passage is to enforce the strict limits of the visible world of experience upon the creative mind.

[11] "Neither let it be deemed too saucy a comparison to balance the highest point of man's wit with the efficacy of Nature: but rather give right honor to the heavenly Maker of that maker. . . ." From here Sidney turns to his argument from the Fall of Man, his version of which leaves man's "erected wit" free to apprehend God's perfection, a perfection whose golden home rests in the ideal world which the brazen world of nature, burdened by man's "infected will," must fail to imitate.

couple the better and the different worlds, since he is more distrustful of the "fairyland of fancy"—what Addison, after Dryden, termed "the Fairy Way of Writing"—"wherein the Poet quite loses sight of Nature." For this would put Young's poet, no longer subservient to the sensory impact of God's nature but rather reigning "arbitrarily over [his] own empire of chimeras,"[12] into a false and pretentious competition with God (a competition that Sidney acknowledged and apologized for, but the consequences of which his metaphysic permitted him to escape). Once Young's poet, indulging his fancy, departs from nature, his creaturely inability to know things beyond the material world must lead him to invent false beings, a very "empire of chimeras": "What painter of the most unbounded and exalted genius can give us the true portrait of a seraph?" No, the metaphysical world is God's alone— and beyond the presumption of the most fanciful of us. Hence the fancy deludes, the expressive poet must deceive, and only imitation can move us toward God's truth, whose revelation is vouchsafed us in nature. Far from approaching expressive theory, Young sanctifies imitation as piety, so long as it is God's nature rather than men's works that we are imitating. In this sense Young represents a retreat even from Sidney's ambivalent half-gestures toward expressionism, while of course Shelley, with no fear of hubris, moves recklessly and by fiat to the totally free-ranging creativity of the man-god who envisions the gnostic mysteries: chimeras that take on the universal status of eternal reality.

As I have shown, what is common to these is the sense that the making of the poem itself is an imitative act, although this fact is not usually so nakedly displayed as it is by Young. He also displays another feature common to the ubiquitous imitationism we have been examining, a feature that contributes principally to its theoretical weakness as an aesthetic: the concentration upon the "objects" outside the poem that are brought, with whatever modifications, into the poem. We might say, more generally, that the mimetic theorist is necessarily concerned with the objects in the poem rather than with the poem as an object. When Young speaks of the poetic genius ranging within the "wide field of Nature," "as far as visible Nature extends," he sees it sporting

---

[12] It is of course true that Sidney is using "chimeras" in its literal, classical sense, a more specific sense than Young's. For Sidney the Chimera is the mythical monster itself, the companion—in his sentence—of Cyclops and Furies as well as heroes and demigods. By the time of Young's usage, it has broadened to include any empty and illusionary creation, any unnatural and phantastic (as opposed to icastic) and therefore monstrous invention that has no correspondent reality. But, once we recognize how uncomfortable Young seems to be with mythological fictions, it is not difficult for us to understand that Young's sense of "chimeras" might—for him—be a logical outgrowth of Sidney's.

with nature's "infinite objects uncontrolled . . . painting them as wantonly as it will." The poet must stick, that is, to objects seen "by his own or others' eyes" and stay away from false seraphs, mere chimeras. The point is that poems are viewed here—much as Sir Joshua Reynolds was shortly to view paintings—as a collection of imitated objects, as if portraiture and natural descriptions were the sole genres for the arts, leading us to their objects. Here is an assumption wholly consonant with Addison's earlier definition of "secondary pleasures of the imagination" as reminders, by way of art, of our original sensory experiences, the "primary pleasures of the imagination." Though there may be significant alterations in these objects and though our response to art may be enhanced by such alterations, still there is no way for such a theorist to define the work of art except as a collection box that holds its imitated objects for our inspection and comparison with their originals in the world. It is no wonder that, in the purest form which mimetic theory achieved in the eighteenth century, poetry was thought of "like a painting," and, despite its own verbal and temporal nature, it could borrow from its "sister art" the static ideals, the spatial form, of portraiture and landscape.

4

From its beginnings in Plato, mimetic theory was tied to its emphasis on objects outside the poem that are transported inside the poem. This emphasis had to work to the detriment of any concern with the poem itself as an integral object, since it was being treated as a composite of objects, a collage. All of Socrates' worries, in Book X of *The Republic*, about the relation of the archetypal bed to material beds, and of both to beds as they are painted by artists, seem to have fixed upon imitation theory this concentration upon experienced objects and the dependence upon them of represented objects. Aristotle's central concern with the "object of imitation" seems one wished upon him by his Platonic inheritance, and most of our difficulties with the *Poetics* derive from Aristotle's restive struggle with this inheritance. Nor should we—even when most entranced by his contributions to organic theory—forget the literal meaning Aristotle gives "imitation" in his early use of the term in Chapter 4 of the *Poetics*, where it means little more than aping ("reproduced with minute fidelity").[13] This observation should

[13] He speaks here of man's "instinct of imitation," the imitation through which the child "learns his earliest lessons." And while Aristotle reminds us of the pleasure given us by accurate reproductions of even painful objects, he remarks on the special pleasure we take in recognition ("saying perhaps, "Ah, that is he." ". . . if you happen not to have seen the original, the pleasure will be due not to the imi-

give us pause before we too easily broaden and liberalize his sense of "imitation" to make it almost synonymous with invention. This initial use may remain naggingly to enforce our awareness of some duality that persists in him.

Let it indeed be conceded that Aristotle, in those exciting portions of the *Poetics* that have most profoundly influenced the aesthetics of the past two centuries, enunciates the principles in accordance with which unified plots—plots with sufficient order and appropriate magnitude—can be constructed; still, we are prevented from claiming that such passages represent the whole of Aristotle by that existence of his rather literal concern, elsewhere in the *Poetics*, with the object of imitation. Thus in that most important but most ambiguous Chapter 9—which can be used by commentators of all persuasions to support any claim they wish—the distinction between poetry and history, between the inventing of plots and the borrowing of plots, is consciously blurred while it is being asserted, indeed even while it is being asserted that it is the function of Chapter 9 to make just that distinction. And the agent of our confusion is that term "imitation," which appears here as an echo of Aristotle's repeated definition of the object of imitation in tragedy: he several times speaks of tragedy as "an imitation of an action that is complete, and whole, and of a certain magnitude," as if the qualification applied to the action prior to its being imitated (a complete, and whole, and of-a-certain-magnitude action that is there for tragedy to imitate).

I have been suggesting that Aristotle was obliged to borrow some of the assumptions and terms of Plato as he answered the latter's attack upon poetry. Although he accepted the centrality of Plato's term "imitation," Aristotle was impelled to accommodate that term within the framework of his own philosophy of process. The term could spring easily, even obviously, from the stasis of Plato's metaphysic—with its concern for ideal archetypes, as defectively mirrored in single physical things and separate artistic images of those things—but, having picked it up, Aristotle had to work it into his own conceptual structure, which was built on the notion of growth and movement. Plato's static ideality, based on individual entities, whether physical or metaphysical, gave way to Aristotle's dynamic teleology. The psychology of audience response, and its moral consequences for audience and society, changed from one philosopher to the other accordingly.

---

tation as such [sic], but to the execution, the coloring, or some other such cause.)" Separating "imitation" from "execution," Aristotle has clearly restricted it to subject matter. Could "imitation" ever be given a more unqualifiedly literal meaning?

In contrast to Plato's unchanging austere ideal, for Aristotle the imperfect political realm is also in motion, as is man's capacity to improve it, along with himself. Thus Aristotle must reject Plato's argument against poetry based on the unworthiness of its objects of imitation. Instead of the "monkey see, monkey do" psychology assumed by Plato for the spectator of art, which was to provide only ideal objects for him to imitate lest he be contaminated, Aristotle implicitly provides for man's capacity to purge himself of those imperfect elements whose imperfections dramatically unfold and finally explode before him. The entire poem, as an object, has a structure that transcends and judges the individual object within it: man can learn by seeing examples of what *not* to do, and not just by seeing ideal objects of emulation. It is, as has been pointed out by others, Aristotle's homeopathic medicine replacing Plato's allopathic. Our biologist has provided for an inoculation theory. Consequently, he can allow a central place for emotion in poetry—for it is what is to be purged—without, like Plato, condemning poetry for representing it so prominently. The heat and illusionary power of myth, with its "working power" over our emotions, need not be forsaken for the cool immobility of the philosopher's claim upon *the* Reality. For our pragmatic psychologist does not, like Plato, dream of doing away with our emotions so much as he accepts our need to live with them. Still, despite the radical changes which Aristotle's commitment to process and growth worked upon Plato's metaphysical fixity, the term "imitation" remains to serve the former as it did the latter. Consequently, in Aristotle's hands, now it changes, now it doesn't.

It is little wonder that, as Aristotle grapples with the term (whose very meaning arises out of the notion of fixed objects and images of them) to make it reflect his own world in motion, he cannot make it stand still for himself: when he speaks of the "object of imitation," he seems, like Plato, to be talking of a single fixed thing,[14] although, as he maintains that it is an *action* that the tragedy imitates, he converts the spatial object into the temporal movement.[15] As we move from the

---

[14] It is very likely this habit in Aristotle, largely influenced by the Platonic limitations on this notion of imitation as imitation of an object, that led Butcher to his overly Platonic interpretation of Aristotelian imitation in his distinguished commentary on the *Poetics* [S. H. Butcher, *Aristotle's Theory of Poetry and Fine Art with a Critical Text and Translation of the Poetics* (New York, 1951), esp. chaps. 1 and 2].

[15] One might argue that even Aristotle is only deceptively temporal in his appeal, since the teleological structure of the action—the inevitability of its architectural pattern—constitutes only a frozen motion, a sequence that is fixed rather than free flowing.

fixity of the objects of imitation in Chapter 4 of the *Poetics* through the criteria for properly managed actions in Chapters 7, 8, and beyond— though with what might appear to be momentary reversions to the fixed notions, for example in Chapters 6 and 9—we find the burden of Plato not altogether discarded, for, whatever the change in doctrine, the very word "imitation" itself seems to carry the notion of single, fixed "object" with it to weight the theoretical discourse.

Nevertheless, many will insist that I am forcing difficulties upon Aristotle by overemphasizing his fealty to literal imitationism. Is it just for me to maintain that Aristotle, however trapped between his heritage and his philosophical inclination, is seriously inconsistent (or, at least, that the fragmentary nature of the *Poetics* and its questionable status as a finished treatise allow it to appear so)? I would say he (or it) is, because I believe the literal notion of imitation in Chapter 4 carries over to the central passages of definition, when he speaks of tragedy as an imitation of an action that would, before being imitated, seem already to possess certain characteristics of order and magnitude. Yet Chapters 7 and 8 turn order and magnitude over to the poet's plot-making power. Can we, then, ignore the difference between literal imitation and the expansion of imitation to cover a creative act, a difference that is really as troublesome as I have suggested? Should not the literal sense of the word in Chapter 4, with its echoes elsewhere, make us hesitate before smoothing over the identification (or confusion) between imitating and making that occurs, for example, in Chapter 9, where we are hard put to determine whether the form of the tragedy is given the poet or created by him?

The passage in Chapter 9, as I have suggested, makes it difficult to make out in Aristotle a specific and single-minded attitude toward an opposition between history's casual-ty and poetry's causality, though he seems determined to establish just such an opposition. It must be admitted that, in discussing the tragedies in his tradition, Aristotle was dealing with works that for the most part treated common stories derived from legendary history, so that the notion of a tragedy imitating a preexistent action could make literal sense to him. So Aristotle begins Chapter 9, which undertakes to distinguish history from poetry, by separating the casual from the causal: that which has happened from that which may happen according to the laws of probability and necessity. But he then must cross his categories when he tries to account for the fact that tragedies usually deal with historical figures. He justifies this fact, "the reason being that what is possible is credible."[16] He suddenly seems on the verge of literal imitationism.

[16] ". . . what has not happened we do not at once feel sure to be possible: but what has happened is manifestly possible: otherwise it would not have happened."

But this line of argument—the particular and historical-possible as the support for the universal and artistic-probable—would collapse the distinction that it is his intention to establish in this chapter; so he must reject his retreat to this momentary collusion between poetry and history. Consequently, he argues that fictitious names can also work: we must not hang onto the same old stories "at all costs," since often most of the audience cannot recognize the imitative effect produced by familiarity anyway. Let the poet be the maker of his plots, then. Finally, however, Aristotle retreats once more to allow history and poetry to reinforce rather than to oppose one another: "And even if he chances to take an historical subject, he is nonetheless a poet; for there is no reason why some events that have actually happened should not conform to the law of the probable and possible, and in virtue of that quality in them he is their poet or maker."

We seem to have moved, in this argument, from the imitated possible (history) as philosophically inferior to the invented probable (poetry), to the possible as the basis for the probable, back to the superiority and independence of the probable, and finally to the happy union of the possible and probable in that lucky historical sequence that fortuitously has taken the form of art. It is an ingeniously sinuous trail leading to a cake that one can both eat and keep. The final sentence quoted above shows the making activity (by virtue of which one is the poet) as identical with the imitating activity in the case of that lucky historical plot in which the possible and probable are one. The poet copies his plot from history and—lo!—he has made a proper poetic construct. Literal imitation and artful making are one because simply to copy historical sequence is to construct rightly. Our theorist has, by fiat, obliterated the need for the either/or that lies at the source of his distinction-making intention.

But earlier in this passage we can note that making and imitating meet, as identical activities—and not on the imitative side (as in the final quoted passage) but clearly on the creative side. And they meet in a way that makes us doubt whether we can ever think of imitation as literal reflection in the static manner of Plato, as I sometimes have, taking the lead from Chapter 4: "It clearly follows that the poet or 'maker' should be the maker of plots rather than of verses; since he is a poet because he imitates, and what he imitates are actions."[17] While I can hardly see how this claim "clearly follows," it is clear that the

---

[17] Here, as elsewhere, I have used Butcher's translation. But, after having compared half a dozen often quite varied (and all responsible) translations—and those of several manuscripts—I assure the reader that in the crucial passages I have been pointing to, in which key terms are defined and juxtaposed, there are no theoretically significant differences from the Butcher.

equation between imitating and making here is unequivocal, and it occurs on making's grounds; that is, we cannot—from its use here—view imitating except as the invention of a sequence of episodes that becomes a proper action.

It is because of passages like this one that some influential recent interpreters of Aristotle do not see his doctrine of imitation as curtailing in any serious way his commitment to the poet as the maker of his plots.[18] All that imitating may mean in this context is that the poet, though creating freely, is giving us actions that are like the actions of men—that are, in other words, recognizable as the way men behave. A play is an "imitation" of men in action as in real life. It appears before us *as if* we were witnessing a happening: though a mock event, it is an imitation-happening.[19] Now, as a theory of imitation, this is only minimally demanding; and while it does away with my concerns about Aristotle's conflicting doctrines, it also denies any sufficiently literal meaning to "imitation" that would oppose it to "invention." Aside from claiming that the poem's generally representational quality is the extent of the poet's imitative responsibility, this minimal doctrine of imitation leaves the poet free to invent in accordance with the principles of his art.

It is what the poet imposes as an artist that characterizes his product as a work of art rather than nature. This interpretation begins by calling attention to the fact that, for Aristotle (as seen in his *Physics* 2), art also imitates the method of nature, in that the process of creation is an imitation of the natural process. A natural object bears its principle of development immanently within itself as its *telos:* the acorn, to use the well-worn example, has the form of the oak within it. Its ultimate form is the natural outcome of the growth latent in its material. But the stone does not bear a statue within it, nor do the words of the English language bear *Hamlet* within them in the manner of the acorn and the oak. It is the role of the artist to impose upon alien and unformed material—impose from the outside—a form that is not native to it, a form that, left to its own devices, it would never grow into. Further, the artist must ape nature in that he must so impose his form

---

[18] I think especially of the distinguished Aristotelian scholar, Richard McKeon, who had a profound effect on the literary neo-Aristotelians of the University of Chicago. See "Literary Criticism and the Concept of Imitation in Antiquity," in *Critics and Criticism, Ancient and Modern,* ed. R. S. Crane (Chicago, 1952), esp. the carefully argued pp. 161–63. An extension of this position can be found in Kenneth A. Telford, *Aristotle's Poetics: Translation and Analysis* (Chicago, 1961), esp. pp. 62–68.

[19] This rather bedrock assumption of "imitation" is pursued at length in my Chapter 6, below.

that it takes on the inevitability of a natural form: his object is to reveal a realization of internal purposiveness that we find in an ideally developed organic entity in nature. Indeed, if he does this he improves upon nature, since the natural object is likely to possess accidental imperfections, irrelevant to its teleological form, which the product of human art can avoid. The *telos*, forced on the materials by the artist, ends by being utterly embedded so that a total flowering, with the realization of every potentiality, can occur. No wonder we sometimes speak of a sculpture by Michelangelo as if it grew naturally out of its stone, or feel, as proper Aristotelians, the sheer inevitability of the climax and denouement of the successful tragedy. So the poet imitates the natural process by imitating (in another sense of the term) certain human relations that obtain in the real world and by subjecting them to his own form in order to convert them into his own replica of teleological perfection.

We come, then, to understand McKeon's claim, and it is a tempting one because of the confusions it obviates: imitation may require the poet to borrow his preliminary superficial forms (what McKeon calls "perceptible" as differentiated from "substantial" forms) from nature, but, since they come to him divorced from their natural materials in life, what counts is the way he recreates them in response to the demands of the materials and the formal principles of his art. Still, what makes art imitative is the fact that the artist does take these initial forms from the outside world.[20] The general resemblance to reality is what makes art recognizable to the rest of us. But what makes art artful is the fact that the artist imposes his own matter upon these forms in a way that gives them another responsiveness to another inevitability, a new necessity and probability. In effect, of course, it is forced to develop a new form. For surely we cannot (McKeon to the contrary notwithstanding) *transfer* a form from one matter to another, making it responsible to another set of necessities, without having to *transform* that form into another, and a new one. McKeon's insistence (required if he is to save "imitation" as a meaningful term) that the form is one as it is carried over from life into art betrays a primitively mechanistic doctrine of the relation of form to matter in art, a doctrine happily belied by the profound organicism he brings to his Aristotelianism.

From an organicism of our own, are we not justified in asking whether the original perceptible forms that were imitated from life are any longer seriously relevant to the finished product, once it has

[20] McKeon, *op. cit.* p. 162: "Art imitates nature; the form joined to matter in the physical world is the same form that is expressed in the matter of the art."

achieved a form and an inevitability of its own, responsive only to its artistic medium? In other words, is there any advantage in using the doctrine of imitation to characterize a theory in which imitation is so preliminary and minimal a matter, a theory whose formal center is so evidently in the organic and expressive tradition? For few theorists, if any, would deny that art has its beginnings in some relation to experiential reality, however it may take off on its own from there. If this is imitation theory and Aristotle's, then we are in danger of losing any distinction between Aristotle and Coleridge.

It seems to me that this anxiety to collapse imitation into making deprives Aristotle of a concern that reveals itself, if only here and there and incompletely, in the *Poetics*. It is true that he often—and probably at his best—speaks of imitation as if it is consonant with the invention of plots, so that we are properly tempted to see imitation in its most general and least restrictive dimensions: as keeping the poem more or less lifelike, and only that. At times this is the only reasonable interpretation possible. But it is also likely that, perhaps because he is in part answering Plato or because he is dealing with a dramatic tradition that used commonly received stories from supposed history, Aristotle at times—though fitfully—means imitation quite literally, as an alternative to creativity. It is difficult to look at the entire history of the mimetic tradition, in which imitation *is* taken seriously, without finding some source for it, however minor and sporadic, in Aristotle.

We can speculate about radically different interpretations that might reconcile the poet as imitator with the poet as maker. For example, we could define Aristotle's "imitation" in the quite limited way of Plato in *The Republic*, Book III,[21] as the converting of narrative into speeches by many voices. Thus, to imitate an action might mean no more than to borrow the story (that is, the plot or sequence of incidents) from history (or earlier mythic versions of history) and convert it into dramatic form. But this limited meaning would seem clearly out of keeping with the spirit of Aristotle's claim that the poet is the maker of his plots and that it is in this making that his poetic function principally consists.

However, one could still use this restricted notion of "imitation" to reconcile Aristotle's dual interest in the poet's making forms and borrowing forms by seeing the poet as engaged in a two-step operation:

[21] We must remind ourselves that this narrow and idiosyncratic sense of *imitation* in Plato, as the splitting up of the dramatic poet's voice in its disguised versions (the many voices of his characters), is subsidiary to Plato's more common use of the word in its standard meaning. I refer the reader to my discussion at the start of this chapter, in which I argue that the narrower meaning is consistent with the broader one, being just a more extreme version of it.

first, he rearranges the incidents of a well-known story (ideally, a piece of history on which the human instinct for form has imposed its mythologizing shape) into its most effective structure; and, second, he "imitates" it by turning it into the consecutive speeches and actions of drama. Hence, tragedy becomes "an imitation of an action that is serious, complete, and of a certain magnitude," that is, the "imitation of an action" that already (prior to its being given "imitative" form) had been given its appropriate order, completeness, and magnitude. Even in this reading, however, the poet's prior act of making the bare plot seems less significant than his making the play, though it must be acknowledged that Aristotle seems clearly to want it the other way round. In the case of either of these two heterodox readings, the action has its attributes of order, completeness, and magnitude before being "imitated" (whether those attributes are derived from history or imposed by the poet's creative process), and that structure of action (as "object") is then "imitated" (in Plato's restrictive sense) by being turned into drama.

Thus, although either of these daring readings might solve some problems—by reconciling what seems to be unreconcilable in the *Poetics*—it leaves us with others, perhaps more serious. For the second as well as the first would elevate the speech-writing and portrayal of incidents in the play to being the centrally imitative activity of the poet: in effect, it would turn the structure of the action itself into a merely material cause to be shaped into drama, despite the fact that Aristotle wants the plot (the result of the shaping of the incidents into the structure of the action, prior to any specific speech-writing) to be the formal cause, with the presentational elements reduced to the less significant material cause (see especially Chapter 14, as well as Chapter 6). No, as we have seen, the poet is a poet, for Aristotle, because he is the maker of his plots, and it is the making of his plots themselves that constitutes his imitative nature, the writing of the play (as a sequence of speeches and gestures) being clearly subsidiary. If this creative obligation conflicts with the poet's need to be an imitator in the literal sense of Chapter 4, or to imitate actions that have order and magnitude prior to his coming upon them, then Aristotle must live with this potential inconsistency, as we have lived these millennia with him.

Aristotle will not permit us to extract him from his difficulty by our limiting "imitation" to the turning of narrative into drama (whatever the precedent in Plato for this meaning), any more than by our broadening "imitation" to mean any representation of recognizable creatures and their moral dimensions and their existential crises—much like those of us all. This generic reduction might explain the sense in which (as I discuss at length in my Chapter 6, below) the drama is an imitation of life by virtue of being a make-believe, encapsulated form of actual happenings that we are permitted to witness (the characters more or less acting like real people in real situations, reacting typically as real people would for their real reasons); but the formative power of "imitation" has gone out of the word if it means no more than this lowest common denominator. For Aristotle makes it continually his point (though *not* in Chapter 4) that the power of the imitation arises precisely out of its more-than-reminiscent quality: it arises out of its freedom from fact-bound historicity. And we cannot unlock that secret by tying "imitation" to our generic recognizing power. Yet, as we try to be precise and to be honest with ourselves and with Aristotle while we confront him all at once, we find the conflict the less reconcilable. The history of critical theory has essentially, if not always consciously, accepted it as such, pressing sometimes one emphasis of his and sometimes another.

So I return to my own difficulties with two versions of Aristotle. If I have been a long time with these difficulties, it is because here, at the dawn of the Western aesthetic, in this single work, the issue seemed so crucially joined, and the price of rejecting imitation in order to free man's formally manipulative powers seemed so clearly stipulated. At the heart of these difficulties with Aristotelian mimesis is the fact that the "object of imitation" must be just that, and, at the same time, as an action that has certain attributes, like wholeness or proper magnitude, it must be the all-important "formal cause"; and it is by virtue of his active role in producing this formal cause that the poet-maker proves himself worthy of that title. It seems that Aristotle, whose central interest is to create a theoretical model for the plot of successful tragedy as an organic whole, is forced to do so while struggling against the burdens of an inimical Platonic jargon. We have seen the very phrase, "object of imitation," to carry within it the implication of an entity already fully formed and, in that form, waiting to be imitated. How different it is—especially given the meaning of imitation in Chapter 4— to say "tragedy is the imitation of an action" already endowed with certain characteristics (completeness, wholeness, and so on) rather than to say, for example, tragedy is the making or constructing of an action in which episodes will be so manipulated as to create certain patterns relating to its completeness, wholeness, and so on. The spirit of most of Aristotle as we have him in the *Poetics* may be straining to say the second, but his language constrains him to say the first; what must follow are certain lingering inhibitions that blunt the force of his remarkable and pioneering contributions to organicism.

5

This sense of "object" in "object of imitation" survives to haunt mimetic theory and, for two millennia, to direct it way from the central thrust of Aristotle himself. We now can see that the redirection to the more distinctively Aristotelian would have to come through turning from one sense of "object" to another: from an object *in* the work to the work *as* object, that is, from imitated objects collected in the work to the work as an integral, created object that transcends, as it transforms, the objects within it. Even Coleridge himself, whose conception of the primary imagination we have seen behind Shelley's grandiose claims, seems concerned with the imitation of objects in that primary imagination as well as in what he terms "fancy."[22] He sees the fancy, which can play only with "fixities and definites," as bound by the limits which the empiricist places upon memory, so that, like memory, "the Fancy must receive all its materials ready made from the law of association." These materials, the fixities and definites, would clearly seem to be sensory impressions, objects as they appear to us. And, in speaking of the primary imagination as "the living Power and prime Agent of all human perception, and as a repetition in the finite mind of the eternal act of creation in the infinite I AM," Coleridge is requiring it to bring to objects a subjective vitality, thereby bestowing life upon them.

In his Thesis VII of Chapter 12, the preceding chapter, he proclaimed that "every object is, as an *object*, dead, fixed, incapable in itself of any action, and necessarily finite." He reminds us of this claim in his definitions of Chapter 13 when he asks the application of imagination, as the life-giving ("essentially vital") force, upon objects which "(*as* objects) are essentially fixed and dead." In the world of the empiricist they remain only objects, remain fixed and dead, as the "fixities and definites" which are the "materials" received "ready made from the law of association" by fancy, which can do nothing except combine them in their lifeless state. The godlike, life-giving power of the primary imagination, through the subjective breakthrough of the I AM, brings a vital warmth to "that inanimate cold world," of which Coleridge spoke in "Dejection: An Ode," a poem about the failure of imagination. He concludes that poem by wishing for his friend a universe as blessed as that of the restored and rejuvenated Ancient Mariner: "To her may all things live, from pole to pole, / Their life the eddying of her living soul!"

It is these "things," the objects which have been thus I AM-ized,

---

[22] This discussion of Coleridge refers to the famous definitions in the sketchy Chapter 13 of *Biographia Literaria*.

objects no longer dead and thus objects no longer, that the poet with primary imagination imitates by bringing them into his poem. The role of the secondary imagination, then, as the poem-making power,[23] would seem to be that of turning the self-assertive visions of the primary into a literary work. Thus the secondary imagination is "an echo of the former [the primary], co-existing with the conscious will. . . ." Insofar as it is an echo, we remain clearly within the precincts of mimetic theory, although with an internal object of imitation. For his immodest pronouncements Shelley will not have to go far beyond this.

But Coleridge also claims, in the sentence immediately following, that it (apparently the secondary imagination) "dissolves, diffuses, dissipates, in order to recreate" (apparently) the materials of the primary. Now this activity (dissolving, diffusing, dissipating), in the making of the poem, differs vastly from the claim in the previous sentence that the secondary imagination is an echo of the primary. If an echo is a second coming of the original in essentially the same form, then how can that form be dissolved in order to be recreated as a new form by the secondary? Echo or recreation? Does the essential act of creation occur in the secondary or has it already occurred in the primary? Is the secondary imagination imitative or is it active in an original way? That is, does the form of its product preexist its operation or emerge out of it?

Coleridge only adds to the confusion when he adds, "Or when this process [the dissolving, diffusing, and dissipating, in order to recreate] is rendered impossible, yet still at all events it struggles to idealize and to unify." Surely this refers to a conscious activity of making; it suggests an organic product whose form is hardly limited to the forms the primary imagination provides for the making activity to echo, though it is these forms which it rather seeks to dissolve. Which secondary imagination shall we accept? The ambiguity is of a piece with Coleridge's simultaneous attraction to both mimetic and expressive—Aristotelian and Platonic—traditions, reflected in his twin but carefully distinguished definitions of "poem" and "poetry" in Chapter 14 of the *Biographia Literaria*. With Coleridge (as with Aristotle, whom in this he resembles) we must do what we can with profoundly conflicting doctrines, since he does not enlarge elsewhere on this inadequate and opaque introduction to his distinction between primary and secondary imaginations, a distinction that nonetheless has had an overpower-

---

[23] Though one can hardly claim that Coleridge was indebted to Addison's distinctions between Primary and Secondary Pleasures of Imagination, empirically and mimetically bound as these were, it must be noted that the distinction between primary and secondary—in Coleridge as in Addison—is based on the difference between our general perceptual activity and the making activity of producing art.

ing influence on critical theory.[24] Nowhere in critical history have a couple of paragraphs aroused more extensive commentary and debate.

Let us return to the active rather than the passive view of the secondary imagination. It recreates its world, or struggles to unify its object—perhaps much the same thing. The new form that the secondary imagination consciously creates in language is different from the less consciously created forms that it has dissolved. Thus its is a form responsive to language, one that has emerged out of the poet's struggle to write his poem and that is not reducible to the forms he had before he started going to work, though it may have been these forms which prompted him to undertake his labors. This notion of the secondary imagination differs as profoundly from the primary as Coleridge's definition of "poem" (as an organic piece of work done) differs from his definition of "poetry" (as instantaneous vision). This is a matter for our next chapter. But the other notion of the secondary imagination— as mere echo of the primary—is rather appropriate (and, because of Coleridge's ambivalence, appropriate as a conclusion) to this chapter which has recorded perhaps too many varieties among the imitative meanings attributed to poems.

---

[24] The fact that the primary-secondary distinction within imagination occurs nowhere else in Coleridge has been frequently noted. It undoubtedly puts an extremely heavy strain upon the commentator who would—as I do in the next chapter—place weighty theoretical emphasis on the distinction and would extend it and pursue its implications. Yet I do believe such emphasis is warranted— especially in view of the poetry-poem distinction in Chapter 14 of *Biographia Literaria*, which seems in important ways parallel to his two imaginations. For a most helpful source study and an important analysis of the threefold (fancy, primary imagination, secondary imagination) versus the twofold definition (fancy, imagination), see Thomas McFarland, "The Origin and Significance of Coleridge's Theory of Secondary Imagination," in *New Perspectives on Coleridge and Wordsworth*, ed. Geoffrey H. Hartman (New York, 1972), pp. 195–246. He does not deal with the Addison question.

V
Form and the Humanistic Aesthetic

1

Side by side with the imitationist theme that for so many centuries appeared to dominate the Western aesthetic, there has been in literary theory the celebration of form as a human invention. If the (philosophically) realistic spirit of imitationism requires us to see the presiding forms of art as something given from the outside—something that had been there before the work was made—the alternative must be for us to see these forms as emerging out of man's capacity as maker. The central question would seem to ask whether we would predicate order or chaos of the prehuman world—that is, the world before man and his forming capacity come upon it. Is the given world, the world prior to human perception, already formed so that we have but to copy it for our own works to have form? Or does man, using his form-making power—the prime feature of his humanity—impose order upon a chaotic world? Is order, then, natural and innate or human and imposed, the product of art? If it is the latter, how does man's formal impulse lighten the weight of the unformed world?

In the preceding chapter we have seen the two motives emphasized, at times in oddly conflicting ways, even in Aristotle's *Poetics*. He seems to see the poet at times as an imitator of an already formed action, and at times as an imposer of form upon historical episodes that possess no inherent form. By "form" here Aristotle means teleological pattern, in accordance with his doctrine of "final cause." And, whether it is a cosmological or merely aesthetic affair, form will, after Aristotle, retain this teleological character. The question, for Aristotle, is whether history, as the subject (object of imitation?) of poetry, has a purposiveness immanently within it as its principle of organization (in which case poetry need only imitate history) or whether history is mere accident, a casual sequence of incidents that must be reordered into purposiveness by the teleology of the poem. There may be no question

98

about the *telos* that for Aristotle exists in nature, but there are many questions about the extent to which such potentiality of final purpose is realized in the casual intricacies of human enterprise. It is precisely the function of poetry to create a temporal sequence in which potentiality *is* realized, utterly.

With whatever doubleness we have seen Aristotle undertake these questions, it should by now be clear that he is at his best and most useful in his prescriptions about how to construct successful tragic forms. It is these prescriptions[1] that lie at the heart of the *Poetics* and have allowed it to serve as the prototype for theoretical treatises in the West. In the midst of such prescriptions, all of which rest on the assumption of the tragic action as an utterly fabricated formal structure, the more static inheritance from Plato, both philosophic and terminological, keeps Aristotle fastened to more literally mimetic notions while he moves into his dynamic and organic theories. And we have noted that he retains a stubborn, if sporadic, faithfulness to the more reactionary doctrine throughout the treatise.

Let me now, however, simply waive further concern with any doubleness of intent and turn exclusively to the Aristotle who is the father of poetic inventiveness. And, however we finally dispose of his concept of imitation, it is surely when Aristotle identifies poetic power with a created formal unity that the obsession of the Western aesthetic with humanistic form can be said to begin. Once he characterizes the action of tragedy as possessing completeness together with an appropriate magnitude, his commitment to form (and ours after him) is irrevocable. His organic delineating of how he means these terms is impressively lucid and deceptively simple—indeed, is itself inevitable. As he develops it, the mere insistence on unity for him becomes enough. For Aristotle, the tragic poet must convert a chronological line of development into a logical one: he must, that is, convert *post hoc* into *propter hoc*. Thus Aristotle's definition of formal wholeness requires him to set up, in Chapter 7, his own definitions of the beginning, the middle, and the end of an action. And it is logic rather than mere sequence that determines the meanings of these terms. "A beginning is

---

[1] He arrives at these prescriptions through exhaustive analyses of possible alternatives. For example, he tries to decide (in Chapters 10 and 11) between the respective virtues of simple and complex plots as well as the effectiveness of peripety and recognition, singly or in combination. Or in Chapter 13 he tries to determine which is the most effective among the several possible kinds of tragic heroes, men better than, as good as, or worse than ourselves, and among the kinds of action that befall him, fortunate or unfortunate, deserved or undeserved. Or in Chapter 14 he tries to discover the most effective sort of tragic incident, between people related or unrelated, friends or enemies, performed in knowledge or in ignorance.

that which does not itself follow anything *by causal necessity* [my italics], but after which something naturally is or comes to be." If, then, a beginning has logical consequences but no antecedents, a middle has both antecedents and consequences, and an end is the result of all antecedents but has itself no further consequences. Clearly these words have little chronological force as they are employed here: the slice-of-life novel, a chunk of history that intersects the normal chronology of experience at a random place and stops at another one like it further on, can hardly have a beginning, middle, or end in Aristotle's way.

As I have said before, what the Aristotelian poet does is to transform the empirical world's "casual" into art's "causal" (and what new worlds are opened up by the simple transposition of the "su" of "casual" into "causal!"). He marks off what, from history's viewpoint, may seem like a mere line segment, plucks it out of its empirical sequence, away from what comes before and goes after, and turns it into all the time there is or has been or ever can be. In effect, he bends the line segment into a circle, a mutually dependent merger of all beginnings, middles, and ends; and the self-sufficient world of his poem is enclosed by it. We can never be further from mere imitation of history, from the dependence of internal sequence upon external sequence, than Aristotle is here. As Plato was dedicated to destroy the claims of myth-making as obstacles to the search for truth, Aristotle answers by defending, enlarging, and cherishing man's capacity to convert historical truth to myth, to the anthropomorphic categories of inevitability imposed by the power of *poesis*. Can we help but sympathize with Aristotle's attempt, in Chapter 9, to make history coexist with formed legend, seeing history *as* legend or legend *as* history?

Every before-and-after sequence, then, must be transformed into a chain of cause and effect, in which the final effect is indeed dramatically final, so that, as Dr. Johnson puts it, "The end of the play is the end of expectation." If nothing just comes casually, at random, after something else, but is caused by it and is in its turn the cause of something to follow, then everything functions with respect to the ultimate purpose, a purpose that can be discovered to be the total collusion of these several functions. Clearly such a concatenation would require that each portion of a work—episode, character, metaphor (or even word?)—be turned into an indispensable factor contributing to what that work is and does. Aristotle is perfectly explicit about claiming this total indispensability of parts to the whole.[2]

This commitment to the spirit of what later generations would

---

[2] From Chapter 8: ". . . the plot, being an imitation of an action, must imitate one action and that a whole, the structural union of the parts being such that, if any one of them is displaced or removed, the whole will be disjointed and disturbed.

call "organic form" (drawing, as Aristotle did, on the biological meta-phor) follows from Aristotle's attempt to find criteria to govern the proper magnitude for this unified whole. How large should a work be if it is to succeed as a single and complete entity? The answer, large enough but not too large—which, in the case of a poem, means neither too long nor too short—sounds like an obvious and circular evasion, although it is the only answer the structural organicist can provide.[3] Whatever so-called Aristotelians, in the Renaissance and later, may have claimed about a restrictive "unity of time" that Aristotle placed on drama, Aristotle himself must reject any arbitrary "limit of length."[4] He wants as great a length as possible to the optimum point beyond which it is too long to be grasped as a unity by its audience: "The greater the length, the more beautiful will the piece be by reason of its size, provided that the whole be perspicuous." And the limits in each case are to be placed by the need for the unified action to play itself out: "And to define the matter roughly, we may say that the proper magnitude is comprised within such limits, that the sequence of events, according to the law of probability or necessity, will admit of a change from bad fortune to good, or from good fortune to bad."[5]

For a thing whose presence or absence makes no visible difference, is not an organic part of the whole." It should by now hardly be necessary to point out how consonant the use of "imitation" in this passage is to McKeon's reading. There is surely no opposition here between imitating an action and creating a dramatic whole. Aristotle is never further from the spirit of Chapter 4.

[3] It is, however, only just for us to balance Aristotle's emphasis on the autonomous organic structure of each poem (e.g., Chapters 7, 8) with his emphasis on class criteria for tragedy to which each individual representative of the genre must be subordinated (e.g., Chapters 13, 14). This conflict between immanent form and a transcendent, universal form suggests another area of possible inconsistency, one that is reflected in the work of the recent neo-Aristotelian school. But my interest in seeing Aristotle as the source for the conception of man as teleological form maker leads me to play down his generic emphasis for the emphasis on the poem as a unique structure. R. S. Crane, for the most part, makes the same choice.

[4] "The limit of length in relation to dramatic competition and sensuous present-ment, is no part of artistic theory." For he rejects regulation "by the water-clock" (Chapter 7). It is true, however, that Aristotle does acknowledge, in Chapter 5, that "Tragedy endeavors, as far as possible, to confine itself to a single revolution of the sun, or but slightly to exceed this limit; whereas the Epic action has no limits of time." This latter limit of time, of course, has to do with the time represented on stage rather than length of performance. Further, Aristotle seems to refer here to an historical convention more than a theoretical necessity; so he allows that "at first the same freedom was admitted in Tragedy as in Epic poetry." Certainly the organic spirit of Chapters 7 and 8 would militate against any single imposition of a universal length (whether of represented time or of performance time) as having a theoretical sanction.

[5] Let me emphasize here what I have suggested in note 4: although Aristotle is speaking of the length of time that a play takes to perform, his principles of internal regulation can be applied with equal justification to the length of time that a play

The decision about length, then, is one that is wholly subject to the way in which probability and necessity require the action to work itself out. We can never know that in advance; it is a rule that each work sets for itself, as it develops itself in accordance with its internal necessities. The most faithful gloss of this passage which I know of was given to us by that faithful Aristotelian, Ben Jonson, in his *Discoveries:* "And every bound for the nature of the Subject, is esteem'd the best that is largest, till it can increase no more: so it behooves the action . . . to be let grow, till the necessity ask a conclusion."[6] "To be let grow, till the necessity ask a conclusion": we cannot put it better than that. It suggests a biological description of an ideal pregnancy as much as it does a prescription for play construction. This is precisely my point, of course. The poet builds the inevitabilities of form into the materials of his work. That form, as a structure of potentialities and their realizations, of probabilities and their resolutions, represents the way in which the poet reproduces the organic process in nature: by imposing upon otherwise inert materials an ideal entelechy—one that admits of no errant elements—that appears to grow from within. Thus for Aristotle the formal cause, loaded with finality, automatically brings about the realization of tragedy's final cause—the effect the tragedy must produce upon those who subject themselves to that all-productive formal cause. One ultimate purpose (the intrinsic emotional effect of tragedy[7]) lies enfolded within the totally contingent purposefulness of the interrelated moments that constitute the single form, the tragedy itself.

Here, then, in Aristotle we have found—despite uncertainties that tend in other directions—the beginnings of the dedication to form, to the forceful, even austere, imposition of convergent unity upon casually diverse materials as a theoretical first principle. The aesthetic requires the utter rejection of the random, or rather requires the trans-

---

represents as having passed in the course of the action. How much time? As long as is needed to do its special job. And we cannot say a priori or from the outside how long that will be (although we can say after the fact whether it was not long enough or too long).

[6] True also to his neoclassical spirit, Jonson adds, rather inconsistently, the arbitrary proviso "that it exceed not the compass of one day."

[7] It is also in the emotional effect of tragedy, which is its final cause, that Aristotle appears to be responding to Plato's attack. If Plato accuses poetry of arousing unhealthy emotions in the citizens of a rational republic, Aristotle suggests that, in tragedy, the emotions of pity and fear are aroused, but aroused in order—through formal controls—to be purged. So poetry is a form of therapy, which contributes to the health of a citizenry that has emotions (whether or not Plato wants them to have them) and that is more likely to flourish, not when these emotions are suppressed, but when they are brought to the surface and gotten rid of, through the efficacies of form.

formation of the random, the beating of it into causal shape under the supervision of an insistent, if humanly invented, notion of necessity. The total functionalism among the parts, their mutual contingency that establishes their all-inclusive purposiveness, requires that form be seen as the imposition of a human teleology that is a reflection of the teleology latent in nature. This is why, in the language I have used before, the poet may be said to have made, not a collection of imitated objects, but an ultimate object, uniquely *his* object.

As we have seen, the special value of these humanly created forms, these aesthetic objects, lies in the contrast between the total realization of entelechy in them and the aborted realizations of normal experience. These are other words for the contrast between the order of art and the disorder of life. What is required, then, is the assumption of a randomness in existence to which art provides a corrective. Whatever Aristotle feels about the ultimately telic nature of reality, it is clear that he sees our experience as full of incompleteness: this is the particular and casual character of historical sequence which requires the poet to introduce, by way of his necessity and probability, the universal and telic character of poetic sequence.

2

What alternative ways are there of relating the poem to reality so as to account for its order? To repeat the alternatives I suggested earlier, we can either postulate an original orderliness and purposiveness in our external reality, in which case the poem has but to subject itself to that order, so that it achieves its formal nature by imitating an existential *telos* that preexists it; or we can postulate an atelic or even chaotic character to external reality, in which case the poem becomes an original source of a telic order, one that imposes aesthetic categories to clarify what in preaesthetic (or anaesthetic) experience remains inchoate, pointless, confused. In other words, if art has a unified and purposeful structure as its primary attribute, it must attain this structure either by borrowing it from what has already existed (as in the first instance) or by inventing it anew since it has had no existence prior to art's coming into existence (as in the second instance). The first of these alternatives is clearly the mimetic, while the second is consistent with the formalist side of Aristotle that I have stressed in this chapter.

(There is, of course, a third alternative, which denies the assumption that art has a unified and purposeful structure: One can agree that there is no order in existence-prior-to-art for art to imitate, but that art's obligation is still to existence rather than to itself [and to any independent order it might achieve], so that art should nevertheless be imitative and reproduce in itself the random and atelic character of existence. This view, in fostering an antiformal conception of art, in effect becomes an antiaesthetic: it sees that art's duty is to destroy itself by merging with what it conceives to be life's murky meaninglessness. It is to exchange its created word for the given world. It is as if art were to do precisely what Plato originally accused it of doing, except that the world of petty appearances in which it was locked was all the world there was. This doctrine of art's randomness [though I have already asked how one can dedicate himself to the random without losing that random quality at once] represents an utter departure from my conception of the Western aesthetic tradition as humanistic. It is a departure that has recently gained a considerable following in all the arts and in the antitheory that supports them.)[8]

Centuries after Aristotle, the rigidly neoclassical aesthetic represents the first of these alternatives. Unlike Aristotle's, it provides for a poem that is at once totally formal *and* totally imitative. The faithfully neoclassical poem is surely a model of order, though it is to be an order that is thoroughly reflective of a rational cosmic structure. All parts of the poem, all decisions made by the poet among the possible choices within any part, are subservient to an overriding purpose, though this purpose seems dictated by the rigorous demands of an equally purposeful cosmic reality outside. A theoretical statement like Alexander Pope's is an obvious example of this philosophical assurance concerning both poem and world. If we put together the claims about poetry in *An Essay on Criticism* and the claims about cosmos in Epistle I of *An Essay on Man*, we find the thoroughly consistent and comfortable position of the rational poem within the rational universe of life and art that surrounds it. Despite the considerable distance of years between the two poems, the sort of poem (and of criticism) that Pope calls for in 1711 is just the sort that the universe envisioned more than two decades later would both require and justify. Indeed, the earlier statement of poetics would positively require as its primary assumption a universal construct of the dimensions put forth in the later *Essay*. Since the universe itself is conceived as an aesthetic construct, its mutuality with the aesthetic realm is to be expected.

The major insistence that the poet, in pursuit of order, has no choice but subservience to nature's prior order is put forth in the key

---

[8] See, for example, Ihab Hassan's many writings announcing the obsolescence of what he calls "aesthetic modernism," the final inheritor of the formalist tradition, in the face of an energetic post-modern antiart. Or see Antonin Artaud, who carries into the theater a considerably more violent attack on art in the name of the act. My interests in this book, however, preclude me from tracing or analyzing the antiaesthetic alternative to the various theories that begin by assuming the unity of the poem.

couplet early in Part I of *An Essay on Criticism*: "Nature to all things fixed the limits fit, / And wisely curbed proud man's pretending wit" (lines 52–53). Nature must be permitted to set the bounds to man's would-be inventiveness, which, if not "curbed," would—in its pretension—go beyond nature. Perhaps this is what Pope has in mind when, in Part II, he speaks disparagingly of poets who, too dedicated to the false inventiveness of extravagant conceits, create only a "wild heap of wit," which reflects, not nature's order, but "one glaring chaos" (line 292). This "pretending wit," with the "wild heap" that is its product, is clearly distinguished from "true wit," which, as the well-known couplet has it, does no more than dress an already existing natural order to its advantage, giving it an expression that graces it as it has not been graced before (lines 297–98). As Dr. Johnson observed in his *Life of Cowley*, Pope's doctrine of wit is thus limited to "happiness of language." Poetic invention apparently is not to go beyond these new bottles for old wine, so locked is the poet within the domain of an already fully ordered nature, indeed fully and visibly ordered. It is an order which is to serve as an archetype for poetic imitation.[9] And it is a proper archetype, complete, perfect, and unchangeable:

> *First follow nature, and your judgment frame*
> *By her just standard, which is still the same:*
> *Unerring nature, still divinely bright,*
> *One clear, unchanged, and universal light,*
> *Life, force, and beauty, must to all impart,*
> *At once the source, and end, and test of art.*　　　(lines 68–73)

But if nature, in its orderly perfection, is unchanging ("still the

---

[9] Such limitations as are imposed by the conservative Pope should not surprise us, who have already observed even the later, Whig liberalism of Young allowing the poet to range only "as far as visible Nature extends." What Young was to see as the chimeras of fancy resembles the wild heap of conceits of Pope's "pretending wit." Both are false invention, as both try to defy the limits of nature. (Thus the conceitful Metaphysical Poets are often condemned as being fanciful rather than imaginative.) If pretending wit is fancy, then true wit is proper imagination. We have here the descendants of that distrust of the fanciful evasion of the natural world which has been with literary theory since Plato's castigation of "phantastic" poetry, which our tradition has seen echoed (to speak only of theorists discussed in this volume) in Mazzoni and Sidney. It will take Coleridge, in Chapter 14 of *Biographia Literaria*, to overwhelm this opposition by showing that his kind of poetry, coming at human reality from the phantastic world of the supernatural, is as legitimately the product of imagination as is Wordsworth's, which comes at it from our commonplace world of every day. But Coleridge is a revolutionary link in this humanistic aesthetic tradition, seeking only to serve the human capacity to create new forms. For him, fancy seems too slightly rather than too strongly imaginative, utterly subjected to nature rather than striving to break free from her. Yet even Coleridge, with more inconsistency than his period prejudices could have allowed him to recognize, sadly relegates the Metaphysicals to the merely "fanciful" poets.

same"), then what need for poems to change from age to age? Indeed, what presumption if they dared! So there can be—nay, must be— eternal regulations for poetry, regulations that are patterned on what proper theorists discover to be nature's eternal pattern: "Those rules of old discovered, not devised, / Are nature still, but nature methodized." The theorist discovers the rules for his art in nature much as Columbus discovered America, lying there all the time, just waiting to be found. No wonder that Aristotle, as the scientist, becomes the poet's rule maker: poets willingly "received his laws," because it was appropriate (" 'twas fit") that "Who conquered nature, should preside o'er wit" (lines 651–52). The laws, once given, are given for good. All works at once imitate the same nature (being forbidden to pretend to go beyond it) and obey those rules made in response to that nature: these are perhaps two ways of describing what for Pope should be the same activity. Surely, then, these works must end by resembling one another. When Virgil undertakes to imitate nature as his own man, his "true wit" forces him to see nature so keenly that what comes out is both similar to Homer's imitation of nature and consistent with Aristotle's rules about how to imitate nature:

> When first young Maro in his boundless mind
> A work t' outlast immortal Rome designed,
> Perhaps he seemed above the critic's law,
> And but from Nature's fountains scorned to draw:
> But when t' examine every part he came,
> Nature and Homer were, he found, the same.
> Convinced, amazed, he checks the bold design;
> And rules as strict his laboured work confine,
> As if the Stagirite o'erlooked each line.
> Learn hence for ancient rules a just esteem;
> To copy nature is to copy them.   (lines 130–40)

Here, then, is a totally enclosed situation for the poet, hemmed in by a rule-bound similarity of all poems, indeed an identity ("the same") tied to a timeless identity of nature's essence.[10]

---

[10] At the same time we must remark the exceptional liberality of the lines immediately following (141–68), in which "vulgar bounds," necessary for the poet pursuing the "common track," are to be leaped by the Pegasus poet, who "boldly," "with brave disorder" [sic] pursues "a grace beyond the reach of art," one of the "nameless graces which no methods teach." One would think that once such a breach is made in the closed universe, in which all has been discovered once and for all and nothing essential can ever be truly created, that universe can never be resealed. Indeed, it is even being condescended to ("common," "vulgar"). But, like many of his contemporaries, Pope permits this intrusion of a Longinian moment without

It is this unchanging essence, nature's purposeful order ("A mighty maze! but not without a plan"), which Epistle I of *An Essay on Man* expands upon in a similar spirit. As the best of all systems formed by infinite wisdom, the universe reflects necessity and realization of purpose wherever we look, if we but look rightly. Necessity, as the divine plan, converts—by a priori reasoning—every *is* into a *must:* whatever exists has to exist precisely as and where it is. (Thus, ". . . in the scale of reasoning life, 'tis plain, / There must be, somewhere, such a rank as Man" [I, 47–48]; and the argument proceeds to show that he had to be "placed" just where he has been.) The entire chain of existence— from highest to lowest link—has this graded, mutually supportive nature which requires the all to depend upon the each, although the each receives its character only because of its place in the all. That is why it is looked upon as a chain.

> *Vast chain of being! which from God began,*
> *Natures ethereal, human, angel, man.*
> *Beast, bird, fish, insect, what no eye can see,*
> *No glass can reach; from Infinite to thee,*
> *From thee to Nothing.—On superior powers*
> *Were we to press, inferior might on ours;*
> *Or in the full creation leave a void,*
> *Where, one step broken, the great scale's destroyed:*
> *From nature's chain whatever link you strike,*
> *Tenth or ten thousandth, breaks the chain alike.* (I, 237–46)

This description of cosmos requires a mutually supporting relationship between part and whole much like what we saw, earlier in this chapter, to be Aristotle's prescription for a properly teleological aesthetic structure. The claim, in Chapter 8 of the *Poetics*, was that "the structural union of the parts [must be] such that, if any one of them is displaced or removed, the whole will be disjointed and disturbed." But displacing or removing any item in Pope's world similarly disjoints or disturbs the whole. So Pope now is making Aristotle's aesthetic claim, but he is making it, not merely about a work of art, but about the dependence of the entire cosmic chain of being on the existence and proper placement of each link: any change would "leave a void" "in the full creation," "Where, one step broken, the great scale's destroyed." "And," he goes on, "if each system in gradation roll / Alike essential

---

discomfort and lets the inconsistency stand. He suggests the freak-of-nature analogy ("some objects . . . out of nature's common order") while leaving that order or the metaphysics behind it essentially undisturbed.

to th' amazing whole, / The least confusion but in one, not all / That system only, but the whole must fall" (I, 247–50). Here is a disjointing and a disturbance indeed![11]

With such analogous and yet dependent relations between microcosmic and macrocosmic structures, all based on similarly rational principles of necessity and purposiveness, it is clear that the Aristotelian work of art would be seen by Pope as a mini-world properly in imitation of the orderly world around us. The teleology of the one is echo to the teleology of the other. What we have seen Aristotle attribute to the poet's powers of construction—the transformation of the casual into the causal—is attributed by Pope to the divinely architected universe itself, there for the rational philosopher to prove and for the neoclassical poet to imitate in works whose order is discovered in the nature of things rather than invented in response to the nature of mind.

This cosmos, then, is as stripped of the casual as is a carefully built work of art. It is no step at all from here for Pope to proclaim the universe to be just such a work of art, which our erring perceptions—poor readers of the cosmos, all of us—may fail to comprehend in the way an Aristotelian critic should comprehend an Aristotelian tragedy. Yet the world is tailor made just as exclusively for our understandings as the tragedy was for his: indeed, for Pope tailored it that way. Hence his famous concluding lines of Epistle I:

> All Nature is but Art, unknown to thee;
> All Chance, Direction, which thou canst not see;
> All Discord, Harmony not understood;
> All partial Evil, universal Good:
> And, spite of Pride, in erring Reason's spite,
> One truth is clear, whatever is, is RIGHT.

Once nature has become art, every *is* is a *has*-to-be, every casual possibility a causal necessity.

With this conclusion to Epistle I, Pope has brought us full circle with respect to where *An Essay on Criticism* began. It began with his justification of art through appealing to the natural order; so he is now enabled to justify this view of nature by appealing to aesthetic principles —in effect, by treating it as a work of art ("All nature is but art, unknown to thee . . ."). In short, he limits art by referring it to nature and

[11] And with dire consequences felt even within heaven's precincts: "Let earth unbalanced from her orbit fly, / Planets and suns run lawless through the sky; / Let ruling angels from their spheres be hurled, / Being on being wrecked, and world on world; / Heaven's whole foundations to their centre nod, / And nature tremble to the throne of God" (lines 251–55). All these dire consequences from this slightest void caused by the breaching of a single step in the smallest system-within-system.

limits nature by referring it to art; and he can do both because nature is from the start defined in accordance with the aesthetic principle of teleological order. Pope's tightly closed system collapses any distinction between art and nature, but collapses it on art's side—collapsing, that is, nature into art. Nature is the work of the Master Artist, with our mini-works, each of them a microcosmos, responding to the same rules, the same principles of order, of an indwelling and fully realized purposiveness.

3

I have said that Pope would have us read nature's order with the same awareness of immanent principles of order as an Aristotelian would have in reading an Aristotelian tragedy: in both cases the objects of study have been constructed in a way that is exclusively matched to the readers' understandings. The principles of order in the external universe projected by eighteenth-century rationalism turn out to be— happily for man—precisely those of the human mind. And, I suggested, it ought to be that way, since Pope would fashion his cosmos (and it *is* his) no other way. If we look at this cosmos through the skeptical eyes of what was later called "critical philosophy"—through the eyes of a Hume or (as influenced by Hume) a Kant—we see that the form of Pope's universe *is* (whatever Pope's claims or his hopes) a humanistic form after all, just as much as was one of the poetic forms of Aristotle's it so resembles. The form's immanent teleology, which creates necessity as the primary criterion for including any entity within it, is "critically" viewed as an indulgence in dogmatic anthropomorphism. Critical philosophy views this as a self-deceptive practice in which we take a form within which the categories of mind find it comfortable to live— a form that is in con*form*ity with our mental habits—and project it outward upon "objective" reality *as if* it were reality's form and not ours, *as if* it were a feature of nature and not of our mind, so that we are to imitate it (as having been there before us) and not to view it as our creation.

It is just such anthropomorphism that Northrop Frye celebrates when he sees the world of human imagination as "nature given human form." But Frye, heir of Kant, expressly warns about the self-deceptive dangers of what he terms "existential projection," which occurs when we reify the humanized form that we have imposed on nature, and claim for it the metaphysical sanction of an ontological reality. The myth may answer man's desire—indeed his need—to live in a world cut to the dimensions of his mental and verbal measuring instruments; his drive for sanity may force him not only to see the world as a reflection of himself but also to believe in it, to ask himself to reflect that self-reflection as if it were a moral obligation. In all this he is a form-making artist, even such a one as Aristotle called for, though he is anthropomorphic in measuring the world to himself and dogmatic in insisting, with metaphysical solemnity, upon its independent and indifferently existing structure outside himself, outside us all.

There is a sense in which, as I have argued elsewhere,[12] Pope himself may have viewed his cosmos as a structure created by man's aesthetic and formative capacity. Indeed, I have suggested that "The Rape of the Lock," as his symbolic tribute to man's creative power, dissolves the objectively grounded universe into the airy world of art. This view implies the existence of a real and resistant world outside that world of artifact or artifice, a threatening chaos that rational man—in defense of his sanity—must escape by imposing upon it his own invention, which he then comes to worship as if it existed solely outside him. The struggle between that chaos and the art that would—through metonymy—tame it out of existence is pessimistically, indeed apocalyptically, traced in *The Dunciad*. The relation of eighteenth-century man to his universe—whether it is seen as a cosmos grounded in God's reason or as the rationalist's intellectual construct—is a complex one in which allegiance is mingled with human doubts, the drive to abstract order undercut by the awareness of immediate disorders. But, for the dedicated rationalist, the greater the existential challenge, the more securely complete is his answering structure. He may claim, as Pope does in *An Essay on Man*, that man overvalues himself and should subject himself to external and ontological form; but his very project is the most persuasive testimony of the impulse to form within himself, an impulse so overwhelming that he has accommodated his entire sense of reality to it.

When we view the mighty dogmatic structure of eighteenth-century rationalism this way, as an "existential projection" of a common human metaphor, we may not find it so profoundly out of accord with Humean and Kantian denials after all. The dogmatic nature of this structure may be shown to be an illusory anthropomorphism by the probings of "critical philosophy," but the formal needs of human reason are only being reaffirmed by them. The critical philosopher may take the structure of our reality (that is, the reality we require in order to operate successfully in the world) away from a world of things-in-themselves and put it into the formative categories of the human mind as that mind seeks to impose itself on the phenomenal, history-ridden

---

[12] See "The 'Frail China Jar' and the Rude Hand of Chaos," in *The Play and Place of Criticism* (Baltimore, 1967), pp. 53–68, and "The Cosmetic Cosmos of 'The Rape of the Lock,' " in *The Classic Vision* (Baltimore, 1971), pp. 105–24.

world that surrounds and would confound it; but, ontological questions aside, these constructs appear to dominate our visions, as we relate ourselves to our world, no less pervasively after Hume than before him. The presiding structure by means of which we shape our responses to our experience may be predicated of reality as something existing independently out there and exerting an objective claim upon us, *or* it may be seen as a projection out of the subject of knowledge: it may be the ground for an ontological concern or the product of a merely epistemological concern. Even after the eighteenth century exchanges ontology for epistemology, however, the formal and formative constructs continue to dominate our sense of the world in which we conduct our business.

As a consequence of the bifurcation between subjective and objective realities, for which Descartes is usually given the credit or the blame in the history of Western thought, the Enlightenment world had come to live with its scientific need to work with the assumption of objective and universal truths. And, free (as we had vainly hoped) from subjective intrusions, man was to use his reason to uncover those objective laws that grounded the motley world of our experience. By the later eighteenth century, however, we were forced to confront the possibility that the world of which our reason was to be a mirror was rather the willful creation of our presumptuous (that is, both dogmatic and anthropomorphic) imagination. What had been seen as the pressure of a structured world upon our mental structures, a pressure from the outside to our inwardness, was now seen rather as a pressure from our mental structures to the unformed world, from our inwardness to what lies outside us. In giving the law to nature, we discovered that the forms within which we found nature to behave were *our* forms, not nature's. What we had thought of as the structural ground of an out-there reality was now seen as our metaphor, the mere word that we had mistaken for flesh.

But Hume and, after him, Kant did not deny the eighteenth-century rational construct so much as they denied its objective ground in external reality. At the phenomenological level we respond to the same forms whether we create them or they exist independently of us. So the critical philosophers can account for and undercut the teleological claims of eighteenth-century dogmatism without undoing its formal character. For, like Aristotle, they put the responsibility for this formal character in the form-making capacity of man. Through them we have come to understand the drive of the eighteenth-century rationalist to match his objective world to his subjective needs, that is, to trim the world to dimensions within which he can live comfortably and securely.

It becomes a world ordered in a way he finds recognizable. A world made so like himself cannot be "other," so that he need feel no alienation when confronted by it.

As that world loses its grounding in his eyes and the noumena (if there still can be such things) become unknowable, the subject of knowledge, now shut off from the underpinnings of the objects about him, must come to feel their mysterious otherness and his alienation from them. This is precisely the desperation that Goethe's Faust feels as he tries in vain to crack nature's secret immanent principles, from which even he has been cut off. As he fails to gain admittance to them, to feel any fellowship with them, he tries to duplicate and exceed nature's powers by cultivating the human resources for subjective assertion, for fashioning the world in accordance with his own formative dream. It is the ultimate humanistic dream made fact when, at the end of his monumental strivings, Faust founds a nascent utopia by wresting it from nature's hidden purposes and subjecting it to his own creative intentions. Humanity's moral and social ends have triumphed over a natural order that, in its indifference to man and his purposes, has shut him out: man creates his own future history as one responsive to his ingeniously invented teleology. There is, then, in the shadow of the death of eighteenth-century dogmatism, a radical break between natural and human teleologies. Thanks to the subjective role of human will, in Goethe and Schiller as in Kant, the line seems absolute that divides nature's as the realm of the determinate from man's as the realm of freedom.[13]

Thus man, exploiting his self-conscious freedom, reads his purposiveness into nature, but only for art's sake, creating an object that displays—in Kant's terms—a finality within its form. Kant's is an internal purposiveness, reminiscent of the teleology that operates in an Aristotelian poem, as it occurs in accord with no purpose imposed from outside the work. It is a retreat from the cosmic to the merely aesthetic: no longer able to ascertain a teleology operating within the external world, Kantian man—though as a cognitive creature he must beware of teleology—puts that teleology into his man-made object as a demon-

---

[13] It need hardly be pointed out that this opposition not only is parallel to, but is a general philosophic extension of the opposition between the definitions of the poet's task as imitative and as originally creative. Once the eighteenth-century theorist, in the wake of the collapse of his rational universe, recognizes that we are confronted (so far as we can *know*) by an alien chaos out there, he can hang onto his old mimetic principle only by allowing the poet to imitate the chaos in a formless object. To do so would be to forgo the entire tradition since Aristotle. If there is no form to appeal to but the forms of the human mind, then the theorist can only claim form for the poem by creating a faculty like Coleridge's imagination to put the world together and to replace mimetic with expressionist theory.

stration of his freedom, of his capacity to rise above nature and history in that he can instill a supreme purposiveness within his creations. Still, he will not presume to relate the teleology in the work to any specific or immediate purpose outside the work: hence Kant's finality without final purpose, or purposeless purposiveness, a willful suspension of the will. Man's rigorous delimited aesthetic substitute for his cognitive and practical incapacities produces this new justification of Aristotelian formalism. The facts of man's irrevocable past are there to enslave, but the forms his creative present gives him to live with liberate existence by humanizing it.

It is, by Schiller's own acknowledgment, these notions in Kant that lead to his own concept of the "form-instinct," which leads, in turn, to the "play-instinct" that Schiller sees as inherent in man. Already in Kant we have seen the instinct for form spring from man's need to deal disinterestedly with the world around him, to wrest from it objects that his artistry forces to take on an inevitability, an ultimate purposiveness. It is this ultimate purposiveness that the earlier eighteenth century may have predicated of their universe, but it could now (in Kant) be safely predicated only of the perceptible aspects of man-made objects. Such disinterested dealing with the world becomes "play" for Schiller. It is what saves humanity from savagery, which is defined as the passive submission of man to the forces of nature that exist without reference to him. These would subdue him into passivity by denying his capacity for human freedom. His human response takes no higher form than his aesthetic creations, which, as the product of his instincts for form and for play, are his emblems of that capacity for freedom, expressing himself as an independent authority, separate from nature as a source of value. We are, clearly, on the way to Nietzsche and his worship of man's potential Apollonian grace as a necessary usurpation of what had been the power of the gods.

It is all part of the humanistic dream we have observed realized at the last by Goethe's Faust, when he imposes the form of that dream upon a resistant piece of nature. The form is social and utopist, as it is aesthetic, reshaping what it has wrested from nature's way, and reshaping it in accordance with human need, as defined by human vision. This ultimately humanistic conception, the philosophical and literary equivalent of Beethoven's musical heroism, converts the human into the all-creating man-god whose imprint everywhere transforms the resistant world about him. A century and a half later, in another *Faust* by Thomas Mann, this willful harmonizing of the alien world is shown to issue into the politically inhuman horrors that reveal the falseness of its promise. But the earlier tribute to man's forming powers still leaves open an aesthetic means for man as a subject to recreate the object by infusing it with his life. The tradition being traced and extended in this study, a tradition that celebrates the generative powers of humanizing form, may have proved deceptive as a measure of man's power to create the social forms that tame nature and the nature in himself. But it remains a just measure of man's highest creative accomplishments, those moments, projected and fixed in his objects, in which he most fully realizes what human self-consciousness—in opposition to the inertness out there—can attain. It characterizes, aesthetically if not morally, his power to create order and, through his ordering, to create self-sufficient objects, if only microcosmic ones.

4

The Coleridgean I AM would seem to represent the ultimate claim for man's self-consciousness and its powers.[14] Indeed, Coleridge defines it as synonymous with "spirit, self, and self-consciousness." In this transcendental psychology, the faculty of imagination, which is sponsored by the I AM, is distinguished by what Coleridge calls, in his strange coinage, its "esemplastic" power, the power "to shape into one,"[15] or, in other words, its capacity to impose an all-unifying form upon our fragmentary experiences in the alien world. So what is emphasized is self-consciousness, self-consciousness that creates new forms. These conceptions (of the I AM and the special notion of imagination that it allows) may be seen as the high point of the development I have been tracing, the growing differentiation of human consciousness and the forms it creates (in response to itself) from all that it finds outside itself, which, as objects, are *un*responsive to its orders.

From the violent break between subject and object in the *Cogito ergo sum* of Descartes, the separation had proceeded to its logical extreme in Kant, who was one of the dominant voices heard in Coleridge. But Coleridge, under the influence also of the Kantian revisionists Schelling and Fichte, had to attribute divine transformational powers to man's forming capacities. No object could withstand the all-absorb-

---

[14] Throughout this discussion I attribute to Coleridge what might more properly be claimed for Schelling and, in places, to A. W. Schlegel. But it is, I believe, more profitably pursued in Coleridge because of the unique way he turns these notions to critical use by combining them with other aspects of his theory, whether original or also borrowed (if not, as many would with justification argue, stolen) from other sources. Norman Fruman (*Coleridge, The Damaged Archangel*) to the contrary notwithstanding, Coleridge extends his probings into the imagination (or imaginations) to important critical and theoretical distinctions and syntheses left undetected by those who detect plagiarism, mainly because they find his theoretical claims uncongenial, to the extent that they are able to follow them.

[15] See the opening lines of Chapter 10 of his *Biographia Literaria*.

ing subjectivity of a metaphysically ordained egoism. Coleridge recognized, then, that he required a monmumental change from the dualistic assumptions of the Cartesian notion of subjectivity: with Coleridge the first principle is reduced from the *cogito* (from which the Cartesian *sum* was derived) to the *sum* itself, as an irreducible affirmation.[16] While Descartes' self-conscious thinking divided the subject from the object of thought, assuring that the object would "as an object" be "fixed and dead," Coleridge sees the primal *sum* as an act, the act that affirms the aboriginal identity between subject and object.[17] In the I AM,

> *and in this alone, object and subject, being and knowing, are identical, each involving and supposing the other. In other words, it is a subject which becomes a subject by the act of constructing itself objectively to itself; but which never is an object except for itself, and only so far as by the very same act it becomes a subject (Thesis VI, Chapter 12).*

Though an object, then, if an object only for itself, the I AM thereby affirms itself as an absolute subject: "It has been shown, that a spirit [synonym for the I AM] is that, which is its own object, yet not originally an object, but an absolute subject for which all, itself included, may become an object" (Thesis VII).

This is indeed an "act," the act of reconstituting the world of objects through the infusion of the spirit of the I AM. This is also the spirit of absolute idealism in the form it is given by Schelling. It inspirits the objective universe with the ego raised to cosmic power, until that universe is objective no longer. This act of absolute self-consciousness raises to new heights the human power to make forms; for it is also the act of Genesis performed anew each time by the man-god. Without this power to engender life by his fiat, he is, like the becalmed Ancient

---

[16] See Thesis VI, Chapter 12, *Biographia Literaria*: ". . . the ground of existence, and the ground of the knowledge of existence, are absolutely identical, *Sum quia sum*; I am, because I affirm myself to be; I affirm myself to be, because I am." His quarrel with Descartes's *Cogito ergo sum* appears in a footnote to this passage. The embarrassingly close indebtedness of all these theses to German transcendental idealism, particularly to Schelling, has been well established, indeed was well established, especially among German and comparative scholars, long before Fruman's work.

[17] In my final chapter, through my treatment of Paul de Man, we shall observe the persistence of Cartesian dualism as a Romantic alternative to this Coleridgean monism. Wordsworth himself is seen as an example of the Romantic who accepts the separateness of the subject from its object, with no appeal to the all-absorbing I AM. Wordsworth's resistance, as a lingering British empiricist, to the German organicism in Coleridge stems from this difference in their confidence in the subject's power to overcome his alienation.

Mariner, reduced to a dead man presiding over a deadened world, a world marked by his failure to infuse it with the vitality bred by his own creative self-consciousness. This failure, at once cosmic and personal, produces the state of "Dejection." Coleridge's ode to that state is his negative tribute to the I-AM-izing faculty, the "shaping spirit of Imagination."

But we observed toward the conclusion of the previous chapter that, for Coleridge as literary theorist, the power of the imagination might be centered either in the epistemological visionary power or in the more mundane power of making poems. It is as if he is matching his Neoplatonic side with his more businesslike Aristotelian side. It depends, I suggested, on whether the seat of the poet's creative power is in the primary or the secondary imagination, whether (to put it another way) the secondary "dissolves, diffuses, dissipates" the materials created by the primary "in order to recreate" them, or whether the secondary is a mere "echo" of the primary[18] that translates its materials in accordance with "the conscious will." Coleridge never does choose definitively between these possibilities—or, rather, chooses them alternately at one or another point in his theorizing—so that subsequent theorists can make the most of the side of him they prefer. I maintained also, in my preceding chapter, that his overlapping but distinct definitions of the two entities, "poem" and "poetry," in the chapter that follows his twin definitions of imagination, reflect this two-sidedness.[19]

If I tried to emphasize, in that discussion, the Coleridge of primary vision, for whom the making of the poem itself seemed to be an imitation (or "echo") of what was formed in the mind before that poem came to be made, my emphasis here must fall on the formative power of that making itself. It is this second Coleridge in whom contextualist theorists have found an original source for their development of the formal tradition, while the first Coleridge is consonant with the interests of recent visionary and "consciousness" criticism. So this second Cole-

---

[18] "Identical with the primary" in "kind" and "differing only in degree, and in the *mode* of its operation." The conflict in Coleridge's theory between seeing and making, between the idealist philosopher and the poet-aesthetician, foreshadows the similar conflict in that most extreme idealist, Croce, between "intuition" and "externalization," with his mysterious middle term "expression." The question of dominance between primary and secondary imaginations in creating the poem is much the same for the two theorists. See my discussion of this conflict in Croce in Chapter 3, above.

[19] It is surprising, in view of Coleridge's explicit intention to distinguish "poem" from "poetry" in Chapter 14 of *Biographia Literaria*, how many commentators have failed to mark this distinction and have made unjust charges of confusion or inconsistency based on their failure to see these as two entities, each term being used by Coleridge with care and discrimination.

ridge (second also in being the Coleridge of the secondary imagination) makes a unique contribution to modern poetic theory, while the first (the Coleridge of the primary) is just one of the many voices raised to celebrate man's general epistemological creativity. It is, then, worth probing the second to uncover the Coleridge whose special value raises him beyond those of his contemporaries whose ideas (or even wording) he has been charged with pirating.

Coleridge takes great theoretical pains with his definition of "poem." It is a three-part, dialectical definition. That is, he begins with one superficial definition, and then a second one, both of which he appears to reject, except that they return, profoundly reinforced and justified, as part of the final definition. His first differentia is the artificial arrangement of meter and/or rhyme, which is a purely mechanical matter, introduced, a priori, from the outside and thus troublesome to the organicist unless it can be justified from within. The second differentia is the immediate objective (Aristotle's final cause) of pleasure rather than truth, although he must acknowledge that nonmetrical work can also be addressed to this end. What, then, if one added meter, or meter and rhyme, to a nonmetrical work that had pleasure as its immediate end? Can *it* then be called by the honorific name of "poem"?

> The answer is, that nothing can permanently please, which does not contain in itself [my emphasis] the reason why it is so, and not otherwise. If metre be superadded, all other parts must be made consonant with it. They must be such, as to justify the perpetual and distinct attention to each part, which an exact correspondent recurrence of accent and sound are calculated to excite.

In his final definition, then, the poem is marked by the immediate end of pleasure and, it is implied, by special phonetic arrangements as well, provided it proposes "to itself such delight from the *whole*, as is compatible with a distinct gratification from each component *part*." The "all" is in the "each" as much as the "each" is in the "all." So the first two superficial differentiae are retained but put to the service of the organic principle, which deepens them by making them internally justified, indeed "necessary," in the sense Aristotle has made familiar to us.

The organicism, which is to convert the "casual" into the "causal," which makes the work earn internally all that is externally adventitious to it, is very much in the spirit of Aristotle. But there is a crucial difference. Aristotle argued for organic form, but everything he said about the imposition of human structures that convert the apparent materials of history into poetic necessity refers to creations of plot rather than to creations in language. Indeed, so much does the plot come first for

Aristotle (as "the first principle" and "the soul of a tragedy"—Chapter 6) that it appears to have a disembodied form (almost Platonic?), prior to and independent of words. In its essential nature, then, a plot should be freely translatable. In Chapter 6 Aristotle makes it clear that all matters of diction are subsidiary, as the material cause is subsidiary to the formal cause. His discussion of diction, style, and even metaphor in Chapters 19 through 22 consistently aims at the objectives of lucidity and appropriateness, on the assumption that there is an already existent something that is to be expressed lucidly in words, a something to which diction and all verbal devices are to be made appropriate. It should not, then, be surprising that the discussion, in Chapter 14, of the proper source of the tragic effect should place it solely in the plot, which "ought to be so constructed that, even without the aid of the eye, he who hears the tale told will thrill with horror and melt to pity at what takes place. This is the impression we should receive from hearing the story of the Oedipus."[20] The plot synopsis, as the "soul," must be enough to do the job, though the fleshing out in the minor elements of diction, melody, and spectacle is surely an aid to our response and an intensification of it. It is no wonder that Aristotle can make the shift from drama to narrative in Chapter 23 without theoretical difficulty or any major adjustment. The essence of the tragedy subsists, as an architectural blueprint, before a word of its speeches has been written. The major decisions that will produce the tragic effect have been made with respect to the action alone, whose structure determines all the decisions about diction but which can itself in no way be altered by such material details.

The organicism of Aristotle, then, extends to plot alone; it does not characterize the relations between plot and diction, since the dictation flows in only one direction so that no mutual transformation is theoretically possible. We can, indeed, charge that Aristotle's conception of the role of diction, forcing it to be subservient to the preordained plot, is an unhappily mechanistic one. Coleridge might well have made just this charge. We have seen that, like Aristotle, he conceives of a wholly functional, give-and-take relationship between part and whole. But the parts, for Aristotle, are the incidents as they create the architectural whole that is the plot; for Coleridge the part must be the minimal element in the final poem *as* written—the word or combination of words.

---

[20] It must be granted that Aristotle, at this point, is arguing against the role of spectacle, a superficial role as he sees it, in making a primary contribution to the tragic effect. But his argument here leaves little doubt that the role of diction is similarly secondary.

By including the phonetic character of the word at the start of his definition of the poem, as at its end, Coleridge forces the totality of the work to depend on the actual configuration of words as it finally emerges out of the poet's struggle with them. Whatever the poet at first mechanically imposes—even for the most superficial of reasons, like the desire to create an "artificial arrangement" of sound, meter, and rhyme—he must end by earning, by creating the illusion of its internal necessity. Whatever form, then, is given from the outside must, through transformations within the poem, seem to be growing inevitably from within.[21] The creation of an apparently indwelling form indeed sounds Aristotelian, except that, as we have seen, Coleridge is primarily concerned with transforming our usual prosaic language into a language that is made to deserve the special care that metrical language has had bestowed upon it.

Very likely he felt compelled to provide this theoretical basis for his answer to Wordsworth's claim that "between the language of prose and that of metrical composition there neither is, nor can be, any essential difference." Coleridge answers that, whatever the language starts out to be—with the words taken, as they should be, from our everyday speech—there must be something different about it once it has been made into the language of the poem, as he defines "poem." For, we recall his general dictum, "nothing can permanently please, which does not contain in itself the reason why it is so, and not otherwise." And he finds this nowhere truer than when we give to words the special claim upon our attention that occurs when they are given phonetic and metaphorical prominence.[22]

Coleridge's definition of "poem," then, makes it coextensive with the wholeness of the object, composed of its self-justified parts (parts here meaning words as well as Aristotle's larger structural units). He

---

[21] This distinction between "mechanical regularity" and "organic form" is explicitly developed by Coleridge, though in close imitation of August Wilhelm Schlegel, in that part of his lecture on "Shakespeare, a Poet Generally," in which he claims "Shakespeare's Judgment equal to his Genius." It is, he maintains, wrong to say, as the eighteenth century did, that Shakespeare is saved by his genius from his formal errors in poetic judgment; for it is only a mechanical notion of form that would condemn the internally justified forms he has created.

[22] Thus he puts his counterargument to Wordsworth's in Chapter 18: "Metre in itself is simply a stimulant of attention, and therefore excites the question: Why is the attention to be thus stimulated? Now the question cannot be answered by the pleasure of the metre itself: for this we have shown to be *conditional* . . . I write in metre, because I am about to use a language different from that of prose." He is speaking here, not of a "poetic diction," "a class of words in the English, in any degree resembling the poetic dialect of the Greek and Italian," but of words that the poet has transformed into a different language to merit the badge of meter.

must, then, leave room for a second definition, "poetry," which appears to refer to that pure burst of primary imagination, which occurs where it will, irrespective of the compositional requirements that govern the wholeness of made objects. It is as if he must balance the Aristotelian emphasis on making wholes with the momentary breakthroughs of the Longinian sublime that have marked the Romantic theoretical tradition that Coleridge carried forward.

(Were I tracing sources for their own sakes, rather than for their use in advancing my argument, I would dwell at length on Longinus. What I have referred to as the conflict in Coleridge between Neoplatonic and Aristotelian strains may also be seen as the conflict between the Longinus and the Aristotle in him—between, that is, the interest in the living isolated passage in a work ["poetry"] introduced into the critical tradition by Longinus and Aristotle's interest in the work as a living whole ["poem"]. Longinus's exclusive concern for the sublime passage, echo of the "great soul" whose imagination created it, has long been credited with responsibility for the line of critics that leads to the invention of "poetry" as an entity distinguishable from the "poem." I should mention here, however, that the shadow of Longinus may be seen casting itself on Coleridgean organicism as well. One cannot read Chapter 10 of *On the Sublime* without being struck with Longinus's anticipations of the organic-contextualist tradition: his tribute to "the systematic selection of the most important elements and the power of forming by their mutual combination, what may be called one body," or his attributing to Sappho the power of "uniting contradictions" to produce "a concourse of the passions," or his attributing to the successful poetic phrase the power to "force into union" elements not usually found together, to "torture" words into the unique expression that the passage requires but that language normally resists.[23] But we must not overstate the influence: we must remember that even here Longinus is speaking only of passages and not of entire works. Still, we do see the advance elements here of Coleridge's attitude toward imaginative rather than merely fanciful metaphor—for example, in the lecture on Shakespeare with examples from *Venus and Adonis*—and of the inherited attitudes toward metaphor of his twentieth-century followers after I. A. Richards.)

[23] The organic implications of this chapter are reinforced by the distinction Longinus draws in the chapters that follow (11 and 12) between the sublime and "amplification," the rhetorical pseudo-sublime that he rejects. In characterizing amplification quantitatively, by its "abundance," he distinguishes it from the true sublime as the mere "aggregation" of details differs from a true union. This is just the distinction Coleridge urges, in his running argument with Wordsworth, between fancy and imagination.

The definitions of "poem" and "poetry" in Coleridge are neither mutually exclusive nor complementary, though they are possibly overlapping: one refers to work done, an object made, and the other to the direct reflection of a faculty, unmediated by aesthetic or rhetorical requirements. "Poetry," then, may appear outside "poems," and what makes a "poem" worthy of its name does not derive from its "poetry." Coleridge explicitly declares that "poetry of the highest kind may exist without metre, and even without the contra-distinguishing objects of a poem." So poetry frequently appears in nonpoems: Plato, many portions of the Book of Isaiah, and Bishop Taylor are presented as writers of poetry who put that poetry in works that are not poems, as Coleridge defines poems. For the criteria that permit us to characterize a passage as poetry have nothing in common with the criterion of organic self-fulfillment that permits us to characterize an entire object as a poem. It follows also, then, "that a poem of any length neither can be, or ought to be, all poetry." While a poem is an obvious receptacle for passages of poetry, it will usually have long passages of nonpoetry as well. If poetry is seen as the direct reflection of imagination, the rest of the poem must be seen as the reflection of the poet's inferior faculties.[24]

The poem, then, would appear to be a largely routine sequence of moments of nonpoetry interrupted by high points of poetry or, at most, a sequence of high poetic moments held together in a nonpoetic glue. We must wonder whether we are reading for the pleasures of the total work or for those sublime breakthroughs. Are we to choose between such Aristotelian and Longinian pleasures? No, for Coleridge's organic principle, by which he defines poems, will hardly permit a poem to be a mere collage of the reflections of primary imagination (the poetry) and the reflections of other faculties. The totality of the poem is still the poet's primary responsibility: "If an harmonious whole is to be produced, the remaining parts must be preserved in keeping with the poetry." But how? This harmonious adjustment can be produced only "by such a studied selection and artificial arrangement, as will partake

[24] Though he does not carry forward his single attempt at a distinction between primary and secondary imaginations (see note 24 to Chapter 4), Coleridge's sense of poetry as the direct reflection of the poet's imagination would seem to limit it to the expression of primary imagination, that is, would see it as occurring prior to the poet's willful operation as maker: it results more from transcendental psychology than it does from the poet's struggle with his growing object. "My own conclusions on the nature of poetry, in the strictest use of the word, have been in part anticipated in the preceding disquisition on the fancy and imagination. What is poetry? is so nearly the same question with, what is a poet? that the answer to the one is involved in the solution of the other. For it is a distinction resulting from the poetic genius itself, which sustains and modifies the images, thoughts, and emotions of the poet's own mind."

of *one*, though not a *peculiar* property of poetry [or does he perhaps mean "poem" here, in accordance with the first of his earlier three-part definition?]. And this, I repeat again, can be no other than the property of exciting a more continuous and equal attention than the language of prose aims at, whether colloquial or written." The non-poetry, lacking the primal magic itself, must be given the trappings of poetry in order to persuade the reader that it too belongs in the poem, along with the poetry. Lacking the poetry itself, it must take on the superficial resemblance to it, so that it may coexist in harmony with it. The trappings we are routinely prepared for are those provided in Coleridge's earlier definition of "poem," the kinds of "artificial arrangement" aimed at calling more attention to the language than we find in prose.[25]

So the poem would seem to be composed of patches of pure poetry (reflections of imagination in language that calls attention to itself because they deserve and require such a language) on a background of pseudo-poetry (reflections of other faculties that are made to resemble poetry in their superficial verbal arrangements). But we must contradict Coleridge with Coleridge: his organic principle, which controlled his definition of the poem, cannot permit any pseudo-poetry to remain poetry in appearance only. We need only invoke his dictum, which we observed earlier, "that nothing can permanently please, which does not contain in itself the reason why it is so, and not otherwise. If metre be superadded, all other parts must be made consonant with it." So if the poem maker forms and combines words that force us to view them as resonant objects in themselves as well as mere tools of communication, what those words are doing "must be such, as to justify the perpetual and distinct attention to each part, which an exact correspondent recurrence of accent and sound are calculated to excite." Thus the non-poetry in the poem, having taken on a superficial "property of poetry," must—if it is part of a proper poem—transform itself into that which justifies the form it has been given. In short, it must transform itself into poetry. The harmonizing activity of the poem maker, with such a conversion of the nonpoetry, would force the poem to become *all* poetry. No wonder we have been witnessing a blurring of the line between poem and poetry: the organic principle has converted Coleridge's labored distinction into an identity.

The agent of this conversion is, of course, the imagination, though

[25] I repeat that, in that earlier definition, Coleridge claimed this to be "*one*, though not a *peculiar* property" of the "poem" rather than of "poetry," since the latter need not have meter or any of "the contra-distinguishing objects of a poem." The firmness of his poem-poetry distinction clearly weakens here, as it becomes advantageous for him to blur it by allowing "poetry" to become specially arranged language that deserves, indeed requires, this special arrangement.

in this case probably the secondary. The imagination, then, has two functions, and the poet is a poet by virtue of either or, preferably, both. I have suggested earlier that the imagination—probably the primary— is directly in charge of the production of poetry, the sublime expression of vision that has no regard for the making of objects. Poetry, thus characterized, "is a distinction resulting from the poetic genius itself [shades of Blake], which sustains and modifies the images, thoughts, and emotions of the poet's own mind." The poet is most obviously and immediately a poet by virtue of his indulging this power ("What is poetry? is so nearly the same question with, what is a poet? that the answer to the one is involved in the solution of the other"). But imagination, this time the secondary, has another responsibility: it provides the harmonizing principle that produces the all-and-each interrelations that make a poem worthy of the name. Whatever is "superadded" it must transform so that it may be subsumed. The poet, as maker of the poem and not just of its poetry, must relate the imagination to the other faculties as well as to the products of its own immediate operation: he

> brings the whole soul of man into activity, with the subordination of its faculties to each other, according to their relative worth and dignity. He diffuses a tone and spirit of unity, that blends, and (as it were) fuses, each into each, by that synthetic and magical power, to which I would exclusively appropriate the name of imagination.

This poet is the poem maker who uses the secondary imagination to rule over even the poetry created out of the primary imagination by absorbing it within the poem's harmony of faculties and their products—all of the latter, of course, remade into the poem's (the secondary imagination's) equivalent of poetry. "Finally, Good Sense is the Body of poetic genius, Fancy its Drapery, Motion its Life, and Imagination the Soul that is everywhere, and in each; and forms all into one graceful and intelligent whole."

The secondary imagination, we must remember from its initial definition, coexists with the "conscious will." In the passage in Chapter 14 from which I have been quoting, we are told that the imagination— in its all-subordinating, all-harmonizing function within the poem— is "first put in action by the will and understanding, and retained under their irremissive, though gentle and unnoticed, control . . ." Under this control it can manage the restless surges of passion that are the products of the poet's instinct. Thus, in the famous passage dealing with the "balance or reconciliation of opposite or discordant qualities," the imagination is shown to be lord over the contraries of passion and will, blending "a more than usual state of emotion, with more than usual order; judgment ever awake and steady self-possession, with enthusiasm and feeling profound or vehement . . ."

For Coleridge this harmonious interaction between passion and will is central to the way in which the secondary imagination can convert poetry (together with what was originally nonpoetry) into the unique organic forms that are poems. In Chapters 17 and 18 he returns to do explicit battle with Wordsworth on the role of meter in the contrast between the language of prose and the language of poems. We have seen that, while Wordsworth sees poems as prose with the superaddition of meter (that apparently changes nothing else), Coleridge requires that whatever has meter superadded to it must be transformed to earn that superaddition. Whatever the poetry may be for Coleridge, there is no question that the imposition of meter upon the poem is a conscious act by the poet who knows what he intends to be doing. Thus, Coleridge tells us, meter originates from "the balance in the mind effected by that spontaneous effort which strives to hold in check the workings of passion." It comes about "by a supervening act of the will and judgment, consciously and for the foreseen purpose of pleasure."

The decision to use meter, then, is an imposition by the will upon the materials of passion. The fact that meter is required (or deserved) should tell us at once that the materials to which it is being applied are of sufficiently passionate a nature to need this restraint.[26] But, once the language exists within the restraints of meter, the orderly controls of the will (however "gentle and unnoticed," though also "irremissive") must share the stage with passion:

> . . . as these elements are formed into metre artificially, by a voluntary act, with the design and for the purposes of blending delight with emotion, so the traces of present volition should throughout the metrical language be proportionately discernible. Now these two conditions must be reconciled and co-present. There must be not only a partnership, but a union; an interpenetration of passion and of will, of spontaneous impulse and of voluntary purpose.

This union of will and passion spreads beyond meter to justify other impositions by the will as well. Thus the poet will also use, in a poem far more than in prose, "a frequency of forms and figures

---

[26] ". . . as the elements of metre owe their existence to a state of increased excitement, so the metre itself should be accompanied by the natural language of excitement." In this discussion Coleridge seeks to carry out his earlier claim (in Chapter 14) that the poem must "contain in itself the reason why" meter should be imposed upon it.

of speech" for the same double purpose: at once to point up the emotional power in the materials being imposed upon and to hold those materials in some check by this demonstration of the power of the will to produce order and even artifice, even as it converts both for the sake of pleasure, "that pleasure, which such emotion, so tempered and mastered by the will, is found capable of communicating."[27] With these figures, as with the meter, the imagination must operate to harmonize the products of passion with the products of will. Coleridge puts it magnificently when he refers to the figures, as they exist in the completed poem, as "originally the offspring of passion, but now the adopted children of power." The metaphor may be the natural child of passion, in that the impulse to metaphor springs from the extraordinarily emotional motive for writing this poem; but, once taken up by the poet's voluntary purposiveness, it can, with the intercession of imagination, become an adopted child of its unifying power. Though it also retains its original paternity, it is not an alien foster child, nor is it regarded as a changeling. For the spirit of these pages in Coleridge assures us that it must be not only adopted, but thoroughly domesticated. Not only has the will provided it a home in the poem, but the imagination, whose poem it finally is, has allowed it to be at home in the poem and to find there the source of its "power," which raises it beyond "passion." For the poem has been adapted as much as it has been adopted. This is as true of the meter as it is of the figures, or of any of these superficial evidences of the poet's self-conscious will. All that begins as artificial must end as inevitable.

The supervising and transformational agency is the secondary imagination, although the evidence for the critic lies within the observable elements of the poem, from the words to metrical and figurative relationships among the words. We have indeed come a long way from the self-sufficiently visionary claims for the primary imagination.[28] Still a faithful idealist, however, Coleridge himself will warn us not to mistake the effect for the cause, or the manifestation for its spiritual creator. The true creation of imagination cannot be mistaken for the

---

[27] Of course, the entire process fails where the sufficiently worthy materials are not present for the emotions, so that double labors of the will are not justified. And the reader will sense it: "Where, therefore, correspondent food and appropriate matter are not provided for the attention and feelings thus roused, there must needs be a disappointment felt; like that of leaping in the dark from the last step of a stair-case, when we had prepared our muscles for a leap of three or four."

[28] Yet many recent critics, perhaps more in the spirit of Kant than of Coleridge, have satisfied themselves with distinctions between poets and other agents of vision, or distinctions among poets, by referring to the translatable visionary frameworks themselves. But this is a point to be argued in the sequel.

false, no matter how much the latter may wear the verbal trappings of the former. So completely, in Coleridge's mind, has the imagination domesticated its "adopted children" that it views such children as its own: it becomes "the prerogative of poetic genius to distinguish by parental instinct its proper offspring from the changelings, which the gnomes of vanity or the fairies of fashion may have laid in its cradle or called by its names." One can judge true poems not by external characteristics, but only by the abiding spirit of imagination that fills these.[29] "The *rules* of the Imagination[30] are themselves the very powers of growth and production. The *words,* to which they are reducible, present only the outlines and external appearance of the fruit. A deceptive counterfeit of the superficial form and colors may be elaborated; but the marble peach feels cold and heavy, and *children* only put it to their mouths." The rules of imagination *are* reducible to words, so that the words of the poem are all we have to judge by; but we must not be fooled by the pseudo-poem, which lacks the power that should inspirit it with life. It is next to this life that the marble is seen as cold artifice. The idealist in Coleridge warns us from leaning too heavily on the material reality of the poem's language, although the critic in him—wary of the distinction between primary and secondary imaginations—knows that the words, in their manipulated configurations, are all we have to start with as we try to move from them to the life within.

In Coleridge we have seen glimpses of the farthest extension of the claim to man's formal power, the celebration of a humanistic Genesis. Moving, as Schelling did, beyond Kant's limited faculties of will and understanding, Coleridge yet goes beyond Schelling: he finds the evidence of organic union, under the aegis of imagination, in the language of the poem, as the words come—with the internal life that has been bestowed upon them—to earn from within what the Kantian faculties have imposed upon them from without. The raw materials of unmediated passion come to be mediated by a conscious act of will: devices like meter and figures of speech, at once stimulants of attention and conductors of order, are introduced "*artificially,* by a *voluntary* act." The secondary imagination itself is "first put in action by the will and understanding, and retained under their irremissive, though gentle and unnoticed, control." Yet it transcends both as it supervises the

[29] This notion resembles the argument Coleridge makes for the conversion of the nonpoetry in poems by having the poet first impose meter and then work, via imagination, to transform that which he has imposed upon.

[30] These must be *rules* given from within (as Coleridge uses the italicized word almost ironically), since he has just said, "Could a rule be given from *without,* poetry would cease to be poetry, and sink into a mechanical art."

"interpenetration of passion and of will": its I AM creates an interior life for the words, and without this life the will would produce only a metered pseudo-poem.[31] At the same time the imagination cannot altogether lose its character as mediator, which it has borrowed from the will and the understanding; otherwise the passion comes through undistilled, a "spontaneous impulse" unwed to "voluntary purpose," a mere agitation not transformed to power.[32]

So the original language of passion has had superadded to it the metrical and figurative artificialities sponsored by will, and what might have remained a mechanical combination of antagonistic forces is synthesized by imagination into a language everywhere animated from within and yet functioning in response to a self-willed purpose. The imaginative vision the poem permits us to see is the product of the verbal work that has been made. Whatever may be the spirit we are to see behind the poem, it is only by way of its discernible verbal form that we can see through to it. So the poet's creation is, finally, a verbal one, and the critic's object is the same. For it is by virtue of what the poet does to the language of passion, after his will imposes its order upon it and his secondary imagination works upon both, that the proper critic determines the extent to which he should bestow the clearly honorific title of "poem" upon it.

As it shapes any poem, the I AM of the imagination, this discussion makes evident, should surely be thought of as "a repetition in the finite mind of the eternal act of creation."[33] For it is the finitude of human imagination—and, therefore, human genesis—that persuades Coleridge to move from poetry to the poem, from transcendent vision to the work-

[31] We must remember that, in Chapter 18 and elsewhere, Coleridge condemns as "a pure work of the *will*" those poems of "wit" which, for all their poetic show, reveal no inner life. We should remember also that, much later, Yeats, in the spirit of Blake, scornfully defined rhetoric as "the will trying to do the work of the imagination."

[32] Surely this is an echo of Wordsworth's paradoxical notion that poetry, as "the spontaneous overflow of powerful feelings," must yet have its "emotion recollected in tranquillity." The recollection is again the mediating element, though, as in Coleridge, the intensity of emotion—in its second coming—must not be mediated out of existence.

[33] I am aware, unhappily, that Coleridge predicates this qualification of the primary rather than the secondary imagination, a fact which weakens the force of this argument. But I must make it anyway, since it is the sense of finitude that I must insist upon as the dominant feature of the secondary imagination, tied as it must be to its workings in language. The extensions I claim to find in Coleridge are often, I admit, mere glimmerings, sometimes contradicted, for which I am seeking to provide a theoretical structure. I am trying to justify the importance of Coleridge to this theoretical tradition by showing what it is in his work that adds significantly to it.

ing out of vision through the manipulation of words. Far from forgoing a medium, man's creative triumph depends upon his acceptance of mediation, and with it his rejection of "the unmediated vision."[34] For the Coleridgean poet, the usual world and our usual language, as mere objects, are lifeless affairs; but the particular object out there and the words we normally use to talk about it can be remade by the poet's double act of imagination. By his actions the poet does not reject the world before the I AM, though it has been the hopeless victim of mediation, for the I AM will breathe life into it anew.

But for man the breath of life is language, the very debased language that has produced the deadening consequences he has come upon, so that it is the language itself that his formative power must remake, forcing it to become a unique object. Yet it is also an object, though one created in a medium, that gives dynamic life rather than mechanical death. The dynamics within the object would seem to defy its fixed, mediated form as object, and it is only the miracle of imagination that frees it, instead of just freezing it. Still this is only a human act of genesis: man, even with his aspiring imagination, cannot create *ex nihilo*, but must work by means of one of his languages, in whatever corrupted form he may come upon it. His restlessness, his creative resistance to that corruption, is his assertion of a life-producing freedom that gives us our world anew, a genesis the second time around, perhaps more precious than the first, if surely more limited. For only God's creativity is absolute. The rest of us must do with what we have; and the poet shows us how much man can do.

The visionary theorist, who sees language only as a debaser of the preciously special image he sees, would hardly limit the primary imagination, as Coleridge does, by subjecting it to the secondary. More unqualifiedly idealistic, he will not accept man's finitude, and will not restrict the godlike nature of man's creativity. Gnostic man, here the absolute poet, legislates his world out of the forms of his mind. The all-conquering human subject overcomes all otherness by fiat and, like the future society seen by Goethe's Faust, lives in domestic comfort with his creations. This flight from otherness becomes a flight from language, as the limiting medium, in its search for that unmediated vision. It is a flight from the world itself as other, disdaining all that impedes the airy leap.[35] Its arbitrary claim to power bypasses all strug-

---

[34] My reference is, obviously, to Geoffrey Hartman's book of that title (New Haven, 1954).

[35] See my treatment, in these terms, of the opposition between Northrop Frye and the New Critical tradition: "Northrop Frye and Contemporary Criticism: Ariel and the Spirit of Gravity," in *Northrop Frye in Modern Criticism*, ed. Murray Krieger (New York, 1966), pp. 1–26.

gle, dislodges all burdens. Such a subject hardly need wrestle with objective properties, as does Coleridge's secondary imagination, in order to gain a subjective victory on objective grounds—by creating a new and free object, one bound to its world of readers.

The visionary theorist, as celebrant of exclusively primary imagination, sees all matter as alien and dead, and language as a part of matter. Like Poulet's characterization of "the Mallarmean *Cogito*," he "sees himself where he is, in the moment when he is. Existence gathers together into one point, into one instant, into an act of thought."[36] In such pure subjectivity surely this thought, as an act, is hardly conditional, hardly dependent upon words, lest it simply become an act of language, mediated and thus no longer properly instantaneous. And, as theorizing from Shelley to Bergson to Poulet reveals, words are seen to inhibit uniformly and universally, though we can strike through the veil they create to the quick subjective realities beyond. Nor can such theorists have the Coleridgean sense of what a poem can be as an object (thanks to the *secondary* imagination), an object that can claim exemption to the deadening curse of objects generally, or of objectification. It is, for verbal objects, a curse produced by the generic, mediating properties of language, which freeze into spatial molds the flowing temporality of subjective consciousness. Language enslaves, and the instantaneous return of thought upon itself liberates. No objectively discernible forms can avoid death by freezing, and poems are just others among such forms. They can become sources of organic life only if we deny their fixed, objective, formal characteristics and pierce through to the breathing consciousness behind the frozen mask. The logic of this argument requires that all forms of discourse be equally open to such penetration, so that poems, just one among many sorts of systems, are in no way elite objects. All discursive objects, as objects, are equally inimical to the flow of consciousness.[37]

As we consider what, in the past century and a half or so, has become of man's humanistic dream of encompassing and controlling the alien outside world by means of the forms he has created and projected, we can understand his temptation to flee from those structures which have hardened into external threats to his internality. Goethe's dynamic vision freezes, as we move through Hegel to the post-Hegelian world: forms become fixed into universal structures that

---

[36] *The Interior Distance*, trans. Elliott Coleman (Baltimore, 1959), p. 264.

[37] The subject's need to resist objectification as a form of murder is a standard notion in the existentialist and personalist ethic: anyone or anything on our horizon, seen as thing and thus as other, as object, is thereby killed and, in turn, in order to save himself (itself), threatens our death by trying to convert *us* into objects within a world of things.

enslave man's world and the private man himself. As the nineteenth century proceeded, man came to place too much confidence in the determinate power of his formative categories, thereby producing an overmediation of nature. He overimposed upon the external flux the rational orders that, created in response to his will, believe too completely in their own rigid objectifications. Dogma is reinstated by fiat, even if without any but an arbitrary metaphysical basis. The humanistic dream has turned into nightmare: what begins with Goethe's Faust emerges as Thomas Mann's. Schiller's "Ode to Joy," the shrilly sweet moving spirit of Beethoven's "Hallelujah Chorus," turns to the bitter "Ode to Sorrow" in *The Lamentation of Doctor Faustus* of Adrian Leverkühn, written as an accompaniment to and explanation of the Nazi horrors, Goethe's social utopism now gone awry. The mediations produced by human will have returned upon man as structures oppressively ugly, perverse, apocalyptically destructive.[38] It is no wonder that, by way of reaction, man yields to his antimediating impulse, to the cultivating of a subjectivity that remains internalized; that he rejects all that takes the form of an external object and embraces only the amorphous forms of interior consciousness.

But the Coleridgean tradition, as I characterize it, asks whether the poetic imagination may not create an alternative to those deadly objective embodiments of the will, those demanding structures projected by man's broadly symbolizing powers. Through its willingness to work with language in an attempt to reawaken it, indeed to remake it, and to make it live by endowing it with substance, this imagination can create a unique object that bodies forth the forms of subjective consciousness without deadening them while it fixes them. For the object, though finite and closed, yet contains the dynamics of endless movement within its being. The imagination, forgoing direct vision to accept the limits of man's condition, contents itself to create a particular (utterly particular) object, single and complete, in which symbolic systems and media are remade into what is still a system and a medium, though these escape the antimediator's objections.

This is the ultimate humanistic formalism, one that emphasizes not man's general power to make forms for his world but his power as poet to remake his world by remaking his language into a newly made object. Such an act requires him to accept his bondage to a routinely received language and a routinely received world, but only so that he can work to assert his freedom to reshape both. His central concern with language is at the center of his humanistic mission, since it is

---

[38] I refer the reader to my note 11 to Chapter 6, below.

his language that distinguishes him as man and that characterizes his mind and his culture. But he can remake language only by struggling with it, forcing his organic purpose upon it to defeat the mechanistic tendencies he finds in its dead forms that he picks up from others. It is, I say again, a repetition of genesis in the finite mind since, by lifting up anew the language that ties him down, the poet takes on the incarnating power, the power to turn words into living substance, into breathing flesh itself. I have suggested that, in contrast to the Coleridgean, the visionary theorist has reasserted the subject-object dichotomy in order to reject the authoritarian object for the free subject. But the Coleridgean theorist, cherishing his own myth, still tries to unite the two by calling for an object that is dedicated to the life of the subject by creating a new verbal sequence to celebrate it. Here is a formalism indeed, as the conclusion of a lengthy tradition we have traced from Aristotle. But it is no empty and ornamental or escapist formalism, such as is charged by impatient antiformalists who create a parody of their antagonist. Rather it is a vital formalism, in that its forms claim to be the forms of an organic life and its living language.

5

The concept of the all-unifying imagination, which Coleridge worked so hard to apply to poems as unified objects projected out of that imagination, also sponsored claims for the unification of consciousness. Indeed, as the supreme faculty in a transcendental psychology, the imagination, when it was picked up by later nineteenth-century thinkers, could be expected to characterize the mind more than its works. Its capacity to produce psychic balance and reconciliation[39] was consistent also with the doctrines of disinterestedness, breadth of fusion, and play in earlier writers like Kant, Goethe, and Schiller, respectively. And when a critic like Matthew Arnold found himself the child of the thought of all these people, he concentrated upon the unity of consciousness, viewing poetry not as it related to its own nature so much as it affected the sensibilities of its readers. In the search for a disinterested unity of mind that might serve a disinterested unity of society, Arnold looked to poetry to perform a necessary psychological function. This function called for poetry to be free from specific allegiance to beliefs, called for it to indulge in free play, much as Schiller

---

[39] From Chapter 14 again: The imagination "reveals itself in the balance or reconciliation of opposite or discordant qualities . . ." It is by means of this "power" that the poet "brings the whole soul of man into activity," diffusing "a tone and spirit of unity, that blends, and (as it were) *fuses*, each [of the faculties] into each. . . ."

had conceived of poetry as play. This was a disengagement that was to lead to the celebration of poetry's fictional power for its own sake—a power that led poetry away from the empirical world and from claims to cognition such as less inhibited Romantic theories were fond of asserting. This celebration of poetry as a fiction takes us down an alternative path to the one indicated by Coleridge—toward Northrop Frye rather than the New Critics.[40]

We see, in the opening paragraphs of "The Function of Criticism at the Present Time," that Arnold has retreated from any cognitive claim to the modest acknowledgment that the poet can create only poems, not ideas. He distinguishes sharply between the functions of criticism and of poetry-making, drawing upon an equally sharp distinction between the materials of each. And both distinctions seem founded on a pessimistic determinism borrowed from the historicist tradition extended through Taine and Sainte-Beuve. It may well be argued that Arnold is invoking these distinctions—and arguing for the primacy, indeed the greater creativity, of the critical rather than the creative—in order to justify, to himself as well as to others, his own decision to turn his career from poetry to criticism. For surely there seems to be in this distinction an implied criticism of his own poetry that his critics have shared. In any age insufficiently stocked with mature ideas, the poet finds himself burdened with the need to create, as well as to combine, ideas; puts on himself the role of critic as well as the role of poet; and in part fails at both. Thus Arnold implicitly apologizes for the excessively bare, prosaic, ideational nature of his verse, as he signals his turn to criticism.

It is the critic's responsibility, then, to create the ideas that must be made available to the poet. These the poet can only combine: they are his received materials, but their creation is not under his control qua poet. The critic's task is "analysis and discovery," the poet's is only "synthesis and exposition." So, in historicist and determinist fashion, "two powers must concur, the power of the man and the power

---

[40] I am, of course, pressing one tendency in Arnold at the expense of the more sober Victorian critic we usually see in him. We must not forget his dedication to the "higher truth" and "higher seriousness" of great poetry—his dedication to "poetic truth"—though he means these only as his English rendering of Aristotelian virtues in accord with Chapter 9 of the *Poetics*. The element of Victorian didacticism might well seem to tie him to the world's truths rather than leading him away from them, playfully toward fiction. But the tendency in Arnold that is picked up by his most exciting followers in our century does leave him open to the (perhaps unbalanced) reading I am making, looking back at him through the eyes of writers like Richards and Frye. By the end of my treatment of him I hope to have made sense even of terms (hardly in the fictionalizing tradition) like "idea" and "poetic truth."

132

of the moment, and the man is not enough without the moment; the creative power has, for its exercise, appointed elements, and those elements are not in its own control." In an age not supplied by ideas, an age for which criticism has not paved the way, the poet—rather than being insufficient as poet—should sacrifice himself to the poets of the future by turning critic and creating the needed materials that can turn a nonpoetic age into a prepoetic age, into at least a forerunner of a poetic age. It is in this sense that I suggest that perhaps the "critical power," as the only inventor of ideas, is more creative than the "creative power" for Arnold, so that his forgoing of the creative for the critical in his own career may not be such a "sacrifice" after all. He must not fail the future, he argues in self-defense, as the Romantics failed him.

There is another, less unfavorable (to the poet) side to Arnold's shutting off the poet from the genesis of ideas, thus making him dependent on previous ideas "current at the time, not merely accessible at the time." As Arnold puts it, it is true, the prohibition against creating ideas may seem to throw a pall over the poet's creativity, even as it unleashes the creativity of the critic (still a self-serving act at this stage of Arnold's career). But, once freed from obligations to new ideas, the poet can turn to the special powers of poetry-making itself. And this is a form of creativity that carries with it emotional, if not intellectual, consequences that can heal the stricken sensibilities of a world victimized by its chill, unpoetic knowledge, now totally the product of science. Its very independence from immediate worldly truth can become a virtue empowering the poem to do what it does for us. Arnold's elevation of the affective power of fiction beyond the deadening world of fact becomes the central influence that moves critics like T. S. Eliot and I. A. Richards to build their apologies for poetry on its separateness from the poet's beliefs about the world, trading beliefs for feelings and giving those feelings words. Finally, it is not that they are uninterested in poetry's capacity to have meaning, but that they see its meaning as *sui generis* and not to be confused with the worldly meanings that constitute the realm of prepoetic beliefs. The function from which the poet willingly cuts himself off, once set aside, becomes a limitation that opens him to a function that only he can fulfill.

But the limitation seems to be rather firmly imposed. For Eliot as for Arnold, the poet is not licensed to poach on the territory of the philosopher. Eliot praises his idol, Dante, despite (or rather because of) the fact that "when [he] has expressed successfully a philosophy we find that it is a philosophy which is already in existence, not one of his own invention. . . ." He and Lucretius "both drew their material from the work of philosophers who were not poets."[41] How closely this resembles Arnold's assignment of their respective functions to the critic (critical power) and the poet (creative power)! And when Eliot, by contrast, laments the unavoidable failure of Blake, we see the unhappy consequence of a single figure trying to encompass both powers in his poetry:

> *What his genius required, and what it sadly lacked, was a framework of accepted and traditional ideas which would have prevented him from indulging in a philosophy of his own, and concentrated his attention upon the problems of the poet. . . . The concentration resulting from a framework of mythology and theology and philosophy is one of the reasons why Dante is a classic, and Blake only a poet of genius. The fault is perhaps not with Blake himself, but with the environment which failed to provide what such a poet needed; perhaps the circumstances compelled him to fabricate, perhaps the poet required the philosopher and mythologist. . . .*[42]

We may well sense here an echo of Arnold's implied judgment of himself as poet. And we understand why, in his Dante essay, Eliot speaks glowingly of "the advantage of a coherent traditional system of dogma and morals like the Catholic."

Of course, these statements are also the consequences of Eliot's well-known traditionalism—if, that is, they are not rather the source of it. Eliot's famous criterion for beliefs, that they be "coherent, mature, and founded on the facts of experience," is his way of saying that they must be the consequence of one of the great traditional systems of belief, since their staying power is the proof of their serving the requirements of coherence, maturity, and adequacy to experience. Otherwise Eliot could not see how they would be likely candidates for the allegiance of a substantial following of people for many years. (Shades of Dr. Johnson's dictum that "nothing can please many, and please long, but just representations of general nature.") Clearly it is on this conservative basis that Eliot can distrust the more esoteric sets of beliefs and the sort of poetry stemming from them, as he moves to his lamentation for such as Blake. While it may be that Eliot's traditionalism causes him to deny the poet a role in creating new beliefs, it may also be the other way around: that so puristic a conception of the poet's role must

---

[41] "The Social Function of Poetry," in *Critiques and Essays in Criticism, 1920–1948*, ed. R. W. Stallman (New York, 1959), p. 107.

[42] "William Blake," in *Selected Essays*, new ed. (New York, 1950), pp. 279–80.

lead the poet to search out the comforts—with the freedom they allow for his intellectual irresponsibility—of a fully formed and easily borrowed tradition. In either case the fact remains that Eliot as traditionalist is quite at home with the Arnoldian separation of ideas and poetry and that Eliot's objective correlative comes to depend on this separation.[43]

The poet, we are told, is only to show us how it feels to hold certain beliefs rather than to present the beliefs themselves to us for our assent. Thus Dante, assuming that we are instructed in the beliefs presented by Saint Thomas Aquinas (which Dante borrows for his own), gives us the emotional equivalent of those beliefs. But the poet also gives us "words for [our] feelings"; that is, he gives us, not the feelings themselves (which, according to the impersonal doctrine of the objective correlative, must be kept out of the poem), but the objective or verbal equivalents for those feelings. So to take these equivalences to the second power, as Eliot does, we may say that the poet is to give us the verbal equivalent of the emotional equivalent of the beliefs he borrows from his intellectual environment. In thus eliminating the ideological responsibility of the poet in this Arnoldian manner, Eliot enables himself to utter such strange judgments as his claim (which, despite its initial impression upon us, he meant as unqualified praise) that Henry James had a mind too fine ever to be violated by an idea. He is rarely any more liberal in what he allows or denies the poet than in the following passage:

> *I believe that for a poet to be also a philosopher he would have to be virtually two men; I cannot think of any example of this thorough schizophrenia, nor can I see anything to be gained by it: the work is better performed inside two skulls than one. Coleridge is the apparent example, but I believe that he was only able to exercise the one activity at the expense of the other. A poet may borrow a philosophy or he may do without one. It is when he*

[43] It seems clear enough that roots of Eliot's objective correlative can be traced to Arnold's 1853 "Preface to Poems." Eliot's infamous complaint against Hamlet as suffering from "the buffoonery of an emotion which can find no outlet in action" ("Hamlet and His Problems") is all too reminiscent of Arnold's rejection of his "Empedocles" because it is a representation of a situation "in which the suffering finds no vent in action." Arnold goes on, in language suggestive of the language Eliot is to apply to Hamlet: such situations are those "in which a continuous state of mental disease is prolonged, unrelieved by incident, hope, or resistance; in which there is everything to be endured, nothing to be done." Obviously, what the Aristotelian Arnold here requires to head off such "morbid," "monotonous," and hence "painful" rather than "tragic" representations is an objective structure of action (Eliot's call for "a chain of events"?) that can justify externally (become the objective equivalent of?) the otherwise unvented subjective expression.

philosophizes upon his own poetic *insight that he is apt to go wrong.*

Eliot's relegation of the poet to the world of emotion, after having exiled him from the philosopher's world, has of course obvious similarities to the emotive (as opposed to the referential) function to which Richards restricts the poet. Eliot's apparent colleagueship with a natural ideological enemy like Richards in their attitude toward "poetry and beliefs" was clearly a source of discomfort, or at least embarrassment, to him. We have only to look at the lengthy, half-apologetic note he appended to his essay on Dante. Eliot must feel as little comfort in an assertion of momentary brotherhood with the early Richards as he would feel in being even more intimately related—as a child—to the theories of that alien secular humanist, Matthew Arnold. The positivistic Richards must have reminded Eliot how repelled he was by Arnold's notion, adopted by Richards, that poetry could take the place of religion. If poetry or anything else could replace religion, then this would only emphasize the fictional basis of the theological claim. Eliot properly sensed that this was Richards', as it had been Arnold's, claim, although he was less aware of the extent to which his own theory also supported it.

Eliot was far more concerned to protect the orthodox basis for the unified mind of man, although here too there are significant points of contact with Arnold and Richards, who are anything but orthodox. Though the poet is to keep his beliefs separate from his poetry, for Richards as for Eliot, he still is to preserve behind both beliefs and poetry the psychic unity that enables him to work one within the confines of the other. Both Eliot and Richards dwell on this unity of consciousness—in the poet and, thanks to the poet, in his reader—though their grounds for establishing it differ, with Eliot's being historical-theological and Richards' being psychological. Eliot develops his notion into his central doctrine of the unity (in opposition to the dissociation) of sensibility. One might have predicted that so sharp a separation as Eliot maintains between poetry and belief in the poetic function would be seen to flow from a dissociated rather than a unified sensibility. Yet Eliot insists on having it the other way around: apparently the mark of the poet of unified sensibility is his capacity to feel his beliefs with an emotional immediacy that frees him from the self-consciously intellectual need to conceptualize them (although, as we have seen, we cannot be sure whether for Eliot this unity is found in the poet's capacity to contain his belief or in the coherent and mature belief's capacity to contain its poet). In either case, what counts is the poet's sense of being so at home in his world of beliefs, so comfortable in them and so secure in their unchallenged sway, that he is free to poetize without intruding them self-consciously, argumentatively, from the outside. For they are inside, inside him, informing the emotional complex that seeks verbal objectification as the unimposed-upon poem, the poem that guarantees the unified sensibility behind it.

Eliot's notion of the unified sensibility is clearly indebted to Arnold's nostalgic admiration for the unity in the Middle Ages of the senses of conduct, beauty, and knowledge. It is the splitting up of these senses, and the rivalry among them—now with their separate ends and methods—that mark the divisiveness of the modern world. (This is Arnold's equivalent for Eliot's dissociation of sensibility.) It is this desire for unity, for the enfolding of the practical within the coordinate Kantian virtues of the true and the beautiful, that is the basis for Arnold's call for disinterestedness (also Kantian). Hence the Arnoldian insistence on the separation, in our intellectual life, of the sphere of ideas from the sphere of practice. The overpowering need is to keep our ideas free of the personal intrusions of interest and desire. It is these ideas, after all, which are to feed that ripe critical moment that can sustain the poet's creativity. This disinterestedness that preserves the purity of the world of ideas leads, in the domain of criticism, to Arnold's attack on the "personal estimate," surely a forerunner of Eliot's doctrine of impersonality, the notion that poetry is "an escape from emotion" rather than "a turning loose of emotion," that in the poem there must be an absolute separation of "the man who suffers and the mind which creates." The submerging of the poet's personality in his poem, like the submerging of his beliefs in their emotional equivalents and the submerging of his emotion in its objective equivalent, is permitted by the unity of his sensibility and that in turn by the unity of his culture, external or interior. These are the ways he can absorb ideas and contain them in his work, disinterestedly in order to objectify them, rather than to be taken up by them in a manner that would sacrifice his status as poet.

This impersonal union of elements in poetry that properly flows from the properly fused sensibility—backed by a properly fused culture—may be a Goethean ideal that Eliot adapts from Arnold. But it seems to be allied—if not confounded–with the psychological unity he derives from the Coleridgean imagination. Thus, in speaking of Marvell's union of levity and seriousness, of the self-consciousness of wit and the devotion of imagination, Eliot can invoke the all-inclusive claims of Coleridge's "elucidation of Imagination" (the capital "I," which doesn't appear elsewhere when Eliot uses the word in the essay on Marvell, is significant).

> *This power . . . reveals itself in the balance or reconcilement of opposite or discordant qualities: of sameness, with difference; of the general, with the concrete; the idea with the image; the individual with the representative; the sense of novelty and freshness with old and familiar objects; a more than usual state of emotion with more than usual order; judgment ever awake and steady self-possession with enthusiasm profound or vehement. . . .*

This passage, with much else in Coleridge, came also to influence I. A. Richards, and, through either or both of these masters of Cleanth Brooks, came to exert its force on an entire school of criticism. It may be at such points that divergent influences like the Coleridgean and the Arnoldian are crucially joined, perhaps in ways not unlike the joining in our own day of the even more divergent influences from Eliot and Richards. Be this as it may, the fusion of ideology in the poetic complex must be seen—thanks to the poet's unified sensibility sanctioned by Arnold or thanks to the poet's organic imagination sanctioned by Coleridge—as a victory over ideology, a disinterested freedom from it. The freedom from the self-conscious creation of ideas, like the freedom from the practical service performed on behalf of ideas, is a freedom to play with them, the sort of play that Schiller, as Kantian aesthetician, used as the defining quality of art. And art as play leads inevitably to art as fiction.

In freeing the poet from responsibility for ideas and from the burden of his private feelings, Eliot is directing him toward the unity of his poem as an impersonal object, a unity that can be seen—from the perspective of Arnold's influence on Eliot—as reflecting the poet's sensibility and its reflection of the unity of the culture he inherits. Poetic unity is thus grounded in psychic unity: consciousness has come to the foreground as that which enfolds everything else. It is here that we see the point of union between Eliot and the early Richards as the common heirs of Arnold. It is true that we find the early work of Richards marked by a far narrower selection out of the broad range of Arnold's concepts, so that we perhaps feel that work to be far less in the Arnoldian spirit, even a distortion of that spirit in its excessive concentration and in the partiality of that concentration. If, unlike Eliot, Richards adapts only one or two of Arnold's points of emphasis, he attaches himself to them with an intensity that almost persuades us (but, in the end, only almost) that these may after all be the very center, the reduction of, Arnold's varied plenty. The reduction is created out of that notion of psychic unity that Arnold wistfully attributed to the outworn faith of the Middle Ages. This created or discovered center of Arnold, what Richards believes to be Arnold's indispensable definition of the capacities and limitations of modern culture, and poetry as its spokesman, is found behind the selection that Richards quoted for his epigraph to *Science and Poetry:*

> The future of poetry is immense, because in poetry, where it is worthy of its high destinies, our race, as time goes on, will find an ever surer and surer stay. There is not a creed which is not shaken, not an accredited dogma which is not shown to be questionable, not a received tradition which does not threaten to dissolve. Our religion has materialized itself in the fact, in the supposed fact; it has attached its emotion to the fact, and now the fact is failing it. But for poetry the idea is everything. . . .

Richards could have added the last two sentences of this paragraph in Arnold, sentences that foreshadow the mood of George Santayana: "Poetry attaches its emotion to the idea; the idea *is* the fact. The strongest part of our religion today is its unconscious poetry." And, in the same spirit, he could have added words also from the next paragraph in that essay, "The Study of Poetry":

> Without poetry, our science will appear incomplete; and most of what now passes with us for religion and philosophy will be replaced by poetry . . . our religion, parading evidences such as those on which the popular mind relies now; our philosophy, pluming itself on its reasonings about causation and finite and infinite being; what are they but the shadows and dreams and false shows of knowledge? The day will come when we shall wonder at ourselves for having trusted to them, for having taken them seriously; and the more we perceive their hollowness, the more we shall prize "the breath and finer spirit of knowledge" offered to us by poetry.

What is central here is the conviction (1) that religion has lost its influence on modern man because of its dependence on supposed facts that turned out to be error and (2) that poetry, so long as it does not depend on facts that have a claim to truth, can take on the role of the now defunct religion. Clearly, poetry must be kept clear of the claim to truth if it is to be spared the fate of religion.

It is the development of modern science, with the revolutions it has forced upon our sense of man's place in the universe, that for Arnold has destroyed the possibility of faith. Arnold sees medieval faith, with

139

its cornerstone in the Church, as providing enormous psychological advantages. Primarily, it is the psychic unity allowed by the hegemony of the Church that related our senses for knowledge, conduct, and beauty to one another as they met in the transcendently controlling domain of theology. Each sense moved only in accord with the others, with a watchful eye keeping it from straying too far on its own, in response to its own objectives. The autonomy of the free pursuit of knowledge awaited the grand breakup of disciplines that marked the Renaissance. The explosion of inductive knowledge, with each science unleashed to create its own methods for authenticating its own discoveries, responsible to no authority or inhibition beyond its own orbit, led to fantastically impressive results, but at an enormous cost. For what was being exploded was not just the previous unity of "supposed" knowledge, but the psychic unity required for human emotional satisfaction. Lost, then, were the great psychic advantages of the unity of our senses of knowledge, conduct, and beauty. This is to say that the Middle Ages—to the extent that they created a theocratic unity of arts and sciences—had the advantage of being everything but right. No less than does a positivist like Thomas Henry Huxley, Arnold concedes that the supposed knowledge that was humanly comfortable, warm, and wishfully complete and rounded, turned out to be utterly false, disproved by the empirical criteria of sciences whose only authority derives from contingent experience below, not from dogmatic necessity above.

Once exposed to the convincing verifiability of the knowledge of modern science, for all of the psychic comforts it precludes, man is no longer able to will his return to those wrongly supposed facts—source of his prior faith—which sustained the psychic unity needed by man to sustain *him*. However discomfited by the new facts that coldly put him in his cosmic place, man will not deny them or their consequences as they affect his psychic security. So Arnold is one with the positivists in conceding to laboratory-controlled science the sole access to truth. But he will not concede, as did the Huxleys, that the human psyche can live without the satisfactions, now forgone, that the now outmoded supposed facts had afforded. If, then, the need is constant and the supply is cut off, some substitute way of supplying that need must be found. Poetry is to be that way.

The special usefulness of poetry to perform this function stems from its power to unify our sensibilities without founding this power on supposed fact. Psychological power founded on supposed fact will collapse as the supposed fact crumbles under the impact of proven counterfact. Poetry must then be prevented, by the very nature of its assumptions and the modesty of its presumption, from exposing itself to the fact of science. We remember that for Arnold it was religion that "materialized itself in the . . . supposed fact . . . attached its emotion to the fact and now the fact is failing it." Hence religion becomes "but the shadows and dreams and false shows of knowledge." What is needed instead is the power of fiction to serve the soothing escape from the reality of science, which is the only nonfiction we have, according to Arnold (or the Arnoldian Richards). We must, in other words, retain the psychic efficacy of religion without involving the commitment to those supposed facts that can undermine that efficacy. Or, put from the other side, from the positivist's viewpoint, we must not permit the advance of an independently empirical science to be slowed by the intrusions of the comforting warmth of human needs and the wishful thinking it sponsors. From either side we find a place for poetry, an art that would have to be invented if it did not already exist, which now can come into its own to substitute for religion. Let it perform the psychological function, which science with its new facts is obliged to ignore, but let it leave all claims to knowledge to science, lest it enter into the impossible competition that will explode it as that competition exploded its predecessor. Indeed, we are almost brought to wonder why, in those earlier days when religion could do its job unchallenged, poetry ever did exist!

Viewed from the perspective of Richards' positivism, Arnold's concessions to Huxley seem to have been this substantial. Still, as humanist, his defense of poetry's power to minister to human needs— like his defense of the unchanged nature of those needs despite the changed world produced by science—is unremitting. As his disciple, who read the underlying concession and defense in Arnold's words, Richards may well see himself as spinning *Science and Poetry* out of the quotation that is its epigraph. From this he derives the central separation of poetry from all questions of knowledge, the separation that Richards sees as the freeing of poetry to perform its therapeutic psychological task, created by the heartless but necessary "neutralization of nature." Science marches ruthlessly on, annexing ever more territory in the land of "what is," having long abandoned the proper province of poetry, with its pastoral tending of the nonsensical land of "what ought to be." The latter, however, must not be taken seriously beyond the psychological occasion for which it is invented. For that occasion requires that poetry produce, not the singularity of commitment, but the balance of forces that permits an equilibrium, with its consequence of paralysis that prevents cognitive or practical decisiveness. This equilibrium is again a consistent outgrowth of Arnold's adaptation of Kantian disinterestedness and Schiller's consequent notion of play.

So long as poetry makes no cognitive claims, it cannot be denied. (Shades of Sir Philip Sidney's claim that the poet "nothing affirms, and therefore never lyeth.") Its future as "an ever surer and surer stay" for man is assured, whatever the aggrandizement of cold scientific certainty. Indeed, the greater science's successes, the more we will need the soothing, unchallenging, unchallengeable, "emotive" accompaniments of poetry. Richards' invention of the distinction between emotive and referential (or between pseudo-statement and certified statement) as an absolute dichotomy is inevitable. It is true, of course, that the nineteenth-century Arnold, trapped in an older language, still reverts to archaic phrases like "poetic truth," suggesting to the less committed of us some uncertainty in him about taking the consequences of his occasional insights as agnostic humanist (distinguished from the religious humanist on the one side and the agnostic positivist on the other). He is, we must remember, father to Irving Babbitt as well. After all, he does admit that, if poetry does not, like religion, attach its emotion to the fact, it does attach its emotion to the "idea," which must still strike us as an intellectual commodity. But Richards, systematizing the more radical of Arnold's suggestions by rushing to take their consequences, must see such reversions in Arnold as momentary lapses that may blunt the keen thrust of his pioneer daring without diverting us from its direction.

Though propelled this time by another motive and from another part of Arnold's forest, we find ourselves very close to where Eliot had earlier brought us in consequence of *his* response to Arnold. With Eliot too, poetry was to find its function by turning aside from any direct responsibility for world views or systems of belief. In restricting himself to verbal equivalents of emotional equivalents, Eliot's poet was—not altogether unlike Richards's—to steer clear of the question of intellectual assent. He was to allow his poem to perform its therapeutic task unencumbered by our agreement or disagreement with his beliefs, since these beliefs were not to offer themselves separately for our judgment of them *as* beliefs. No wonder the orthodox Eliot felt embarrassed enough with his obvious similarity to the radically positivistic Richards for him to append the apologetic note to his Dante essay, with its ad hoc attempt to mark off some differences between them.

In his Arnoldian awareness of the distinction between a determined, if neutralized, nature and the emotive act of man needed to save his humanity, the early Richards also brings us toward Northrop Frye.

142

It may seem that we are trying to tame Frye if we temper the influence of Blake on his work with that of Arnold, but his own expressions of such a debt encourage us to do so. For the starting point for Frye is his distinction between the order of nature and the order of words, the first being the world of science and the second the world of language, the imposition of human forms. As we see that Frye's nature is an objectively determined order while his language is an order determined only by the free act of imagination, so we see in his distinction both the reflection of Kant's opposition between the realms of nature and of freedom and the operation of the Kantian categories. With the absolute break between subject and object, there is the total differentiation between that world out there which goes its indifferent way without regard to how we would have it and the world created—as Frye would say—in response to human desire, in accordance with our imagination and the creatures with which it chooses to people its world. Thus we can define the world of nature and the world of human freedom, or, more precisely, nature given the scientific forms of objective necessity and nature transformed by the requirements of human imagination. It is the opposition allegorized by Goethe in his Faust, who, shut out from the indifferent world that exists before man and outside man, must create his human world—in competition with it and beyond it—out of his own subjectivity that wills how man must have what he chooses to live in, his own humanly responsive world. This opposition also furnishes the answer, made in the shadow of Kant and Goethe, that Schiller's sentimental poet provides for the lost naïveté of the simple poet, his defunct ancestor.

All of which, from the point of view of Richards, may seem to be only an inflated way to speak of the emotive, and to authorize it by thus elevating it. To the still existing human needs that, for Arnold as for Richards, prolong the function of poetry in its pseudo-religious obsolescence, Frye adds the mythography of Blake, which authenticates—all but metaphysically—the land of heart's desire. But still the central distinction in Frye between the worlds of nature and freedom, of science and language—for all the heavenly glories of the free word—can be seen to grow out of the lineage that moves from Kant, Goethe, and Schiller to its positivist reduction that, suggested in Arnold, we have seen realized in Richards. The transformation of nature by human creativity is, after all, what is being allegorized at the end of Faust's career in Part II, when he literally remakes nature's waste in accordance with the orders of his human will.

It is this concentration upon man's remaking of science's nature in his own image, upon his continuing act of symbolic construction,

that enables Frye to speak interchangeably about imaginative literature
and other, nonfictional modes of discourse, since, whatever the differences among them, they are equally to be thought of as forms of imaginative projection, as fictions after all. Of course, Arnold had continually treated all the major forms of human expression as coordinate,
if not finally identical. We think of the several kinds of endeavor that
Arnold asks to be concerned with "the best that has been thought and
said in the world," and we recall that he indifferently applied this criterion at various times to what he calls "poetry," what he calls "literature," what he calls "criticism," and, most broadly, what he calls "culture." Frye himself acknowledges the inclusive supremacy of Arnold's
term, although in this regard he clearly separates himself from Richards
and Eliot, who, however Arnoldian in most respects, cherish the role
of poetry more exclusively. Frye's breadth in this matter is explicit:
"But it seems clear that Arnold was on solid ground when he made
'culture,' a total imaginative vision of life with literature at its center,
the regulating and normalizing element in social life, the human source,
at least, of spiritual authority." This concession to culture, which is in
effect the stretching of poetry to include the very process of imaginative
vision, can clearly be seen to have its philosophical sources in the tradition we have traced back through Goethe and Schiller to Kant. Coleridge, on the other hand, is finally less inconclusive. We might say, in
the Coleridgean spirit, that Frye has collapsed the secondary into the
primary imagination, and has lost the distinction between poems and
nonpoems into the bargain.

The basis for Arnold's broad conception of human creativity, what
Frye thinks of as its democratic appeal, is found in Arnold's special employment of that word "idea." It is, though Frye himself may not credit
the word, Arnold's ubiquitous *idea* that makes Arnold—for Frye as for
others—the humanist par excellence who readies man to live, imagina-
tively and self-sufficiently, in a ruthlessly objectified world that lacks all
awareness of subjects. Thus the question of the *objective* reality of God
and of the metaphysical realm can be by-passed as humanistically irrelevant, a mere matter of whether or not we wish to indulge in the
"existential projection" of our humanly created fictions. It is now in a
more profound sense that we return, through Frye's perspective, to
Arnold's claim that "poetry attaches its emotion to the idea," rather than
to the failing fact, as did religion. Further, the troublesome and seemingly retrograde notion of "poetic truth" may now be seen to fall more
consistently into place within Arnold's other claims.

The ideas which his culture must furnish the poet clearly are the
ideas to which he must attach emotion—much in the manner of Eliot's

poet in his search for an objective correlative. But we now understand the sense of *idea* as a human creation, not to describe the factual state of nature (the proper business of science), but to create the conditions under which man chooses to live in that nature. The idea, in the tradition that Arnold as middleman may have passed from Goethe to Richards and Frye, dares make no claim to objective truth, no religious or metaphysical claim. Otherwise it risks obliteration by those self-abnegating, dehumanized disciplines dedicated only to indifferent fact. But those ideas, unfit for attachment to fact, are fit for attachment to emotion. If not true of nature, they can be true of man in his imaginative freedom. Without risking the chance of being false to nature, the idea can become a human truth, a "poetic truth." All ideas, by their very constitutive power, become poetic ideas, poetic truths. Thus the ideas that the poet must have to do his work, the ideas for which Arnold must sacrifice himself as poet so that he may create them as critic, are those which man must invent for himself to live with in the faithless age. Arnold apparently feels that it is better for him to contribute to the invention of such ideas than to lament poetically, though without new ideas, for the loss of faith—which is to say, for the loss of bogus ideas, which naïvely put themselves into hopeless competition with science. Here Arnold most anticipates Frye—if it isn't rather that Frye forces us to reinterpret Arnold. In either case, Arnold can be seen as authorizing the Frye who has man imagine the forms that shape his world in response to human desire, thus creating his culture that has its own authenticity, in distinction from that objectively authenticated world of nature, bound by its ineluctable processes. That culture is our dream. But we are doomed to be creatures of the night, the time of dreams, so that it becomes our truth, the truth of our poetry. And all our ideas are in that sense poetic, even as, from the standpoint of daytime science, they remain fictions.

6

Perhaps, to conclude this lengthy study of doctrines of form, at once diverse and related, we can find a point of union between the Coleridgean concern with imagination as a poem-making faculty and the Arnoldian concern with the poem's fictionalizing—and thus humanizing—power by looking at a key essay by Sigurd Burckhardt.[44] In it the line leading from Kant, Goethe, and Schiller to Coleridge and the New Critics appears to merge with the line leading from Kant, Goethe, and Schiller to Arnold and more self-conscious theorists of

[44] "Appendix: Notes on the Theory of Intrinsic Interpretation," *Shakespearean Meanings* (Princeton, 1968), pp. 285–313.

poetic fiction. The essay begins by setting forth a parable of the Western mind in the Hebraic-Christian tradition, according to Burckhardt. In the beginning were the two great sacred Books, the Book of Books and the Book of Nature. The second was seen as an allegory of the first, the *works* of God seen as the projection of His *Word*. Thanks to the union, in the Middle Ages, of metaphysics and science in theology, both Books were assumed to be ultimately and totally interpretable, and thus to be infallible: in the spirit of the Aristotelian poem that converted all apparently chronological details into the teleologically necessary and the probable, both books were "totalized," without hiatus. (The assumption of infallibility, which accompanied total interpretability, required that all observable discrepancies or deviations be so interpreted that they help establish—rather than undermine—universal order.) At the same time, however, faith had to assume both Books to be metaphysically referential texts, though both were to turn out to be monumental fictional contexts.[45]

Since their perfection or the totality of their interpretability rested on their claims to being supported by "the facts,"[46] once they are revealed as fictions only, their hold as sacred books is removed. They fall away at different times, however: when the Bible is seen to be literally untrue to nature and interpretable in many equally valid ways—as after the decline of the authority of Rome—it comes to be seen as just another book and no longer as the Book of Books. But, as under the aegis of Rationalism, the Book of Nature still stands as perfectly interpretable on its own, thanks to its inner "laws." Then it too loses its hold, having been undermined by critical philosophy, as we observed earlier in this chapter. In the secular and skeptical aftermath that followed the loss of the sacredness of these Books, we find the retreat we have already traced from metaphysics to aesthetics: man's fictional power to write such books is retained, though the power of any of the books to become

---

[45] Burckhardt's treatment of the history of the Book and the word has certain similarities to what we find in Michel Foucault's *The Order of Things* (New York, 1970—I prefer for my purposes the French title, *Les Mots et Les Choses*), though it is evident that Burckhardt's is quite independent. Both rely on commonplaces in the history of ideas, but the original use to which Burckhardt puts his parable of the Books is in crucial ways opposed to Foucault. I pursue the difference in consequences between the Burckhardtian and the structuralist commitment to language in Chapter 8.

[46] The Arnoldian temper is clearly reflected here. We have only to recall the passage Arnold quoted from himself to open "The Study of Poetry": "Our religion has materialized itself in the fact, in the supposed fact; it has attached its emotion to the fact, and now the fact is failing it. But for poetry the idea is everything; the rest is a world of illusion, of divine illusion. Poetry attaches its emotion to the idea; the idea *is* the fact."

a literally sacred text is gone. To return to my own example, Pope's *Essay on Man* is now seen only as a poem, a metaphoric construct, no longer as a metaphysic.

From this time, each book of man is seen as potentially a book that is ultimately and totally interpretable and thus infallible: within its context, "whatever is, is right." Give the critic the problematic detail and he will make sense of it. But it is no longer literally a sacred text; it must be seen as a human fiction, though a fiction that testifies to man's power to make it in the perfection of the form he has created for it. Here, in effect, is the "deconstruction of metaphysics" urged by Derrida in what he sees as the spirit of Heidegger—except that, for Burckhardt, man's tendency toward totalization (making and apprehending totality) is not to be yielded up with the metaphysical presumption. The aesthetic force of man's capacity to make and read infallible books is retained as a fiction by the critic-interpreter for whom, consequently, hermeneutics is all: it is this fiction which gives *him* life. Served by the precedent of those great infallible Books which were thought to be written by God and (through God) by nature, but which were discovered to be fictions constructed by man, man's secular gestures toward such book-making come from less demanding creators whose claims are more self-consciously limited to the aesthetic realm. Their constructions that invite our worship rest upon that deconstruction of metaphysics—unless, like Romantic poet-seers, their vatic tempers claim what Frye derogatorily terms "existential projection," and take their fictions for truth. In the latter case they invite the same demythifying fate—as a consequence of attaching an emotion to the "supposed fact"—which Arnold saw befall the outmoded theological "science" and from which he (and in different ways Richards, Eliot, and Frye after him) tried to protect poetry.

The separation of the poem from any external system of belief remains the guarantor of its immunity, bestowed upon it in return for its willingness to retain its modest fictionality, to remain a secular, lowercase book, object of an interpretive approach at once idolatrous and limited in its circumspection. The approach has as its ground the fact that the interpreter's apprehension of the object is an intentional act: he intends it as an interpretable aesthetic object. The potential perfection of the form of each poem—each "book"—which the post-Aristotelian or post-Kantian critic assumes (as his fiction), allows the possibility of the complete interpretation of itself, though it explicitly interprets nothing else.[47] Nevertheless, the form that is given for interpretation is

---

[47] For an opposed view, that which follows from the undercuttings introduced by Heidegger and Derrida, see Joseph N. Riddel's endorsement of William Carlos Williams' wish "to destroy the Book, and with it the view of Literature as a Text

not just a formalist's escape from the world of experience; in the perfection the interpreter-critic finds for it he finds a form that shapes his own consciousness of his experience. The form, after he persuades himself that he has apprehended it, will serve him as a perceptual norm. Surreptitiously and subversively it returns him to the world, or rather returns to him a world as he has never quite known it before. And the fiction is only a play no longer. Coleridgean claims of cognition re-intrude themselves on fictional modesty. Burckhardt himself provides for the effect of poetic form on the development of man's awareness of his world.[48] How can we account for the effect fiction has on our perception of the world of empirical reality it was to supersede? It is a question that deserves more than the chapter I shall now give to it.

---

or Word with total meaning" (*The Inverted Bell: Modernism and the Counter-poetics of William Carlos Williams* [Baton Rouge, La., 1974], p. 257). Riddel's authority here is Derrida, and his reference is to *De la grammatologie.* (See, for example, Derrida's Chapter 1, "La Fin du livre et le commencement de l'écriture.") If modernism in literature is the final reach of the tradition my study is tracing, the postmodernism to which Williams is here seen to point is to "deconstruct" this entire tradition.

[48] See the first half of the two-part article written by Burckhardt and Roy Harvey Pearce, "Poetry, Language, and the Condition of Modern Man," *Centennial Review* 4 (1960): 1–15. These are Burckhardt's pages entirely.

VI
Fiction, History, and Empirical Reality:
The Hourglass and the Sands of Time

O for a Muse of fire, that would ascend
The brightest heaven of invention,
A kingdom for a stage, princes to act,
And monarchs to behold the swelling scene!
Then should the warlike Harry, like himself,
Assume the port of Mars; and at his heels,
Leash'd in like hounds, should famine, sword, and fire
Crouch for employment. But pardon, gentles all,
The flat unraised spirits that hath dar'd
On this unworthy scaffold to bring forth
So great an object: can this cockpit hold
The vasty fields of France: Or may we cram
Within this wooden O the very casques
That did affright the air at Agincourt?
O, pardon! since a crooked figure may
Attest in little place a million;
And let us, ciphers to this great accompt,
On your imaginary forces work. . . .
For 't is your thoughts that now must deck our kings,
Carry them here and there, jumping o'er times,
Turning the accomplishment of many years
Into an hour glass . . .   Prologue to *Henry V*

Shakespeare's hourglass is a splendid figure for what the human-istic theoretical tradition attributes to the form-making powers of man. With modesty this passage justifies the presumptuous play that compacts the real "kingdom" and its "princes," who performed their many actions across the many years and fields of history, into the brief compass of this stage ("this unworthy scaffold," "this cockpit," or, most forcefully, "this wooden O"), and the actions carried out on it by the "flat unraised spirits" of this artificial occasion. Though the modest tone apologizes for the inadequacy of the undertaking, there is the suggestion that this human capacity for symbolic reduction has its own power: "since a crooked figure may / Attest in little place a million." The very notion of number attests to all of the world's plenty that the mind can pour into its symbols; it attests to all that these symbols, in their miniature nature, can capture and contain. The actors onstage and their dramatic actions must be thought of as "ciphers to this great accompt," which then are reexpanded by the viewer's "imaginary forces" into a new reality. Thus the lowly "wooden O" (with its own suggestion of symbolic and reductive enclosure) changes into the graceful hourglass, a figure more than mathematical.

Our problem is to justify how that hourglass becomes itself a sufficient object to be studied by our "imaginary forces," how its creatures become so independent of their historical source that the poet can even stock it, by Aristotle's precedent in his Chapter 9, with characters whose names are not historical and still retain the audience's interest in his "imitation." We must confront, then, the engagingly naïve question that the beginning student has every right to ask—and often does. Why should we interest ourselves seriously in the once-upon-a-time worlds of fiction—these unreal stories about unreal individuals? It has been a persistent question in the history of criticism—ever since Plato first called the poet a liar—and it is a question at once obvious and embarrassing. It is obvious because, for the apologist for imaginative literature, it becomes a prolegomenon to all further questions; and it is embarrassing because merely to ask it threatens to put literature out of business and, with it, all those who treat it as a serious and world-affecting art. Why, then, should we interest ourselves seriously in fictions? However elementary, it is a question that is more easily asked than answered.

Now, one can simply dwell upon the once-upon-a-time element in fiction and justify it as an escape from the world around us. Fiction's made-up, make-believe character is the very feature the escapist celebrates. Indeed, it can be argued that Freud justified literature precisely on such escapist grounds, as a necessary sublimation for the frustrated poet who, as daydreamer, provided daydreams for the rest of us. It can be argued similarly that Northrop Frye constructed his ambitious system as a tribute to the grandiosity of human desire: desire arbitrarily creates its imaginative forms as the world in which it chooses to live, preferring its made-up order of words to the grim given order of nature in which, without imagination, it would be doomed to live. Thus is history exchanged for myth, with the domain of myth limited to that never-never land, not altogether unlike Freud's, in which things happen as we would like them to—that is, in which we control the forces that, in reality, we find uncontrollable.

But, despite the intense seriousness of Frye's system, may we not have found its escapist tendencies frivolous, after all? May it not, then, have been these tendencies that kept that system from catching on with more of us, and for a longer time, than it did? The critical tradition has always resisted—despite temptations in the other direction—any theory that took the literary work away from "reality" (whatever meaning one attaches to that term) and kept it away too long. The tradition has sought, in the end, to return fiction to the mundane truths about us. What else can account for the persistence of some notion of "imitation" and the search for "objects of imitation," however sophisticatedly we maintain, at the same time, the man-made, once-upon-a-time arbitrariness of the fictional fiat? The scholar-critic has traditionally justified his interest in literature by returning again and again to his claim that the literary work must affect the world that precedes and follows it; he must always see in that work, product of human skill and invention, a model of that world, if not a model *for* it. Therefore, to rest in the capacity of fiction to give us a make-believe escape, as a pleasurable alternative to all that really surrounds us, is a temptation that his dedication to the Arnoldian requirement of poetry's "high seriousness" compels him to reject. He must also reject the corollary—in Frye's theory, at least—that art must imitate art rather than life: that poems must, in the end, conform to earlier fictions, to the dominant imaginative structure that absorbs all fictions to itself, instead of keeping its eye on the object of imitation out there in the world, beyond all poems.

We must, then, ask again about our continuing devotion to fiction, once we decide not to use it as an escape from reality even while we attend seriously to it for its own sake. There is, of course, the alternative justification that would have us use the fiction as an exemplum for some moral universal. Since long before the work of conservative sixteenth-century theorists like Julius Caesar Scaliger, we have been called upon to view the poem as that which, in his words, "imitates the truth by fiction." That is, it creates tales that are not accurate chunks of here-and-now reality in order to represent accurately, by allegory, the truths of some transcendent reality. Thus Aristotle's "fable" is changed into Aesop's "fable." But, as centuries of didactic literary theorizing have taught us, this is not to care for fiction as fiction at all, so long as our interest in it is limited to the thinly allegorical. At one point in his *Apology*, Sir Philip Sidney speaks, more ambiguously, of the poet's giving us either a world arbitrarily different from our own or one morally better than our own. It is hardly necessary to add that Sidney, soon after this passage, retreats to the safe confines of didactic justification that would insist upon absorbing the "different" world into the "better" one.[1] We too must make our choice: we must decide whether we want an authentic fiction, self-justified, or a mock fiction whose tenuous and momentary existence depends on its leading us to a transcendent truth whose existence hardly depends upon *it*. And we are likely to decide against Sidney; our historical need for poetry suggests that our fictional urge may be greater, and more primary, than our philosophical urge. Our moral promptings hardly exhaust our interest in those strange works about strangers we'll never meet.

So, now that we have eliminated escapism and didacticism as inadequate answers, we return to that initial and not-so-trivial question: Why should we worry so about fiction, *as if* it made any difference to us in our reality? The "as if" in this question is precisely the issue: how can fiction's "as if," like the "as if" in the question, break down so that, *as fiction*, it does make a difference in our reality, and the question, suddenly converted from "as if" to a statement of fact, must be directly confronted?

Without using the fiction to flee from the workaday world and without denying the fiction's cogency so that we may pursue an unrelated philosophical proposition, we must accept the fictional world as intrinsically worth our time and our concern: this fiction must be made into our truth for now. All the while, of course, we know better, for we do not delude ourselves: although we willfully sustain the illusion that allows us to take it for truth, we know it is not truth. We do not leap onstage to rescue Desdemona from Othello's murderous intent; but neither do we fail to attend profoundly, and with intense emotional commitment, to what must befall them both. From Aristotle, in his response to Plato that is a justification of fiction, to Sidney to Dr. Johnson to Wallace Stevens, the history of literary criticism is filled with the struggles to make sense of this dual awareness, because we have found fictional illusion useful, indeed indispensable, to aesthetic experience and—given the ubiquity of aesthetic experience—to the human economy as it exists in its culture.

Dr. Johnson put this issue masterfully, as he put so many others. He pronounces on it in his "Preface to Shakespeare" in the course of his attack upon the unities of time and place:

It is false, that any representation is mistaken for reality; that any

[1] I remind the reader of my extended discussion of this problem in Sidney in Chapter 4, above.

dramatic fable in its materiality was ever credible, or, for a single moment, was ever credited. . . . It is credited with all the credit due to a drama. It is credited, whenever it moves, as a just picture of a real original; as representing to the auditor what he would himself feel, if he were to do or suffer what is there feigned to be suffered or to be done. The reflection that strikes the heart is not, that the evils before us are real evils, but that they are evils to which we ourselves may be exposed. . . . The delight of tragedy proceeds from our consciousness of fiction; if we thought murders and treasons real, they would please no more.

So he can conclude, "Imitations produce pain or pleasure, not because they are mistaken for realities, but because they bring realities to mind." For a moment—in this passage and for this crucial argument, not quite consistent with the balance of his essay[2]—Johnson, with a call for casuistry, is being an authentic Aristotelian. It is in this sense that the Aristotle of Chapter 9 of the *Poetics* distinguishes poetry from history as what "may" happen differs from what actually happens. It is also Aristotelian to find the source of the difference between poetry and historical reality in the "materiality" of the fable and in the principles of sequence appropriate to that materiality, independent as it is of the materials of historical reality.[3] If it is the materiality of historical events, of empirical realities, that presses us to accept their actual consequences for ourselves with delight or dread, what is there about the substance of that surrogate half-reality of art that compels our response—at once concerned and distanced—to its shadowy consequences for those creatures of another's casuistry?

Ever since Aristotle, theorists have been concerned with poetic fictions as imitations of history, though imitations with a difference. In his Chapter 9, Aristotle struggles, not always conclusively, to estab-

---

[2] In view of the subject of this chapter, I ought to acknowledge that Johnson usually prefers poetry to avoid the artifice of fiction in its proper function of mirroring reality. Indeed, he can at times oppose the falsity of fiction with vigor. Nevertheless, I am here stressing his defense of fiction in this portion of his "Preface to Shakespeare," a defense that is of signal importance in the history of theory. I treat Johnson's several conflicting attitudes toward the fictional and the realistic (as well as the moralistic) obligations of poetry—and especially drama—in "Fiction, Nature, and Literary Kinds in Johnson's Criticism of Shakespeare," *Eighteenth-Century Studies*, 4 (1970–71): 184–98. See also Johnson's *Rambler* no. 4, "On Fiction," where his treatment is far less even-handed, and less probing.

[3] The reading of Richard McKeon is helpful here: "For Aristotle, consequently, imitation may be said to be, in the fine arts, the presentation of an aspect of things in a matter other than its natural matter, rendered inevitable by reasons other than its natural reasons. . . ." ("Literary Criticism and the Concept of Imitation in Antiquity," in *Critics and Criticism: Ancient and Modern*, ed. R. S. Crane [Chicago, 1952], p. 162). See my discussion of this reading in Chapter 4, above.

lish the extent to which poetry does or does not depend upon historical precedent. Although we are mainly attentive to his brilliant definition of poetry in its distinction from history, we must remember also his wavering between that distinction and his momentary concessions to poetry's more literal dependence upon history and legend, or upon history *as* legend. Of course, our awareness of the use of legend, or legendary history, as the source of Greek epic and tragic plots helps explain Aristotle's uncertainties, uncertainties that persist even while he labors so effectively in the service of poetry's formal independence of the world of actual happenings.

The role of history as poetry's object of imitation persists in the Aristotelian tradition, especially in the conservative notions of those who emphasize imitation over invention and thus must exaggerate poetry's historicity. Witness Scaliger, for example: "Then who will deny that all epic poets go to history for their subjects? History, sometimes delineated only in semblance, sometimes idealized, and always with changed aspect, is made the basis of poetry. Is not this the practice of Homer? Do we not do this in the tragedies themselves?" And he goes on to suggest that historians, also imposing some emendations upon actualities, are as much poets as those we normally honor with that name: "For as the tragic poets base their plays upon true events, but adapt the actions and speeches to the characters, so Livy and Thucydides insert orations which were never recognized by those to whom they were attributed." Thus historian and poet become one, and the distinction between fiction-making and chronicling disappears.

Scaliger here reminds us how naïve our conception of history is if we think of it only as brute facts, the flow of events itself. We may conceive of history as phenomena, but we may also conceive of history as a humane discipline. That is, history may be the unimpeded sequence of raw empirical realities or it may be the intellectual form that provides the tune to which the sequence marches. Both the raw materials, the so-called data, and the formal constructs our minds impose upon them may be thought of as history: both the history men live through and the history of historians. And as we read historical data in accordance with one or another cause-and-effect model furnished by historical discourse, we are moving into the realm of the fictions that Scaliger saw as akin to the forms of the poets. History as we conceive it begins as the child of myth and never altogether escapes its parentage. The sophisticated humanist may become unable to constitute *his* historical reality, unable even to *see* the welter of history's facts, except by way of the formative categories that history's disciplines give him as his visionary habit— the discursive habit he resorts to in order to keep from seeing history's facts as brute. The theorist of history can discover classificatory schemes, alternative model histories, much as Northrop Frye did for literature and its critics.[4]

Despite the artfulness that Scaliger shrewdly attributed to the historians, thereby seeing them as sharing with the poets the need to improve upon history as brute fact, we can yet distinguish between the two. For surely we can try, however vainly, to hold the historian responsible to a reality outside his discourse in a way beyond what— from Aristotle's point of view—we can ask of the poet. The historian's discursive model, however elegant, does have an explanatory function, and what it seeks to explain is, at least for the mind not trapped by the framework, outside the system, as positive or negative evidence. Indeed, the very notion of "evidence"—the notion that such a term is relevant even if difficult to agree upon—suggests a criterion, a need for support, for empirical relevance, that is foreign to the poet in his freer creativity. History as "the facts" must somehow serve as the source and "verification" (or—negatively—they at least provide for the possibility of the "falsification") of the history of historians; facts can hardly prove a poem to be false in the same way. It is this accountability "to the facts" (and my quotation marks indicate my skepticism about such naïvely realistic terminology) that inhibits the purity of the historian's formal models, imposing as it does a referentiality upon his work that the poet blithely ignores: "Not to know that a hind has no horns is a less serious matter than to paint it inartistically," Aristotle assures the poet, as he could not assure the historian. But of the differences between the poet's forms and the historian's, more later.

We should better understand Scaliger's persistent attention to raw history as the source for poetry when we consider my own starting point here—the naïve question about our interest in make-believe— and what follows, the joint problems of delusion and illusion. For there *is* an ambiguity in the *apparent* reality of the stories we read or—even more persuasively—in the plays we witness. When we watch a drama, we see particular individuals in a sequence of incidents that conclude in certain consequences. There seem to be a before and after for these individuals with their individual names and destinies, so that surely this is an imitation of history in the very sense that Aristotle meant it. It is an imitation, what Renaissance critics called a "feigning," and what is imitated or feigned is the historical way things happen. (Is it not this sense of drama as feigned or make-believe history that led Italian Renaissance and later French critics toward the literalistic doctrine of

[4] Hayden White has undertaken just such a schematic analysis in "Interpretation in History," *New Literary History* 4 (1973), 281–314.

verisimilitude—the claim that any leaps of time or place on stage, any gap in continuity, would violate our empirical sense of how events proceed?) What appears to be going on before us looks historical and acts historical, although our responses are rather more sophisticated (as Dr. Johnson reminded us) than they would be to a series of actual experiences that we were observing, if rather guiltily, as *voyeurs*.

I have made it clear in my fourth chapter that I find Aristotle's the most useful way of distinguishing poetry from history. There we saw it was significant that, although it is logic that concerns him most, he uses terms we would apply to chronological happenings (beginning, middle, end) to characterize the sequence of incidents onstage. Of course, it is only as he transforms the usual meanings of these terms from the chronological to the logical that he establishes the special character of poetic form. It may be true that we find him centrally concerned with the beginning, middle, and end, as well as the significance of the *post hoc*. In their before-ness and after-ness plays are like our running lives; but, as we have seen, how unlike they are to our lives these terms are made to attest as they are changed to reflect the *propter hoc*. In Aristotle the diachronic becomes the synchronic. The abortive elements of normal experience, its gaps, irrelevancies, or superfluities are thus to be purged from Aristotelian form. Even the life of a single man, bounded as it is by the chronological beginning and end of birth and death, does not qualify as a single action unless the poet has so selected and ordered and interlocked its incidents that he makes it one. Aristotle says as much himself in a passage that reveals he no longer has any ambiguity about the casual nature of history by the time he reaches Chapter 23: here he claims that a narrative poem, like a tragedy, "will differ in structure from historical compositions, which of necessity present not a single action, but a single period, and all that happened within that period to one person or to many, little connected together as the events may be." (Of course, Aristotle's view of "historical compositions" here is more naïve than we have seen Scaliger's to be: he is limiting them to the mere recital of facts.) At this point poetic form has an independence from the external sequence of incidents that seems absolute. Such an autonomy of form is beyond what the historian's model of causality can dare claim if that historian is to claim any historicity for his model—if, that is, he is, despite Scaliger, to claim to be more than poet himself.

But we have noted that the dramatic presentation itself, however tightly bound its Aristotelian unity of form, retains for the viewer the appearance of mere historical sequence. The poet's form has constructed within this sequence the clues of internal relations that the viewer, with his aesthetic habits of apprehension, learns to read, reconstructing the history into the play. The aesthetic work is there, as innocent and as silent about its meaning as are history's random facts about theirs. But these facts have been converted by the poet's form into elements that are anything but random for those who have been taught to disentangle and relate them in more ways than their casual before-ness and after-ness would suggest. So the poem functions as the critic's data very differently from the way in which chronological facts function as the historian's data (unless those facts are seen to come trailing clouds of teleological glory). For teleology is precisely what poetic form boasts as its essential characteristic. It is just the poet's freedom to put teleology where his object of imitation had none that distinguishes him from even the most arrogant historian who would fashion the past in the shapes of his private fancy.

These formal characteristics help set the stage apart from our world, thereby creating that "consciousness of fiction" which keeps us from being deluded about the historical factuality of what is unfolding before us in the play we are watching. There is something rare and striking and finally unhistorical about that sequence of events, that imitation of history: it must happen in a certain order and lead to a certain conclusion—and conclusiveness. This is so both because it always happens just this way in this play and because—if it is a successful work—it ought to, nay must, happen just this way because of its internal necessities. Just as the poet converted the line segment into the circle of a form that feeds on itself, so the sequence of events that apparently have only a before-and-after relation among themselves turns out to be a frozen sequence, with a sometimes maddening identity among its many unfoldings in performance after performance, production after production. If there is too marked a change in the way the play unfolds, we protest that it is no longer *this* play.

When Dr. Johnson, echoing Aristotle's notion that imitation pleases, reminds us that we enjoy fictitious sufferings that it would pain us to observe in life ("if we thought murders and treasons real, they would please no more"), he is justifying our preference for the tragedy we watch to arrive at the customary catastrophe we know it requires. We must prefer the last-minute reprieve that rescues hopes and lives in the real world of our newspapers, although we do not want our tragedies to be changed the same way. It would be more pleasing for a real-life Lear (who of course would then not be Lear at all) to have his Cordelia restored to him breathing truly, and we would cheer the miracle that saved her and, consequently, him. But we must feel that the play—and the pleasure we take in it—is better ended as it is and always has been ended, that Lear's fate is invariably fixed in the fixed form of the italicized *King Lear*. Yes, it is better, for it *ought* to end that way, although Aristotle reminds us that our "ought" is aesthetic and hardly moral. This accounts for his preferring the impossible probability to the improbable possibility, however devoutly we might wish for the latter in a real-life situation. We are now close to the heart of the casuistic, if not the sophistic, element in literature's special reality.

The "materiality" of the dramatic performance, then, requires that it be a fixed sequence performed by impersonators whom we know to be such. The rules by which the *sequiturs* proceed determine that invariable fixity, so radically distinguishable from the always contingent befores and afters of life. And the criteria for our deciding upon the better-ness or worse-ness of the consequences are just as different in the two cases. It was out of this sense of the distinctness of art's ways that the proscenium arch and curtained stage came to be seen as an appropriate development for the theater, serving as the frame for the picture of moving life, as far from our moving lives as the still life is from the actual bowl of fruit. And, just as appropriately, the thrust stage returns as dramas more and more reduce to "happenings" and the line between art and life, stage and audience, comes close to being erased.[5]

I have used the drama because, among the literary arts, it seems, in the most graphically immediate sense, to be an imitation of history, of history—that is—as empirical reality. It has a presence that makes it analogous to actual happenings that we are permitted to witness: long before the cinema, the play was a "moving picture."[6] But, in their own ways, other forms of imaginative literature similarly suggest illusions of factual presentation. That is, they similarly "feign." In each case, similarly, the work displays—often as flagrantly as the proscenium does—those elements of artifice which cut off the work from life and proclaim it make-believe, thereby denying the intent to delude. If we see the play as imitating a real happening, history in the making, we can view the epic, and after it the novel, as imitations of history as discourse,[7] whether narrative history or narrative biography. The lyric

---

[5] This is not to deny that the properly aesthetic can coexist with the thrust stage and its illusion of increased audience involvement. But other, less superficial elements of artifice are then required.

[6] Lessing, for example, suggests that drama, as the moving counterpart to the still pictorial arts, approaches becoming—like painting or sculpture—a "natural sign," despite the fact that, like the other verbal arts, it consists of the "arbitrary signs" of language.

[7] I refer the reader again to the *Poetics*, Chapter 23, where Aristotle explicitly distinguishes the structure of the epic from "historical compositions," which they so resemble and to which we have seen Scaliger later try to restore a structural similarity.

poem or the first-person novel has a greater or lesser presentational resemblance to autobiography or the confession, each of these in its own
way an historical mode, however subjective.

The difference of "materiality," to which Dr. Johnson could point
in distinguishing stage happenings from actual ones, is less apparent
when both the imitation and its object are forms of discourse (epic and
"historical composition" or lyric and autobiography). But, from the
standpoint of aesthetics, the "material" differences are as profound: the
possible relation of discourse to its own conventional forms and to the
internal manipulations of its own elements creates a different responsibility toward those beings and events which it is *about*, or (in the case
of fiction) is *presumably* about. If we may revert to that term from Dr.
Johnson, this is to say that there is still a difference of materiality in
the live or the feigned objects of the discourse. To choose an extreme
case, we must feel that Tolstoy's Kutuzov—or, for that matter, Shakespeare's Henry V—has a different "material" status from that of history's Kutuzov (or Henry). And surely the case is stronger as we move to
characters who are nominally fictional as well. All that recent criticism
has written about the persona argues, similarly, that Hemingway's Jake
Barnes or even the "I" of a sonnet has a different "material" status from
that of an autobiographical subject. Of course, when we think of a
Rousseau or a Wordsworth, the question of when autobiography
merges with fictional pseudo-autobiography, when persona merges with
person, becomes a delicate one for criticism to settle in each instance,
but without threatening the essential usefulness of the Aristotelian (or
Johnsonian) categories.

Of course, Aristotle himself is not quite constant to his devotion
to form as a human invention. After appearing to fight back and forth
with himself about the role of factual history in invented plots, Aristotle—in Chapter 9 of the *Poetics*—finally tries appeasing both sides in
the struggle by suggesting the possible union of history's happenings
and a humanly satisfying form:

> *And even if he [the writer of tragedy] chances to take an historical
> subject, he is nonetheless a poet; for there is no reason why some
> events that have actually happened should not conform to the law
> of the probable and possible, and in virtue of that quality in them
> he is their poet or maker.*

This may seem like hedging in a theorist who will put all his money on
man's formal commitment to improve upon history's accidents by imposing his causality upon the mere casualties of happenstance. Today,
however, we can perhaps feel the cogency of an attempt to merge fact
and art—even to surrender art to fact. Recent commentators have noted

more than once that the facts that constitute our recent history outdo the tame possibilities of the most outlandish fiction, since there is in our reality a sensationalism that the human imagination would not dare match.[8] Indeed, our reality may render all our imaginations—those of creators and readers alike—shockproof. Thus one can see the merger of history and art taking place on history's side as well as on art's side, as Aristotle suggested. One thinks of the so-called new documentary, part of the new journalism, as well as some splendid examples of old history and biography.

What is at issue is whether the writer is appealing to form or fleeing from form by appealing to a random welter of casual happenings, the latter being a flight from form. But form, we know ever since Kant at least, is not fled so easily: the very *pursuit* of the random, as a pursuit, can hardly be a random procedure. The post-Kantian view, if not the Aristotelian, would then obliterate any choice between the discourse that imposes form upon history and the discourse that supposedly tries to do no more than reproduce history's purely casual flow. After all, it is that imagination—as a form-giving power—which must give even history's raw data their intelligible contours, almost as if in accord with the compromise between history and poetry suggested in that fence-straddling quotation from Aristotle. It goes without saying that, if the form-giving imagination cannot help but see form in history's casual sequence, it is largely because its prior intercourse with fictions has conditioned it to perceive such forms. Thus the imagination collapses history into the categories of human form: in effect, it turns history itself into a fiction, much as Scaliger suggested. This was to become the essential claim of Northrop Frye, who, with a Kant-like division between the order of nature and the order of words, saw the latter as the domain of the free imagination, which must cast nature into human form as our myth. (Wallace Stevens follows here as well, except that he more stubbornly reminds us of the deprivations produced by that factual world that lies outside our necessary fictions.)

Beyond these enabling claims for fiction in Aristotle and Kant, however, there is a further theoretical challenge that is not often pursued: the attempt to distinguish poetic fiction, with its special freedoms, from that historical discourse whose nature, however fictional, arises out of an original fidelity to "reality," obliging it to try to drag more of the world with it. For, whatever the degree of semblance to the "is"

---

[8] William Wasserstrom's "The Strange Case of F. Scott Fitzgerald and A. Hyd(Hid)ell," *Columbia University Forum* 8 (Fall 1965): 5–11, is a moving example of this claim. In it the author cunningly shows *Tender Is the Night* to us as but a pallid reflection (and prophecy) of the assassination of President Kennedy.

by the "as if," there are in poetic fictions the technical devices, the patterned juxtapositions, the moments of self-reference, the conventional reminders, and—most crucially—the elements of a form that is a transformation of what might have had a simple empirical reference; and these join to shout "artifact" as they seduce us toward the willfulness of an indulged illusion. Thanks to that transformational form, the feigned reality, with its own peculiar "materiality," takes on a presence that presses us to accept it as our truth for now, indeed as a prior truth, a truth that may be normative of history's truth for us. This is a theme to which I must return later.

It is enough for now to say that the work is no lie and that, without claiming to be true, it interests us for itself. This is, in effect, to say with Sidney

> that of all writers under the sun, the poet is the least liar. . . . he
> nothing affirms, and therefore never lieth. For, as I take it, to lie,
> is to affirm that to be true which is false. . . . He citeth not authorities of other histories, but even for his entry, calleth the sweet
> Muses to inspire into him a good invention. . . . And therefore,
> as in history, looking for truth, they go away full fraught with
> falsehood: so in poesy, looking for fiction, they shall use the narration, but as an imaginative groundplot of a profitable invention.

In using this support from Sidney, I must acknowledge, alas, that for him the "invention" is "profitable" because his fable is more Aesop's than Aristotle's, so that, like Scaliger's, his fiction is the allegorical servant of Platonic truth.[9] But his language and the nature of his argument, taken out of their Platonic context, serve such later defenses of fiction as Johnson's.[10]

[9] To our disappointment, Sidney actually uses Aesop here as an example of profitable fiction-making: ". . . so think I none so simple would say, that Aesop lied in the tales of his beasts: for who thinks that Aesop writ it for actually true, were well worthy to have his name chronicled among the beasts he writeth of."

[10] Indeed, the justly famous *reductio* that Johnson uses in the "Preface to Shakespeare" against the arguments for the unities of time and place can be traced to this very place in Sidney's *Apology*. The brilliant passage whose climax is the sentence, "Surely he that imagines this, may imagine more," is answering the need for the spectator to watch the scene shift from a first act at Alexandria to a second act at Rome, though "he knows that place cannot change itself; that what was a house cannot become a plain; that what was Thebes can never be Persepolis." But, for any such shift to raise itself as a problem in credibility, Johnson tells us, the spectator at the start must really imagine "himself at Alexandria . . . [believing] that his walk to the theater has been a voyage to Egypt, and that he lives in the days of Antony and Cleopatra." In *his* defense of the poet's fiction-making, Sidney himself used Thebes as his example of the make-believe required by a play. "What child is there, that coming to a play, and seeing *Thebes* written in great letters upon

It is necessary, if fiction is to be defended as an alternative reality of its own and not as a controlled disguise for a higher truth, that we focus our attention, as Aristotle did, on the internal purposiveness that justifies the way everything functions within that feigned reality which comes wrapped in its own materiality. And man becomes the form-making animal: his capacity to create forms and to impose them on matter in a way that brings it to organic life can free him from history by allowing him to reshape it as he will.

In my previous chapter I treated Aristotle's dedication to form as the triumph of teleology over the random in history. We saw there that normal experience outside the poem was seen to have an incompleteness, a failure to realize potentiality, that its "imitation" was to transform into the perfection of structural inevitability ("the probable and the necessary"). And we traced this primary commitment to man's form-making power, the power to create concepts or objects that are totally purposive, through the teleological cosmic structure of neoclassical orthodoxy to the rebirth of human teleology in Kant. In this respect Kant can be viewed as a second coming of Aristotle, except that Kant retains a more constant awareness that teleology is to be explicitly limited to man's inventions as an aesthetic creature (and not attributed to nature by man as a scientific creature). Kant thus more centrally provides for what later thinkers will find in man as a maker of fictions. Through the eyes of Kant, we saw, even the universe projected by Alexander Pope could be viewed, not as a cosmic claim to metaphysical validity, but as an aesthetic construct that was a tribute to man's formal powers, if not his ontological insights. Viewed this way, Pope merely joins those form makers who remake a world whose secret internal motions are alien to him into a humanized world answerable to his own categorical impositions. Goethe's Faust, shut out of the natural order, creates an order of his own out of his uniquely human will. Schiller's "naïve" poet, one with nature, loses that natural home and becomes the "sentimental" poet, on his own as man and obliged to exceed nature's order with his human one. In exceeding his own history, the poet—as if still true to Aristotle's injunction—conquers history itself. His aesthetic capacity, the capacity for play and form, creates his own

an old door, doth believe that it is Thebes? If then, a man can arrive, at that child's age, to know that the poets' person and doings are but pictures what should be, and not stories what have been, they will never give the lie to things not affirmatively, but allegorically, and figuratively written." Of course, Sidney was hardly willing to follow the consequences of his argument to an attack upon the unities of time and place, as Johnson was to be.

reality as the object he has made, whatever its metaphysical modesty.[11] The facts of man's irrevocable past remain there to enslave, but the forms his creative present gives him to live with liberate existence by humanizing it, making it fit for human habitation.

Of course, man's shaping habit leads him to impose causal schemata on *all* that presents itself to him as data: everything his discourse touches it touches with its forms—everything, and not just the special materials of poetry and the arts. Thus, as we have more than once observed, history itself must be seen, not as brute facts, but as subject to the forms of the human discourse that creates it as meaningful for the rest of us. All empirical reality, including the raw materials for (and before) our formulations of history (which raw materials I have also termed "history"), is seen as oppressively outside us, a formless continuum that threatens our freedom to create the purposive and causal relations that convert these materials into the humanistic disciplines. Is it, then, that Scaliger was right after all and that the historian and the poet join as humanistic fiction makers in common? Are the forms through which we are to perceive a past moment in our culture a model configuration like that through which the poet asks us to perceive his dramatic episode? Is there, then, a continuum among the various humanistic forms to match the continuum in the pre-formal data of unshaped experience? Clearly I must resist such a notion by once more calling upon Dr. Johnson's claimed difference of materiality between poetry and history.

If we think back to my own dramatic simplification, in my previous chapter, of the ideological impact of eighteenth-century rationalism, and the special form it assumes when viewed from the standpoint of "critical" philosophy, we find me imposing a formal model consistent with the needs of my historical discourse and my theoretical position. In short, it was my mythologized version of history, although surely the

---

[11] This humanistic dream, in which man's creative fiat turns the dream into fact, may be the ultimate projection of the form-conscious tradition in aesthetics (and, by implication, in all philosophic areas from epistemology to ethics). It is, of course, just this dream—with all of its grandly arrogant presumption—which the last century and a half of human history has destroyed, turning it into parody. Thomas Mann's transformation of Goethe's into his own *Faustus* brilliantly creates the fictional dimensions of the humanistic self-deception that produces the self-destructive parody of modern antihumanism (see *The Tragic Vision* [New York, 1960], pp. 86–102). Mann's perhaps is answer enough to those who would turn the post-Kantian aesthetic into a humanistic way of life, and it may mark its obsolescence as a hope to control our living. But I still hold onto the formal promise of that aesthetic tradition as the key to our art and literature, whatever the current drives to celebrate an alternative art and literature in the service of an antihumanism.

163

capacity of its commonplaces to account for the facts (to the extent that we have access to such things independently of competing interpretive discourses) is seriously open to challenge. In this it is like all history, though I do not mean to condemn all of history's schematic or dramatic models as simplistic fictions just because mine may have been so. Yet it is true that in its patterned reductions, its interpretive consistency, every historical model has something of self-referentiality about it, however doggedly we think we are holding it accountable to the "evidence," its raw data. Each systematic model is constructed out of, and in response to, its own forms, its reductions, its historical commonplaces, though these commonplaces do claim responsibility to the data. And this responsibility marks the point at which the historical structure, however it approaches self-referentiality, differs from the poetic structure as the formal tradition from Aristotle defines it. As this responsibility attests, it is a difference between the two "materialities," the empirical and the illusionary.

I must once again, then, claim the poetic fiction to be *dis*continuous with our other fictions: for it is the poem's departure from, and transformation of, the raw materials of history that have marked its growth into an autonomous structure. These transformations point us toward the work's inner teleology, its aesthetic center. As a poetic fiction, it is responsive only to that teleology whose principle of internal relations is independent of its external sources in historical reality. Every element taken from that reality—an incident, a character, an idea, even words and their normal meanings—must be newly justified by the role it must play in that closed teleological pattern. As a result, that element must change its meaning, indeed its very nature and ontological status, by virtue of these interlocked functionings. Let us only recall the special sort of personage Lear must become for us if he is to serve his casuistic role in his tragedy, which responds to rules, behavior, and consequences —and arouses effects in us—so at variance with the "real happening" it may appear to "imitate."

But I have said that it is not only brute historical reality from which the poem deviates and which it transforms; it deals similarly with the commonplaces normally supplied by historical discourse for our understanding of various moments in our culture. As I have already suggested, the history of ideas (or rather the historian's ideas about the history of ideas) are also treated by the poet as his raw materials, ripe to be deviated from and transformed. Like the words he picks up, and his stories and characters and moral attitudes and generic and technical conventions, the mythologized historical notions around the poet—

as the freezing of a culture's internal motions—exist as commonplaces for his work to transform, even violating them if necessary. A fuller, keener, and more humanly illuminating historical awareness must modify the generalized ideology-bound readings made by the historians with the transformations made upon them by the poet. My own reductions of eighteenth-century philosophic rationalism, which I converted into claims of a metaphoric aesthetic (in light of the skeptic's charge of anthropomorphism), could undoubtedly profit from such modification. Pope-the-poet himself gave half-hidden voice to the private person's doubts about the extent to which Pope-the-philosopher's world of airy abstractions made provision for the aging, dying man of flesh and blood.

I have elsewhere treated "The Rape of the Lock" as a masterful expression of this self-dialogue whose intricacies our histories of ideas normally slight.[12] Let me here refer, for the sake of brief, almost prima facie demonstration, only to a single rather spectacular example from that poem. Pope forms his poem out of the tension between the sylph-protected, drawing-room evasions of time-ridden reality and the persistent biological promptings themselves. In several passages his brilliant juxtapositions of the fragile China jar both to actual chastity and to his chaste and bloodless "toyshop" world become metaphorical equivalents for the commonplaces of his period's (and his) dandified metaphysic. But one of these passages takes this common metaphor of China and forces it at once to sustain the entire weight of both the delicate art world and the teeming continent itself.

> *On shining Altars of* Japan *they raise*
> *The silver Lamp; the fiery Spirits blaze.*
> *From silver Spouts the grateful Liquors glide,*
> *While* China's Earth receives the smoking Tide. (3.107–10)

Here is the utterly empty coffee ceremony rendered in a mock-heroic euphemism that seems unintentionally to bring in what this ceremonial world must exclude—the heaped, fleshly realities of birth and death. These are excluded as the decorative crockery from China excludes that peopled place itself: the refinement of the earthen rejects earth. We see "grateful Liquors," heated by "fiery Spirits," gliding from "silver Spouts"—a "smoking Tide" received by "China's Earth." Here is a ceramic charade of coitus, an artful imitation of history's brute facts

---

[12] See "The 'Frail China Jar' and the Rude Hand of Chaos," in *The Play and Place of Criticism* (Baltimore, 1967), pp. 53–68; and "The Cosmetic Cosmos of 'The Rape of the Lock,'" in *The Classic Vision* (Baltimore, 1971), pp. 105–24.

that is also a metonymy that evades them.[13] For it is an imitation that the poet's characters must take for all the reality there is, although the poet has shown us he knows better. And now so do we: in light of this passage, China, suddenly the grand symbol and summation (or rather consummation) of both earthy and earthen, earth-ridden and earth-denying, bodied and disembodied, can never be the same for this poem, and this poem can never be the same for us, as we seek, by means of it, to understand Pope and Pope's time.

In an earlier work I made much the same sort of claim about the way in which the dramatic context of Marlowe's *Faustus* helps us, as historians, to formulate our awareness of Renaissance man—his Faustian aspect, as it were.[14] A more commonplace notion of that Faustian aspect might come from the Faust legend, but it is in the totality of Marlowe's work that the potential of what it is to be Faust is realized for us, so that it can become a normative category for the historian. Or I might use Hamlet as our example, struggling to trace in action and language the unique configuration of belief, skepticism, and the consequences of judgment and action, and then handing my results to the historian to help him enlarge his categories. But, for our purpose here, another brief and obvious word-centered example might better illustrate how the poet can serve the Renaissance historian.

In the context of Shakespeare's Sonnet 87, "Farewell! thou art too dear for my possessing," the word "dear" speaks volumes. We think it is the lover's "dear," only to have some doubt introduced by "possessing," followed by the certainty—with terms like "estimate," "charter of . . . worth," "bonds," and the rest—that it is no more than the merchant's "dear." This clearly ambiguous "dear," pointing in the opposed directions of love and the marketplace, supervises the painful unfolding of the poem, in which the lover must surrender the claims of fidelity to the fact of worldly worth. This is just one of many sonnets in which the old-world values of troth struggle against the new world's

[13] The adjective "grateful" ("grateful liquors glide") is the one word whose animistic character would apply to the sexual rather than the coffee rite (unlike "fiery" or "Spouts" or "Earth," which point both ways). But, clearly, the fleshy reality is suggested only to be excluded by the toy shop's charade. Similarly, the game of Ombre can be viewed as a charade of war, or the very rape of the lock itself as a metonymic charade of the bodily rape. But the precision of parallelism in the ceramic charade permitted by the puns on "China" and "Earth" makes this one the most brilliant metonym in the poem for my purposes: metonym as metaphor. The metonymic way, I shall argue in Chapter 7, is often the way in which the poem as metaphor—as a stand-in for reality—becomes our window upon it.

[14] See *A Window to Criticism: Shakespeare's Sonnets and Modern Poetics* (Princeton, 1964), pp. 60–62.

truth; and most of the them proceed with crass marketplace terms that turn out to be puns for the language of endearment. [Just consider "precious" in the "precious friends" of Sonnet 30 ("When to the sessions of sweet silent thought"), one of the most brilliant in a brilliant group of poems.] But none of these poems is so neatly contracted into a single word as is Sonnet 87 into "dear," which sends forth and yet holds within itself the two sides of meaning that follow. For all his devotion, the lover just cannot escape the language of cold reckoning, and, trapped by it, he accedes to its demands, gives up his beloved to its calculating standard of equivalence, and retreats to dreams—a more favorable unreality which can "flatter" a fidelity that is now seen as unworthy (not worth much materially). "Thus have I had thee, as a dream doth flatter⌐ / In sleep a king, but waking no such matter."

It is as if language itself, as an instrument of love, has been corrupted by the mercantile mind. Whenever the lover tries to use his terms of endearment, they emerge as marketplace puns. The ineffability of his affection requires that he find metaphors for it in tangible reality. But his metaphors, taken from what the world finds "dear," become the very enemy to his love: they turn that love into its material reduction, as the mercantile world turns his metaphors real. The worth or preciousness of his love must be measured in worldly terms, thus destroying it when it becomes "too dear." The flattery in the loving half of the "too dear" of the opening line becomes the grim arithmetic reality of its other, expensive half, which is substantiated through the poem. Love is the victim of a mistaken metaphor of a world whose nature has reduced its language, as much as it is a victim of that fallen nature. It is eliminated by language and the marketplace it serves, so that the lover should be rendered speechless as well as loveless. Yet his love survives, if only in the dream that is a denial of matter ("no such matter"), a denial of all that reality has become. Further, he forces love to have a place in language after all, *his* language, and thus a place in the matter of this poem, by forcing that word "dear" to have his own meaning as well and to sustain it also through the poem. And beyond the poem, and all the *Sonnets*, it touches all that we can know and feel about the Renaissance mind in its struggle with past and present structures of reality and its values.

When we look at "China" in Pope or "dear" in Shakespeare, we have miniature samples of how the poet violates the way words ordinarily function, defining themselves and staying put, as he forces upon them a sustained doubleness, though a double precision and not a mere blurring. I am reminded of Sigurd Burckhardt's claim that proper ambiguity in poetry occurs not when one word can have many meanings, but when "many meanings can have one word."[15] It is at once a reduction and radiation of meanings. This is one major way in which our fiction makers have undone and remade the commonplaces handed them by what surrounds them into a self-sustaining form for their art, which for us can become a special entry into the way they and their culture framed their vision of the world. The hourglass thus becomes the shape of their time, for them and for us.

So—to return to the question with which I began—we can value fiction because of its power, as our metaphorical truth for now, to give us a vision of equivalences and oppositions that less free disciplines must disdain. The deviations and transformations make the poem discontinuous with its reality and with the other kinds of discourse that seek to contain that reality. Yet it supplies the forms that become our norms to frame that reality. Far from being a repository of available ideologies of its period or a demonstration of our historical ideologies about its period, the poem can become a newly constitutive word, a measure of the inadequacy of our older words, those historical formulations which seek to account for all that is thought and felt in a moment in culture. It is indeed presumptuous to claim this primacy for literature, to suggest that the fiction—through the casuistry of its "as if" reality—can give us the eyes we need to see the common reality that has been there eluding us. But the poem, broadly defined, is probably best equipped to create a language to match a vision, since it can remake the language of the rest of us.

Since I have concentrated so heavily upon examples of verbal manipulation, it may momentarily seem as if I am restricting the poem at this point to verse only, despite my broader interest in poetry as fiction, proclaimed from my earliest pages. Though I am anxious for these examples to clarify my argument, I should not wish that argument to rest exclusively upon them, since I *am* concerned to establish the case for *poesis* at large. I acknowledge, of course, that the tightness of verbal structure in verse permits the spectacular remakings of language that furnish especially handy examples, capable of brief treatment, to serve needs such as mine here. But my claim is the broader one made earlier that, from ideology to generic conventions and—often most prominently—words, there are many norms and sources for them serving as raw materials for the poet to deviate from and transfigure in his effort to internalize the form of his poem. The brilliantly tight lyric may seem paradigmatic of the process, but looser and baggier monsters must also

[15] In "The Poet as Fool and Priest: A Discourse on Method," *Shakespearean Meanings*, (Princeton, 1968), p. 32.

be accommodated by any poetic theory concerned to account for poetry as fiction.

The history of criticism provides one example after another of theorists who have tried to account for the power of poetry as fiction to violate what would seem like the norms of other discourse, the power of poetry as fiction to render our usual concepts of consistency—like our usual concepts of reality—inadequate. Aristotle himself insists that the virtue of artistic probability will not ensure a satisfactory plot unless it is accompanied by the less obvious and less predictable virtue of surprise; thus the "complex plot," with discovery or reversal, is preferred to the "simple plot." Similarly, the virtue of character consistency can sustain itself though it contain his apparent inconsistency, and the virtue of probability in plot can establish itself though it contain empirical impossibility. As another example, Plato's earlier distinction between "icastic" and "phantastic" art is adapted (and distorted) by a Renaissance theorist like Jacopo Mazzoni so that the truthful imitation of existing things gives way before the capriciously invented world of the poet (although this world must be a believable illusion: it is verisimilar, *like* truth, though not true). Yet the poet's artful intrusion of the "marvelous" upon the merely "credible" must itself force belief upon the reader, forcing that reader to "accept what [he] did not believe could happen." In this tradition phantasy (or, later, "fancy") imposes itself upon us *as if* it were truth itself, as if it were a discovery made within reality rather than an arbitrary invention that is to be an alternative to our normal reality. Hence the fears of the more literal-minded mimetic theorists like Edward Young, who, still following the lead of Plato, distrust the "chimeras" of phantasy.

By the time of the theory of Coleridge, "fancy" comes to be relegated to the prosaic limitations of empirical reality, so that now it is the organic imagination that represents the poet's alteration of the norms of our experience. In Chapter 14 of the *Biographia Literaria*, Coleridge relates how Wordsworth and he wanted the poet to unite the "faithful adherence to the truth of nature" with "the power of giving the interest of novelty by the modifying colors of imagination. The sudden charm, which accidents of light and shade, which moon-light or sun-set diffused over a known and familiar landscape, appeared to represent the practicability of combining both."

This notion and even these words are echoed in the definition of prose romance as the moonlight genre when later nineteenth-century writers like Hawthorne and James sought to distinguish it from the (presumably "realistic") novel. For example, in the well-known introductory Custom House section of *The Scarlet Letter*, Hawthorne sees himself as the archetypal romance writer, sitting "in the deserted parlor, lighted only by the glimmering coal-fire and the moon, striving to picture forth imaginary scenes, which, the next day, might flow out on the brightening page in many-hued description." Given the mixture of real objects, moonlight, and the fire,

> if the imaginative faculty refused to act at such an hour, it might well be deemed a hopeless case. Moonlight, in a familiar room, falling so white upon the carpet, and showing all its figures so distinctly—making every object so minutely visible, yet so unlike a morning or noontide visibility,—is a medium the most suitable for a romance-writer to get acquainted with his illusive guests.

Hawthorne then lists in detail all the routine items of "the little domestic scenery of the well-known apartment":

> whatever, in a word, has been used or played with, during the day, is now invested with a quality of strangeness and remoteness, though still almost as vividly present as by daylight. Thus, therefore, the floor of our familiar room has become a neutral territory, somewhere between the real world and fairy-land, where the Actual and the Imaginary may meet, and each imbue itself with the nature of the other.

We are told that even ghosts may be welcome here (shades of those "chimeras" distrusted by Young in his eighteenth-century concern about what Addison, after Dryden, called "the fairy way of writing"). Here such imaginative license is granted as the domestic warmth of the coal fire "mingles itself with the cold spirituality of the moonbeams" and all of these are placed "one remove further from the actual, and nearer to the imaginative" by being seen in the reflection of the looking-glass. "Then, at such an hour, and with this scene before him, if a man, sitting all alone, cannot dream strange things, and make them look like truth, he need never try to write romances." Here is a gloriously climactic passage for my brief history of theories about the imaginative transformation of reality, a transformation which, though not true, is in its mimetic character "like truth." The reader is thus to allow his normal daylight sense of how things go to be imposed upon by what Mazzoni called the "credible-marvelous."

Of course, each of these theorists in the tradition I have so briefly traced from Aristotle to Hawthorne wants to have it both ways, maintaining both the deviation from normal reality and a new norm constructed around that deviation. Probability in Aristotle may seem to give way before surprise, but what emerges is a far more impressive probability, one that is earned through the mastery of a major challenge. His consistent inconsistency similarly surpasses the cheap satisfactions of an easy, unveering consistency, but it retains the consistent pattern. For Mazzoni, the "phantastic," in the illusoriness of its private perspective, outdoes the reality-bound "icastic" in the belief it can inspire (which is why Plato feared it). Again, the elements worked upon by Coleridge's imagination are made to be far more intimately related to one another than those more obviously related elements worked upon by his "fancy"; and the American writers who defended prose romance surely treasured the truths behind their make-believe causal relations more highly than they did the cause-and-effect truth of empirical reality.

So in each case what begins as arbitrary ends as inevitable, having first guaranteed—through its inventive power—that our sense of inevitability has been immeasurably broadened. Form, resisting the simplism of common sense, has cultivated its diversionary antagonist—and swallowed it. Form thus reasserts itself by reappearing in shapes more bizarre than, from its trim beginnings, we could have expected. It has converted the most resistant elements of antiformal experience into its teleology. As verisimilar, the poem takes on a reality that surpasses the empirical reality it has transformed. Twentieth-century critics have seen these claims as consistent with Coleridge's insistence on "the balance or reconciliation of opposite or discordant qualities." What is central is both the resistant opposition and the poet's unique capacity to reconcile its elements. Thus the early nineteenth-century motto, "unity in variety," can emphasize equally, though paradoxically, its two antithetical nouns. In Cleanth Brooks, who sees himself as influenced by these notions in Coleridge, the revelation of life's confusions is dependent upon the poem's power to create a total form for them. Such a theoretical emphasis culminates in a critique of form that values it in relation to the antiformal obstacles it has overcome, in relation, that is, to the anaesthetically real and resistant elements it converts into materials for the aesthetic imagination. These criteria, characterizing as they do a notion of strenuous and difficult beauty, dynamic in its subduing its antagonists by absorption, leads to an aesthetic and formal judgment that is more than restrictively aesthetic and formal, for it hinges upon the human power to reorder our experiential world.

This tradition, in our own time, reveals itself in the critic's explicit concern with norms and—more important—deviations from the norm, together with the movement (in Leo Spitzer, for example) toward the new norm *for this literary work,* constructed precisely upon the deviation. In the same spirit, Sigurd Burckhardt, in his brilliant essay that is a blueprint for interpretation of this sort, acknowledges that the "disturbing element" may obtrude and seem to block the easy interpretation we might like to make (though the poem as a whole may resist such facility); but he insists this very disturbance can become the enabling feature of the more difficult interpretation that satisfies a less reduced version of the poem's total form.[16] With its new norm, that form can become normative for us all. There is, in the end, responsibility to the world's norms and no mere escape from them. But the responsibility to the world is on the poem's own terms.

As this theoretical tradition would have it, then, the artful illusion of a truthlike, as-if world produces in us a credibility that outdoes the world that is. Its superiority proceeds from a wholeness whose capacity is not strained by the incompatibles it must accommodate wthout disharmony. Experience outside this poem finds them in fact incompatible, but the illusion of harmony is sustained by the form the poem struggles to achieve. Yet we must not succumb altogether to the fictional illusion we have fostered, lest we mythify the poem in the same way that, as critical philosophers, we have found the eighteenth-century rationalist to mythify his cosmos. If, with Kant, we have reduced the domain of teleology from the cosmic to the modestly aesthetic, we should not re-deceive ourselves by inflating the poem and the extent of its claims upon our belief: we should not, with renewed naïveté, overstate what it is we believe when we believe the poem. For believe it we must.

(These claims, based as they have been on the tradition of humanistic form-making, must confront the counterclaim that has had an increasing influence of late. For mine has been a tradition that has treated poetic fiction as a holistic construct, sacred in its integrity—a "totalization" that Jacques Derrida, for example, would treat, somewhat derogatorily, as the mythification [and mystification] of language. An attitude like Derrida's would prefer a literary model that deconstructs the myth with a language that acknowledges its own incompleteness, its inadequacy to contain and center the world. Thus come the lapses, the gaps, and the vacancies that undo the myth of an immanent teleology, now lost to the randomness of "free play." I shall contend with this challenge at length in my final chapter. Here I would point out only that later versions of what began as the Aristotelian doctrine of fiction see fiction as conscious of its own basis in illusion, as they concentrate on the work's self-referential features. This self-reference suggests, of course, precisely the consciousness of artifice that carries its own de-

[16] Sigurd Burckhardt, "Appendix: Notes on the Theory of Intrinsic Interpretation," in *Shakespearean Meanings*, pp. 285–313.

mystification, like that for which Derrida calls, though it at the same time maintains the order of the holistic fiction—if always *as* fiction. So, at their most mature, writers in this tradition *include* Derrida's concern without undoing their own: they retain their own centered sense of the "totalized" poetic structure while they allow us our awareness of the sense in which it is a false shadow of an *uncentered* reality and an uncentered language. If, with Derrida, we choose to deconstruct the illusion, then we are in part turning away from the game and its self-imposed magic, thereby risking the sanity gained from living within the order it provides. Yet if we choose the illusion, we must play in full knowledge of what it is: that is, in effect, a knowledge of the reality that resists being embraced by our play with an ultimate language. The language of the poem, in providing its own limits, provides this knowledge as well. Art does not undo fact, least of all the fact of death, so that the human mastery art embodies is provisional only. But, though externality and determinateness remain, beyond the myth of a total language and unabsorbable by it, the mastery of the word helps man create for himself where he lives, and for his fellows where they live after he dies.)

We saw in Chapter 4 that, in stressing the illusory nature of art, Plato, in the *Sophist*, condemned the artist for confining himself to how things appeared to him from where he stood. The artist imitated, not the particular thing, but the appearance of the particular thing from his particular perspective: particularity heaped upon particularity. (The dramatist, splitting himself up into his characters, was even guiltier of multiplying perspectives.) Thus for Plato the "phantastic" was identified with the idiosyncrasy of the singular angle of vision, and condemned for it. That it can captivate others is explained by those who, from Aristotle onward, define the power of aesthetic form, with its omnivorous teleology. Plato's distrust of the poet is part of his distrust of the sophists, since he sees the poet as sharing the sophist's power of weaving illusions. As Aristotle and Dr. Johnson will—in their different ·ways—agree, the poet's casuistic world that *may* be threatens to supersede not only the world of fact that *is*, but even the metaphysically sanctioned moral world that *ought* to be.

The world of artful illusion, however, is fostered by the poet in ways far more formidable as well as more devious than Plato could fashion for the poet's philosophic model, the sophist at large. For the poet, disdaining the limits of normal discourse and cultivating his deviations from it, moves—through his patterned juxtapositions and recurrences—from a single dimension of imitation to the manipulated complications of self-reference. From E. H. Gombrich's notion of self-reference to his notion of illusion is an obvious step, one he takes by working out of Plato's *Cratylus*[17] as I have worked out of the *Sophist*. Though the poem as illusion attempts to replace the world of mere fact, it does not deny it: the poem acknowledges—through self-reference—that it is but illusion itself, thereby acknowledging also the persistent reality of those mere facts. Yet it will also itself persist. Since it does not ask to be taken (*mis*-taken) for truth, it shows itself to be too self-conscious and self-referential an artifact to be guilty of mythification. But it is too devoted to its illusionary totality not to insist on our taking it, in its wholeness, as a completed vision. Though it demystifies itself while it sustains itself, if we merely deconstruct it as we do our usual myths, we manhandle it because we remain blind to its formal power.

If Plato originally alerts us to the poet's power of illusion, he does so only to condemn it. For Plato has the metaphysical assurance of a universal reality that allows him to reject illusion as an obvious lie, a misrepresentation of *the* truth, the substitution of a private perspective for what is substantially out there for us all. Though Plato can thus berate the sophistic character of the poet in his traffic with particularized particulars, for the rest of us—lacking Plato's metaphysical assurance and burdened only by the oppressive reality of empirical fact—the illusion is all. Constructed out of the human imagination as its formal answer to fact and addressed to the imaginative capacity for freedom in us all, the poet's illusion raises reality to the responsive precincts of our most intimate self-consciousness, creating categories for our private vision. So the singular perspective may be rejected by Plato as the ultimate particular, but, as constituted by form, it can be most cherished by us. For, once it comes to be materialized in the fixed work of art, it is hard evidence that the illusion itself—though without delusion—has finally become a lasting fact.

I end, as I began, with the "imitation" and the beyond-imitation in fiction, by using some words I have used elsewhere.

Finally there is of course no denying some imitative role to literature: since history pre-exists literature, literature must in some sense imitate it. There can, then, be no question about history getting into literature: it is the very stuff of literature which, after all, cannot be created ex nihilo. *But this history that enters literature as its raw material is the living, felt, pulsing history of breathing men and not the static formulae of ideology. So it is history as*

---

[17] See, for example, *Art and Illusion* (London, 1960), pp. 305–306.

existential force that gets into literature by being there first; it is history as institutionalized in ideology that comes after, thanks in part to what literature shows us.[18]

We may all be subjects in a passing world we dream, and in two senses: subjects in opposition to the things out there which appear to be objects and subjects because we are in subjection to them as they become our determinate horizon. To free ourselves from this passivity, we constitute our world out of these objects, thereby reconstituting *them*, though usually we can do so only by using the categories our culture has given us. Especially, in subduing this world, we relate our present to its past by using the formative categories of our historians, who variously constitute that past for us. But these create a new passivity in us, subjected as we are to the commonplace forms of our culture and its spokesmen, including its historians as well as its former poets. Yet there can be a further liberating breakthrough, thanks to the poet, if he is the uniquely creative one who, in and through his work, frees himself *partly* from this passivity and creates a new language system. This system provides new categorical norms for himself and the rest of us to dream with and through, norms that preserve the forms of inner consciousness that keep our visionary freedom vital. Undoubtedly, nonpoetic spokesmen, like us critics or historians, will again appear and freeze these forms into commonplaces. In so doing we may supply the future poet with those dead objects which become his raw materials for future workings. What we supply him will be returned, though in a form that will surprise and unsettle us. It may even shock us into becoming, momentarily, only slightly less than poets ourselves, as we allow the shaping selectivity of the hourglass to substitute for our unshaped consciousness of the fullness of time.

[18] *A Window to Criticism*, p. 59.

Part Three  A Systematic Extension

VII

The Aesthetic as the Anthropological: The Breath of the Word and the Weight of the World

At several points in Part Two—particularly toward the end of Chapter 6—I have already entered upon some of the extensions I believe can be made in the spirit of the humanistic aesthetic tradition as I have conceived it. Of course, from the start I have meant candidly to admit that it is difficult to know what is latent in the tradition and what is eccentric in my reading of it as I propose extensions to it—especially when I admit also that I may very well have conceived the tradition eccentrically, so that it would appear to lead toward my extensions. Even if one eschews an openly Hegelian-style procedure, some degree of eccentric distortion is locked into the very enterprise of establishing a dominant theoretical force in cultural history and relating oneself to it.

The present chapter represents the other side of the claims I make in "Fiction, History, and Empirical Reality." As the preceding chapter, in summarizing the tradition, emphasized fiction as the imaginative alternative to reality as "given," so this chapter (still embracing that tradition but trying to stretch it) must bring fiction back to that reality. If we are to account for the constitutive role which the tradition has claimed for man's form-making power, those created forms, as alternatives to empirical reality, must be justified on more than escapist grounds, as more than a wish-fulfillment that turns from that reality. Instead, a way must be found for fiction to sustain reality, or at least to help us sustain it—or only bear it. The present chapter will search for it. I would now invoke the weighty, worldly spirit of Dr. Johnson rather than the flighty, airy spirit of Northrop Frye, though this Dr. Johnson would by now have read and absorbed Frye.[1] What emerges

---

[1] See my extended discussion of Frye in the context of this opposition in "Northrop Frye and Contemporary Criticism: Ariel and the Spirit of Gravity," *Northrop Frye in Modern Criticism: Selected Papers from the English Institute,* ed. Murray Krieger (New York, 1966), pp. 1–26.

may be not altogether unlike Wallace Stevens' lingering reality principle, though without the hedonism of the pleasure principle.

Let us begin by recalling the continuing assertion, which I found
in the roll of critics I called from Aristotle to Burckhardt, that the poem
is to break up the pattern of our normal expectations and, by expanding
them to include what before was unexpected and unacceptable, to force
upon us a new and enlarged sense of what is credibly real in our experience. A fiction so conceived surely lays claim to imposing its alternative
reality upon our own in a way that profoundly modifies it, or even
transforms it. Thus, in Mazzoni, for example, the "credible" overrides
the "true" or the "false" as the subject of poetry, in a sentiment not
finally too distant from our own recent tendency, in humanistic study,
to emphasize human consciousness and vision over external, "objective" truth, often seen as the appropriate object of science. After all,
Mazzoni was dedicated to defending Dante's *Commedia*, which was
under attack—for example, by Bulgarini—precisely because, having
no worldly object of imitation, no external action, but taking place only
in the mind of the poet, it was a thoroughly "phantastic" poem, unrelated to the truth of man and history. In response, Mazzoni helped teach
us to turn Plato around and take the phantastic seriously. Despite his
own self-conscious Platonism, Mazzoni had to defend phantastic poetry
in order to defend Dante. He found, consequently, that the freedom of
the poet to create his images in accordance with his "caprice" was conditional only upon his power to make us believe them, in this way altering our capacity to believe. A post-Kantian can see in such a notion
the power of poetry to alter our consciousness, to alter the reality we
constitute for ourselves as the horizons we see as sustaining that consciousness.

Obviously, we have with such notions come a long way from
Plato's view of the phantastic as a warping of an objective reality by the
private perspective.[2] For consciousness, altering with persons and—

---

[2] For Plato, we must remember from Chapter 4, the phantastic (later, fancy) is not
at all as free or capricious as it is to become in Mazzoni and later theorists. Plato's
ontological concern with things independently of their being sensed led him to
deprecate the phantastic as the literal reproduction of sense perceptions, incorporat-
ing the private and diverse angles of vision. From his ontological perspective, this
is already distortion enough, though it *is* tied to what is actually perceived and
how it appears to be. He opposes to the phantastic, as appearance, the icastic,
which would reproduce the thing as it really is, on its own. But once the phantastic
has been thus handed over to the private perspective, in later theorists individual
subjectivity becomes free to grow its visions and move further from the object
(whether as it is or as it is perceived) toward eccentricity, toward the "phantastic"
in our ordinary use of the word. No longer governed by Plato's metaphysical opposition between the apparently and the truly real, the phantastic—later the fanciful
—came to be defined (as in Mazzoni) as the capriciously (and internally) invented
rather than the externally observed.

within persons—with moments, is the enemy to a truth whose ontology is solidly fixed. The diversions and deviations of poems are thus seen to be profoundly subversive. Plato's attack is of course a tribute to the poem's power to alter consciousness and to help turn it into an attractive rival to his calm, universal truth. Persistently, as we saw—in Aristotle, in Mazzoni (dare we not even say, sometimes in Johnson?), in Coleridge, in Hawthorne, in Spitzer, in Burckhardt—the fancy, in cheating us one way, rewarded us in another, incomparably.[3]

This fancy—the unexpected, indeed the marvelous, made credible —is reflected in the inventions of fiction. The conflicting traditions that either cherish or reject such inventions—what Mazzoni saw as having its source in the "caprice" of the poet—are defending or attacking fiction as they defend imagination or attack the "chimeras" of fancy. The defense runs from Longinus through Mazzoni and Coleridge to, say, Spitzer, Gombrich, and Burckhardt in our own day; the attack runs from Plato through the dominant Renaissance voices to Edward Young and more recent literary naturalists; and a mammoth critic like Johnson manages to be on both sides. Although, in the passages I emphasized in Chapter 6, Johnson speaks for the indispensability of poetic illusion and its freedoms, in most other places he has little tolerance for the artificialities and the mythological unrealities of fiction. So, whatever the attitude theorists have had toward fiction, it is one that, clearly, has developed in reaction to the battle, announced by Plato, between the poet's phantastic impulse and the "objective" reality of his experienced objects.

As Plato foresaw, to his sorrow, it is the poet's private deviation from the public, commonplace world (though for "commonplace" Plato would prefer the term "universal")—a deviation now made public in his work—that diverts us and, having disoriented us, reorients our world, no longer commonplace. As I have argued in Chapters 2 and 6, it is the poet's role to impose such deviations upon us by creating the uniqueness of his object out of them. There is a great variety among the kinds of deviations his poetry-making power requires him to pursue and manipulate for his peculiar purposes. We can divide his deviations into two main groups: those which are generic and conventional deviations from our normal reality, the common illusionary properties of fictions like his, and those which the poet creates in order to convert the minimal resources of common fictional deviations from reality into the maximal resources that can yield his unique fiction and its reality. Let us first consider those general deviations from empirical reality

---

[3] By now it should hardly be necessary to note that this "fancy" is closer to Coleridge's "imagination" than it is to his "fancy." We have more than once seen the change undergone by these terms, if not by the concepts.

that all fictions—even those that seem self-consciously "realistic"—conventionally presuppose. We could draw up a spectrum of literary works, running from the least conventional to the most conventional or, put otherwise, from the most apparently "realistic" to the most artificial (or least "realistic"—should I say most "phantastic"?). It would run, then, from those works which appear least conscious that they are not true happenings (in the drama), or true narrative histories (as in epic or novel), or true personal outbursts (as in the lyric), to those works which—in each genre—seem most conscious of their conventional and "merely literary" role, their fictional distance from reality. It would appear to be a spectrum running from those least conscious of themselves as verbal constructs to those most conscious of that fact and most anxious to play upon it. But our critical tradition has become increasingly sophisticated in its awareness of the fact that the spectrum may itself be an illusion—as a spectrum, of course, should be—so that it claims to find self-conscious artifice in all the graded variety of works that make it up. Whether more or less subtle, more or less self-conscious, deviations from normal experience serve—as generic fictional necessities—throughout the range of fictions to mark off the body of art from the flow of life. Functioning as conventions of the poet's genre before this particular poet came along to exercise his powers upon them, they can be found disorienting our response—if we watch closely and without mimetic preconceptions—violating expectations we bring from a commonplace reality outside the common distortions practiced by poetry.

For the "beholder," these generic deviations become the norms of illusion, of fictional—and therefore aesthetic—perception that Gombrich emphasizes in his study of the visual arts, though, by way of my remarks on drama in Chapter 6, I tried to extend his notions to all kinds of literary fictions. As just a single example, the student of painting can remind us of the need to·be attentive to the devices of overlay and perspective by means of which the "representational" artist uses his medium to create the illusion of depth: the illusion that a two-dimensional plane represents a three-dimensional "reality." He can remind us—in other words—that, in Gombrich's pithy expression, "making comes before matching."[4] But of course the Gombrichian student would go beyond this still preliminary recognition to emphasize the elements of self-awareness by means of which the painting fulfills its illusionary role, those elements of self-reference with which it counters its apparently representational objective. Even the most "photographic" of

---

[4] E. H. Gombrich, *Art and Illusion* (London, 1960), p. 99.

182

paintings, for example the still life or—still more extreme—those which would produce a trompe l'oeil, bring about (as Gombrich views them) not a blurring of art and reality but a rousing insistence on their mutual distinctness: the very possibility of our being fooled shrieks the completeness of art's merely illusionary nature and the impossibility of our "really" being confused. The most transparently "realistic" painting thus turns out to be filled with self-reference. Each such work is seen as trying to serve as the case *a fortiori* for the falseness and flimsiness of artifice, whatever its ultimate philosophic claim to truth.[5] Through self-reference it calls attention to its own pretense at deluding us—thus a half-hearted pretense that turns delusion into self-conscious illusion. In an extreme case like that demonstrated by M. C. Escher's "visual paradoxes,"[6] the convention of "realistic" perspective is used to trap us into seeing its illusory absurdity: it forces us to focus upon the painter's art of using the technical devices of his medium to play upon our perceptual habits, and to deviate from reality by doing so.

But, for the sophisticated and learned "beholder" who contributes his "share," the norms he brings with him are more than just those of his elementary habits of naked perception. All of the recognition patterns bestowed upon him by the conventions of the art he has studied—including those of iconographic identifications—are part of what he brings with him to help him "read" the work. And they are, as conventions, the artificial deviations from reality that, like the picture's frame (or the stage's), separate the work from the world around it. These norms, belonging to the medium and history of the art, function in much the same way as the generic literary conventions and *topoi* that scholarship endeavors to make part of our recognition patterns as we read.

The greatest contribution of Rosalie Colie's accomplished career was her conversion of Gombrichian insights into a literary method at once scholarly and critical: the tireless mixing of seemingly innumerable genera assembled from a lore at times mythical, historical, topical,

---

[5] See Gombrich, "Tradition and Expression in Western Still Life," in *Meditations on a Hobby Horse and Other Essays on the Theory of Art* (London, 1963), especially p. 104, and the exciting extension of this notion by Rosalie Colie in "Still Life: Paradoxes of Being," *Paradoxia Epidemica* (Princeton, 1966), pp. 273–99. From the definition of the painted still life as a *vanitas* grows this double sense of its worldliness and its deceptive flimsiness. And the trompe l'oeil is seen, not as trying to make us mistake art for reality, but as trying to accentuate our awareness that, however deceptive the illusion, it is no more than illusion, a tribute to the deft manipulation of the medium.

[6] Gombrich, "Illusion and Visual Deadlock," in *Meditations on a Hobby Horse*, especially pp. 154–59.

183

tropological, linguistic, or conventionally related to fictional genres (in the narrower sense), and the use of these as glasses to condition how the configuration of generic meanings before our vision shall gather and accumulate its meanings.[7] So she sees the art of interpretation as the "filling of gaps" that turns generic cues into the completed pattern that, once we have contributed "the beholder's share," we see as the work. It is indeed consistent with what we saw in Chapter 3 as Gombrich's formula for the beholder's use of "schemata" to construct the illusion that art has provided.[8] Though, as Colie does here, I granted the beholder's share in Chapter 3—however strong my commitment to the ought-ness within the object—like Colie I still wanted to be certain that it was the poet's context that dominated the reader's, that it was the poet's pattern he was completing rather than his own. Colie puts the matter quite unambiguously as she seeks to deal with the way in which the reader is to handle the hiatus within his experience of a poem like "The Garden":

> *the work of art was the unmistakable point of contact between artist and reader, artist and beholder; it legitimately focused attention upon itself, made demands upon both creator's skill and beholder's responsiveness. Decorum did not allow for cadenzas, and space in literary works was not left to be filled by random and idiosyncratic associations or daydreaming. When space is left, then, in such a poem as "The Garden" one is required to see why this is so, to follow the directions given within the work itself for filling that space.*[9]

[7] A most remarkable demonstration of the method occurs in her chapter on "The Garden," in *"My Ecchoing Song": Andrew Marvell's Poetry of Criticism* (Princeton, N.J., 1970), pp. 141–77. Using the Gombrichian notion that the "beholder" completes or fills in the pattern to which the cues point, she claims, "In Marvell's case, we are not lacking for fill: industrious bees, caterpillars, and bulldozers have amassed huge slagheaps of material, from which we have been politely invited to stuff the felt gaps in the poet's work. Bonaventure, Canticles, Plotinus, Horace, hermetica of various sorts, St. Paul, pastoral-in-general, libertinism, and many other ample traditions, concepts, and thinkers have been pressed into the service of Marvell's garden of verses, into the service of 'The Garden' in particular" (pp. 142–43). See also her final and more general statement in behalf of *genera mixta* (the use of and deviation from—or parody upon—received genres or traditional commonplaces) in the posthumously published series of lectures, *The Resources of Kind: Genre-Theory in the Renaissance*, ed. Barbara K. Lewalski (Berkeley and Los Angeles, 1973).

[8] For a discussion in Gombrich of the observer filling in an incomplete pattern in a picture, completing an action within the suspended space of the canvas, see "Moment and Movement in Art," *Journal of the Warburg and Courtauld Institutes*, vol. 27 (1964), esp. p. 302.

[9] *"My Ecchoing Song,"* p. 142.

Out of the leads provided by the poet, the reader was to supply the generic fill for gaps that were perceptual, ideological, or anything in between. The accumulation of such leads, in the eyes of a wary reader,
adds the dimension of self-reference to the poem: those behind-the-
scenes devices, technical or topical, that—enforcing one another—
define the poem as artifice and illusion, however strong the mimetic
impulse in it appears to be. And out of this self-reference, in turn, come
the echoes and juxtapositions that impose themselves as formal or synchronic elements, patterns that shape the verbal and mimetic materials
that flow before the reader, shape them and return them upon themselves.

But to do justice to this aspect of the poet's achievement, we must
move beyond the merely generic deviations with which we have been
dealing to a second and uniquely inventive kind of deviation. Colie herself, in her celebration of the peculiar compound of *genera mixta*, must
finally dwell not upon the common sort of deviations from reality conventionally invented by fictional genres, but upon this second kind: the
special deviations from these generic patterns contrived by the poet for
his peculiar purposes in this work. Though generic patterns deviate
from extra-fictional reality, they remain minimal in the requirements
needed to satisfy their patterns, to fill in their gaps; if maximal opportunities for filling in are to be satisfied, they can be created only by
deviating from the archetype, now seen as stereotype.[10] In effect they
must, out of these latest deviations, create their own newly transformed pattern. How, being unique and thus unforeseen, can they yet
lead the beholder to apprehend them by filling them in the "right way"?
Here arises the poet's greatest challenge.

My distinction between the generic, with its minimal requirements,
and the transformed version of generic elements—the unique with its
satisfaction of newly invented maximal requirements—is perhaps just
another version of the common distinction between sign and symbol.
But there is this difference between most such distinctions and mine:
I put all meanings that are fully assigned prior to this use of them in
this poem under the category of "sign," whether they are arbitrarily
designated (like any verbal equivalent of a thing) or are allegorically—
or even iconically—significant (like the cross of Christianity or a con-

[10] Gombrich himself, it must be admitted, too often fails to deal with this second,
and aesthetically central, kind of deviation; or, if he does, he tends to collapse it
into the first. His central concern is with perceptual norms, and with Colie I view
all varieties of generic patterns as the literary equivalent of these perceptual norms.
The cues that respond to his perceptual requirements often seem only minimal and
generic, although—obviously—it is the manipulation of these norms that permits
superior works of art to take off from merely conventional ones.

ventionally agreed-upon iconographic reference). Since its meaning, as universal, preexists its use in this work, the sign is for me generic, whether it is a counter obviously inappropriate to its meaning or (as may be more apparently the case in the plastic arts than in literature) is appropriate to its meaning, even to the point of resembling it or partaking of it. Although others (Susanne Langer is an obvious example) may prefer to treat the latter group as symbols, my exclusive interest in the poetic remaking of *all* given materials, whether their prior meanings were arbitrarily, ideologically, or aesthetically derived, requires that I see them equally as generic and minimal while they await the poet's transformations. So I would collapse any distinctions among generic signs, seeing such distinctions as insignificant to aesthetics, just as, in Chapter 4, I collapsed the distinction—so important to historians of criticism—between mimetic and expressive theories, and for similar reasons. To concentrate on the transformation into symbols is to move from the generic deviations that our perceptual habits read as universal (and minimal) aesthetic signs—marks of the play of fiction that set it off from our normal experience—to those before-unsuspected deviations that open up the chance for maximal exploitation.

With this second sort of deviation, there would once again appear to be a spectrum among the possibilities, running from those works which are the least obviously synchronic to those whose formal elements most obviously impose themselves on the moving succession of words and represented events. At the one end are works verging on unimpeded temporal sequence, with a minimum of echoes except as these are dictated by generic convention; at the other a multiplication of echoes, an involution of pattern, that sees the work trying to spatialize itself as if in defiance of its temporal nature. But here again the spectrum may prove to be illusory, of course provided we are including in it only works that satisfy the elementary requirement of the critical tradition that—however literal their apparent imitation of history— they finally come to terms with themselves by way of an inner teleology. So long as this criterion holds, in each case the diachronic will at last yield up the synchronic, though in extreme cases perhaps with a grudging and deceptive subtlety.

As Burckhardt helped teach Colie as well as me, the poet wrenches us out of our context and into his, unmakes our pattern by making us construct his, by deviating from the commonplaces, the norms, that are the generic meanings that we bring as our context of expectations to his fictional configuration. It is the jarring and the disturbance that force us to construct patterns that are at variance with our own (as well as with patterns of the generic convention, of course) and which we did not know we could apprehend until we have done so under his guidance. Still it is the generic cues, drawn from so many varied genres of life and art, that point the way. So what scholars like Spitzer, in the European tradition of stylistics, thought of, from the standpoint of the poem, as deviations from the norm, become in Burckhardt, from the standpoint of the reader-interpreter, "disturbing elements."[11] If our first concern above was with generic deviations from extrapoetic "reality," deviations common to all fictional illusion, we now are concerned with those unique deviations with which the poet shocks our generic sense of language and of art and our commonplace expectations about experience.

What I have been calling generic expectations, then, are the patterns or "schemata" that precede this poem and that we bring to it in order to fill in the gaps its reading leaves with us as we seek to turn the poem as read into the poem as interpreted. These expectations, as I have discussed them in detail in Chapter 2, may be drawn from the commonplaces of empirical reality (ours or the poet's as scholarship has informed us about him) or from the commonplace deviations from and transformations of reality that fictional traditions have taught us to recognize and anticipate. In effect (if I may adapt to my own uses the terms we have received from Saussure) they constitute the *langue* behind and before the poem, apparently in control of the poem that serves as its *parole*. The satisfaction of these generic expectations, we saw, requires only minimal cues to produce the stereotyped response in us. The unique deviations from such commonplace and therefore minimal expectations of whatever sort—provided we can discover (or create) a justification for these deviations that points toward and helps constitute the center of a new transformational system—lead to our discovering patterns that only the satisfaction of maximal requirements can fulfill.

In discussing the tradition that culminates in Spitzer and Burckhardt, we noted the devout critic's faith that the deviations in the poem, which, as "discrepancies," become the elements that disturb and distract the routine interpretation, will allow him to transform that interpretation into a more adequate one. We also noted, perhaps more crucially, that this faith rests on the mythology of teleological perfection, what Burckhardt speaks of as the infallibility or total interpretability

[11] One must pay tribute also to those early Russian formalists and their followers in the Prague School, who, with their interest in the distortion or defamiliarization or violation of language norms by poetry, set the terms out of which Spitzer's and, later, Burckhardt's concerns could be formulated.

of the "book," the man-made surrogate for the demythologized sacred books.[12] As I have more than once observed, the notion that every "discrepancy" must be found by the critic to be purposeful—with the reason for this purpose the deep rationale for the surprisingly true meaning of the "book"—is indeed the necessary and supreme fiction that makes this kind of critic's work possible. It is, we have seen, this critic's postulated myth of total interpretability that permits him to see the generic language system behind the poem as first violated and then mixed, the minimal converted to maximal, as discrepancy becomes inevitability, the accidental substantive. He thus no longer views the poem as but another example of *parole*, the particular representation of the never-spoken *langue*: it is not simply an instance of speech in accordance with the elementary structures of the language system. Like all the other generic and minimal elements, the *langue* has been violated to the point that the *parole* appears to have become its own *langue*, a system of which it is the only spoken representation. In effect it becomes its own *micro-langue*, the only *langue* that speaks, the only *parole* that is its own system—the true concrete universal. Not that it is literally incompatible with the existing *langue* of which it is a *parole*, but that the *langue* cannot account for what this particular speech act has performed. The diachronic character of the *parole* gives way to the synchronic transformation of this new *langue* that is revealed in this particular and unrepeatable manifestation.[13] Or so, at least, under the conditions of aesthetic illusion, it claims to be.

However sophisticated this version of the theory has become, it shares with Aristotle—at the very start of this tradition—the need to treat the diachronic in a way that transforms it to the synchronic, so long as the myth of teleological perfection persists as the interpreter's first principle. What makes the present versions more sophisticated is precisely their self-conscious awareness of the mythic and thus fictional character of their aesthetic presupposition, the very existential postulate that permits the critic's function to come into being. We have several times now noted that, just as the poem proclaims its fictional nature by

---

[12] See my discussion of "Books" and "books" toward the end of Chapter 5. Burckhardt of course acknowledges (as I did in Chapters 2 and 3) that man-made books are indeed imperfect, once one drops the mythic postulate, in which case we proceed to substitute an "explanation" of the disturbing discrepancy, which we confess to be no longer interpretable. To explain is thus to give extrinsic reasons (like the loss of control by the poet due to a personal obsession) for what is no longer open to "intrinsic interpretation." See *Shakespearean Meanings*, pp. 293–97.

[13] Of course, though I here use the terms *langue* and *parole*, perhaps metaphorically, I mean to refer to all the elements I have been calling "generic," and not just linguistic ones.

its devices of self-reference, so the critic—in the Burckhardtian mood —makes his assumptions about the "book" at hand only as he acknowledges (at least to himself) that he is speaking of poems only under the condition of aesthetic illusion: that poems do not literally achieve self-enclosed perfection, that the language system in the poem is not in truth discontinuous with discourse at large—and, consequently, that his experience of the poem cannot, finally, be a totally aesthetic experience. He knows that the diachronic has not really, in the end, lost out to the synchronic; that, in the end, the diachronic never loses. The sophisticated critic, though still working within the tradition that begins with Aristotle, needs no demythologizer to remind him of the miraculous nature of his claims, since he has undercut them himself, in imitation of the ways in which the proper poet undercuts *his*.

His self-consciousness is a recognition of the successive deprivations Western man has suffered as he has withdrawn from one ontological claim to another in the many centuries that have led from ontology toward fiction. Such is the sequence I described in Chapters 5 and 6, the retreat of the eighteenth-century rationalistic dogma under the assault of critical philosophy: the retreat from metaphysics to aesthetics, from God's world to the human work, in which the demythologized *is* becomes the *as if*. It is, in short, the retreat from *the* Book to many man-made books. We can distinguish at least a couple of stages in this retreat. First, man as the withdrawing subject abandons the world as an object of knowledge, but only to replace it with the world that he as subject wills. Having given up on the myth of external design, he moves from *Sturm und Drang* humanism through idealism and romanticism to Nietzsche, more and more molding nature to his forms: the aesthetic impulse that swallowed the ontologist's metaphysical impulse is now converted to the ethical, the social-political *act*. Kantian modesty gives way to the new inflation of a post-Romantic Genesis. The impudence of the man-god bestows substance on his aesthetic creations, finding in them a capacious home for objects how and where the arrogant humanist subject would have them. The demythification of cosmos has thus been followed by the mythification of art—the reification, as by Goethe's Faust, of his word as the willed substitute for God's. Man has turned his forms into his created world, a newly solid object of worship and belief.

What follows are the monstrous failures of the creations of our willful utopian visionary, the humanist Frankenstein (traced, as I have claimed, in Mann's recantation of Goethe's *Faust* and culminating in our current march to technological and thermonuclear suicide), and these call forth a second demythifying movement: the subject is driven into a further retreat, in which all he has left is the word, his word-made-form that can no longer create more than a visionary (now only in the sense of an illusionary) reality that is accepted as a fiction. The willful post-Romantic visionary is to be replaced by the skeptical one. If original mythology posited an inspirited external reality, and a de-mythified but still arrogant humanism created the forms of a reified projection that the subject wills to be real and in which he wills to live, this further demythifying of the man-god's belief in his own creations is a final deprivation: only the word as make-believe remains to him. The oppressive reality of external "things" can no longer be seen within its own objective order (as in the original myth), nor is it to be re-constituted within his own willed order (as in the second, subjective myth). Instead, the fictional word is deprived of the power to change that reality, and external "things" remain out there, unknown and in-differently on their own, though this word creates the evasive human categories that permit him as subject to endure the things. As with the characters of *Tristram Shandy,* he uses his language to make a hobby-horsical reality that replaces the objective world, though, like Tristram (and *not* most of the others in that novel), he knows the make-believe nature of the substitute reality he has seized upon, and knows that the other "real" reality—though outside his terms—will yet call upon him to succumb to it.[14]

Beyond this tentative and modest claim for the word there can be no further retreat. For the word, undone as a creator of real worlds, is recreated for fictional play. As the human creator presses this recreated word toward becoming a total object of his own, his new totalization can be retained without the need of being demythologized. Up until this point totalization was always a by-product of mythologizing. The primi-tive myth, as described for example by Mircea Eliade, has about it a sacramental totality, with the whole world being enfolded within it, without residue. So, of course, does the mythological construct of eighteenth-century rationalism: in the world of Pope's *An Essay on Man,* Epistle I, there must be, by a priori definition, a nothing-left-out-ness, a lack of gap, lest the entire construct (seen as objectively grounded) fall apart. Even in the reduced, no longer cosmic claims of post-Goethean humanism, the human constructs that project the formal dimensions in which man wills himself to be contained have about them

---

[14] It is, in light of *Tristram Shandy,* utterly fitting that E. H. Gombrich should have selected the hobby-horse as his example of the aesthetic "substitute" for real objects. See his "Meditations on a Hobby Horse" (which has no reference to Sterne's novel, by the way), in *Meditations on a Hobby Horse and Other Essays on the Theory of Art* (London, 1963), pp. 1–11.

a completeness and a humanly sanctioned sanctity that create an authority that subsequent history requires also to be demythologized *and*
(in the process) returned to the gaps that mark its incompleteness. But
the word-made-form-for-its-fiction's-sake claims neither to find nor to
create a world in which to live: it claims no objective teleology, no
cosmic purpose, and no subjective teleology, no willed purpose. It claims
only the teleology of the word.

There is, then, no place left to retreat if one is to make an even
minimally modest claim to man's form-making powers. Of course, the
poetic object, however self-consciously fictional, still does—in this
tradition—maintain the mythological claim to wholeness, though it is
now restricted to the totalization in the object itself. All that Gombrich
as well as Burckhardt has taught us about the "beholder's" refusal to
acknowledge gaps, his need to fill in anything that threatens the completeness of pattern, reinforces the myth of organic totality that may
also seem subject to the demythifier's attack. We can, for example,
recall Burckhardt's instruction for the interpreter to turn every "discrepancy," each element that disturbs him, into the basis for a new hypothesis more able than any earlier one to account for the poem's completeness. Thus "stumblingblocks [are to be] turned into cornerstones,"[15]
their solid material foundation constructed out of what may have been
perceived as an airy nothing (and, like all words, was indeed just that).
Or we may think back to Chapter 2 and to my own literally mythological
construction (except for my own skeptical disclaimers) of the poem during the creative process as a "developing monster," helping to create
itself as an integral object by imposing its will upon the struggling poet.
I had to postulate that, out of the many selves drawn from a myriad of
centers, there is, as the poem, a constructed self from whose center all
elements radiate and to which they return—and return *us* as willing
reader-subjects. Like the others, this was a necessary metaphor and the
supreme—if reduced—fiction for the theorist committed to the overall
myth of verbal totalization in the poem. So from these significant examples it may seem that I was too optimistic in claiming that, unlike the
others, this minimal aesthetic totalization was free of mythification.

On the other side, however, it can be argued that, so long as the
critic is aware of his dependence on the fictional self he is attributing
to the poem as an integral entity, his totalization can be retained without
the self-deception that renders it vulnerable. He too can accept the
notion that the word as the element that gives our world the continuity
of order—the word in our post-Goethean, post-Kantian mood—*does*

[15] *Shakespearean Meanings*, p. 289.

191

fail. With Lévi-Strauss he can reduce the meaning of our cultural myths to their repetitive structures, with their generic words denuded of their claimed content. But, fighting to recreate the word as fiction in this last humanistic fastness, the traditional theorist can reclaim for the word, now subverted and reconstituted, the power to make a total form that metaphorically contains a world while it skeptically acknowledges that it contains no more than itself. In this doubleness of aggrandizement and self-denial, the humanist's fight for form achieves an invulnerability, if only because it has now been subdued to its final and ironic modesty. Its myth of totality, sustained by the critic who self-consciously supplies what he must to make it work, is proclaimed only to provide the ground in which it can momentarily flourish. With fictions fronting for fictions, personae ducking behind personae, there is little self-delusion here.[16]

The more I speak of self-conscious illusion, however, the further I seem to be moving from making the case for the capacity of fiction to affect our reality. If we stress the miraculous nature of poetic transformation only to admit that it cannot be a miracle unless it is impossible, then our common-sense skepticism undercuts our desire to take the poem as revelation. As we reify our experience of what is before us into an object we "intend" as aesthetic, we may, with our reflexive self-consciousness, prevent the delusion of self-mystification, but only at the risk still of keeping that other, make-believe world of poetry carefully out of touch with our own. If this is the case, then for all the twistings and turnings of literary theory, we are not far advanced from the phantastic-icastic opposition of centuries ago. But I believe that we can move from the deviations we have observed to the metaphors into which they transform their works, and in these we can find reduced versions—at once metonymic symbols and typological figures—of how, during a moment in culture, the world is grasped as reality (or, rather, as-if reality).

As we seek to be disturbed by a peculiarly poetic form, shaken from our prepoetic sets of minimal and generic expectations, we seek for the patterns composed of common directions taken by the deviations. Careful scholarship would permit us to build up many and varied sets of expectations of what the poem would have to mean if it is to be "true to"

---

[16] Burckhardt himself, it must be admitted, does not dwell upon the self-conscious version of the poem as illusion with the explicit theoretical awareness of Colie, with her adaptations of Gombrich. So I have performed some emendation here, though I believe it is thoroughly Burckhardtian in spirit. The self-conscious doubleness of that spirit is immediately apparent in the very title of his first major theoretical essay, reprinted in *Shakespearean Meanings*, "The Poet as Fool and Priest."

this historical and psychological experience, the literary genres, and the generally available language out of which it grows and from which—if it pursues its own integrity—it deviates. The more we know about elements prior to this poem that are reflected in it, and the more elements and kinds of elements we know about, the more open we are to being disturbed if we are attentive to the poem—disturbed frequently and consistently, as the deviations occur. And we proceed—in Burckhardt's way—toward a system constructed out of the deviations, a new center toward which they are seen as pointing.

The myth of total interpretability assumes that the deviations from pre-poetic patterns—whether patterns of life, literature, or language—all help to realize the internally generated teleological system: in each case, as I argued in Chapter 2, the difference between the materials before the poem and their manifestation in the poem is to be justified as a transformation required by the emerging pattern (at least as this process is projected, after the fact, by this myth). So as we put together these differences, each of which is seen as a necessary transformation, they are to constitute a pattern in which we should find the poem's own teleological system. Although there is an endless variety of biographical-historical contingencies that, through all the accidents, mistakes, and connivances of poetic creation, can lead a poet to work distortions in his raw materials—perhaps most of the causes of the differences being local and unrelated to teleological structure—the myth must prefer to overlook all but what lends itself to aesthetic justification. It is not that the local reasons, as genetic accounts, are denied, but that they are of no ultimate interest, since what counts is how the difference serves to create teleology—and serve it must.[17]

Of course, when a deviation can really not be made to serve, despite all the critic's ingenuity, then he is allowed to appeal to the local biographical facts that can account for it, but only because for the moment he has abandoned the objective of interpretation—persuaded by an aberrant work that cannot be talked into coming around—and must in this instance satisfy himself with mere "explanation," the recital of the local facts that prevented interpretation.[18] The need for explanation, then, is accompanied by an implicit negative evaluation, together with the hope—required by the myth—that either he or another critic

---

[17] Once more we must remind ourselves that the critic is not flying in the face of historical evidence, but is relating himself only to his phenomenological construct of the poem as his intentional aesthetic object. The myth springs from this assumption, which really precludes not at all the acknowledgment of the sway of diachronic reality, the casual empirical facts of creativity.

[18] *Shakespearean Meanings*, pp. 293–96.

will one day come upon the insight that permits him to reconstruct the entire interpretation of the work into one that will require precisely this deviation, one that only this deviation can permit him to see. So the compromise with explanation remains provisional and temporary, with the preservation of the myth of total interpretability transcending every failure of poem or of critic.

If the difference between the "matter for" (or before) the poem and the "matter in" the poem (as John Dewey so lucidly put this distinction[19]) is the difference between personally contingent elements and the transformed versions of these as aesthetically necessary elements (with reference to a teleological center), then the poem indeed seems cut off from person and history, so that the impersonal and metahistorical theories of the New Criticism may well follow. But this simple consequence is too simple: even though the purely personal and time-bound event may have to be transformed as it is transcribed into the poem in order to make it work there, still the transforming agent *is* the time-bound poet. As he makes changes in his raw materials to make them fit the emerging pattern that they are also helping to constitute, he can only make them *his* way, bearing his mark. Though the myth may see the poem as an evolving monster that imposes its growing systematic demands upon its poet—demands related only to its needs and not his—it is but a myth: the poem is still written by him and cannot help but reflect his consciousness, even if finally in ways perhaps quite different from what he could have predicted at the outset. The need to transform the prepoetic elements may preclude our using the poem as a simple reflection of the poet and his culture, but the adequate critic must try to discover more subtle reflections, even while he is faithfully interpreting: he must show not only that the transformation is uniquely what the poem requires, but that it is uniquely what this poet requires (perhaps in more ways than he knew), that it is just this transformation which would occur only to him as man and as maker.

The critic, then, cannot help but treat the poem as an expression of the poet's consciousness existing at a moment in culture, although he must do it the hard way—by acknowledging that he can work only with the elements *as* transformed and cannot simply trace them back to their prepoetic sources. How can he find in the poem the repository of man and history while he allows it to have redirected all its elements toward its own center? He does so by treating that center, its own mythic reality, as its constitutive metaphor, expression of what it contains. If its poet's or, through him, its culture's consciousness is to be captured, it

[19] *Art as Experience* (New York, 1934), p. 110.

194

would be there, in that symbolic reduction fed by the deviations, properly read singly and in systematic unison. Attentive to its own integrity, the poem as center yet contains—in that integrity—much that is not itself; but, by capturing and domesticating what is outside itself, it reduces to its order all that is thereby acknowledged to be beyond its dimensions, all that is beyond order and unmanageable in the fullness of its own contingencies, beyond the poem and the aesthetic realm. The aesthetic thus constitutes visionary categories for turning the anthropological into perceptual entities, while its refinements protest their inadequacy for enclosing its bulky object. It contains (holds in, restrains) the object only while failing to contain (enclose) all of it. The existential is aesthetically rendered in its symbolic reduction, except that it does not stop existing, intimidatingly, out there on its own.

The poem-as-metaphor, defined in this way, has to be a metonym as well, the aesthetic part that symbolizes a far less restrictive anthropological whole, an enclosed microcosm that seeks to substitute for what would be the macrocosm except that it is not susceptible of order. The poem is a self-assertive surrogate that arrogantly claims its sufficiency to emblematize reality. This diminutive substitution is necessary because there is no order except in this reduced aesthetic object we make on the principle of *multum in parvo*.[20] Nor does the object overcome the disorder in the world, though what we see as the world through this form of human vision is all order.

Yet there remains, beyond the aesthetic and thus unabsorbed, a motley and undefined welter of experience, on which we normally impose our routine and stereotyped organizations in order to live sanely in it. These are the forms of our normal discourse, the *langue* of our discursive experience, which evades disorder. Yet, beyond the language of our evasions, undistilled experience persists and threatens, and we vacillate in confusion between it and our language. As I have put it elsewhere, "Our pursuit of endlessly diversified experience, veering in its infinitely various and self-aborting directions, our blunting the points we have sharply shaped, our lurching and starting and slowing and gliding and leaping, by turns, all are ways we hide from confrontation of what we dare not confront."[21]

The metaphoric reduction represents such a confrontation. It is the collapsing of the unmeasured, not into the standard, all-too-measured stalls of routine discourse, but into the purified extremity of a measured

[20] Rosalie Colie built much of her criticism on this principle. See especially "*My Ecchoing Song*," pt. 2, chap. 4, and *The Resources of Kind*, chap. 2.

[21] "Mediation, Language, and Vision in the Reading of Literature," in *Interpretation: Theory and Practice*, ed. Charles S. Singleton (Baltimore, 1969), p. 241.

metonym, at once self-assertive and self-conscious about its measured status. This is an extreme vision, one that reads all middling and muddled experience exclusively under the aspect of its casuistic reduction. Within this metonym, which arrogantly assumes its adequacy and its totality, experience is read purely, though the very completeness of its enclosing terms provides evidence of all that remains, unreduced, beyond it. In its extremity, the vision, created as the metaphor that is the poem, helps define its poet's consciousness and that of his moment in culture; but, though locked inside those reduced, metonymic terms, those very terms—with their self-referential awareness of their own artifice—remind us of what is outside as well.

So the poem as a whole serves as a metonymic metaphor in that it has transferred the many-directioned and shapeless materials of reality—the confusing "given" of our experience at any moment in culture—to the diminished terms of its limited but utterly directed and shaped vision: it thus reduces reality, within its own consistent pattern, to its own language and vision, that is, to its language-centered vision and its visionary language. My treatment of "China" in Pope's "The Rape of the Lock," in Chapter 6, can serve as an abbreviated version of this operation. There I emphasized the doubleness of the relationship between the aesthetic reduction and the resistant reality beyond: "China's Earth" (in the line "While *China*'s Earth receives the smoking Tide,") is the polished refinement of art—like that of the poem and of Belinda's toy-shop world. Though it is, in other words, the aesthetic reduction of China, the phrase itself carries in it the meaning of China's flesh, the endlessly peopled earth of that crowded land, but only to exclude it. As purified emblem, the earthenware is the metonym for the earth, a refined representative of it, and yet, of course, not at all like it: its artfulness excludes flesh, its precise manufacture excludes the numberless consequences of the chanciness of nature. Just so the other double meanings ("fiery Spirits," "smoking Tide") suppress what they suggest: the pouring of hot liquid from silver spouts in the coffee rite excludes—as its language, seeming to include, reminds us to associate it with—other "grateful Liquors" pouring from other spouts, filling China's earth as these fill another sort of China's earth. Much of this sort of doubleness—an exclusion whose language seems to spread its meanings to encompass what it, more narrowly, is seen as rejecting— occurs in other rites and games and mock battles throughout the poem, always reminding us what this purified world must neglect, as a prerequisite to its existence. The words seem bent on revealing the limitations of the world they describe, in their doubleness defining it by exclusion as well as inclusion. To return to the China example, we can say that, in reducing one kind of China's earth to another, the poem creates its emblematic metonymy (China for China, earth for earth) as its central metaphor (art for nature), while the fullness of its language denies the existential validity of the reduction. The metaphor, like the world of the poem, is brilliant, with a wrought surface ever admirable, but it is also reminding us constantly that, however satisfying its limited vision, it is not the world.

Yet it is a total metaphor, with its meanings fused into its language. The deviations from a single-file line of meaning are all directed, as they are deflected, into the double-edged reduction, and in the entire poem as in this representative passage. The critic must be careful to distinguish between the use of one entity merely to illuminate another (as in simile or analogy) and the complete transference of a broad area of experience to the terms and the limited but precise vision of a narrow entity (as in what I am terming metonymic metaphor). This distinction between analogy and metaphor, descended from earlier distinctions between allegory and symbol, or fancy and imagination, has been a central issue in organic theory in our century. Critics since I. A. Richards have made the distinction by asking whether the tenor and the vehicle of the figure are separable or are fused. In accordance with my preliminary claims in Chapter 2, I have been assuming in my presentation that the distinction is a meaningful one and that it is only the fully bodied metaphor that is of interest to this theoretical tradition.

Analogy is from this point of view only a rhetorical strategy, in that the poet does not subvert the one portion of experience while comparing it to the other. He completes his analogical comparison with the original portion essentially unaltered. There are similarities between the two objects of comparison, but they remain discrete entities and therefore dissimilar in the main. What was vague in its universality retains its imprecision despite the particularity of the comparison that gives a rhetorical impression of clarity, because it borrows nothing that can change its nature or give it existential authority. Normal language operation is not violated, in that verbal properties remain intact. One is hardly pressing the normal capacities of language by saying that A is like B with respect to characteristic X, since it is quite clear that A and B remain distinct, with many distinguishing characteristics (at most, all characteristics except X). Further, no matter how many additional similar characteristics the poet's ingenuity may discover, the entities of course remain distinct. For he is working in accord with the commonsense logic of language that sponsors the law of identity, the semantic propriety that keeps objects-as-words distinct entities, keeps them from overrunning one another's bounds, from appropriating one another's properties. However elaborate the comparison, it is still within the domain of analogy or simile—and of rhetoric—with the entity being compared still able to withdraw or return from the comparison unaltered.

Poetic metaphor occurs when the poet forces his language to make the case for total identity, A suddenly appearing to become B, in violation of proper language behavior. (I was going to start this sentence with the words, "Poetic metaphor *begins*," but metaphor is always fully there when it is there; for it begins as simile, and metaphor is where it ends.) Ransom, introducing this definition of metaphor, refers to it as a kind of "miraculism," "the same miraculism which supplies to religions their substantive content," a transubstantiation that has the empty sign take on body. Yet, technically, it appears to be no more than "the extension of a rhetorical device"; in constructing it the poet seems to move from an analogy between objects that can relate them to one another only partially "to an identification which is complete."[22] So, in the case of metaphor, the critic, as if he were dealing with rhetorical analogy only, can trace the steps by which the poet has extended his device from occasional similarities to an essential identity, but he cannot return us down those steps or account for the miraculous way in which, at those final steps, the collection of similarities is transformed into equivalence.[23]

What appears as miracle claims to be, in effect, the substantive transfer of properties, as one object is forced to be read as the other, utterly reduced to its terms and no longer capable of returning to itself intact. It may well be that, as Ransom would claim, the development of the metaphysical conceit is the model procedure. How does it move from an increasingly complex rhetorical comparison (which is all that

[22] "Poetry: A Note in Ontology," in *The World's Body* (New York, 1938), pp. 139–40. In *A Window to Criticism*, pp. 4–16, I treat this argument of Ransom's and show similar and supporting theoretical notions in works by Allen Tate, Erich Auerbach, Spitzer, and Burckhardt.

[23] In my discussion of Roman Jakobson in Chapter 8, we shall see that he tries to distinguish poetry from other discourse by claiming that the elements of contiguity (as in his metonymy), which in nonpoetic discourse operate in conjunction with elements of similarity (as in his metaphor), are in the special case of poetry overcome by the principle of equivalence. So in poetry metaphor subsumes metonymy, a notion to which my own may seem similar. But it is important to note in a preliminary way here what will be emphasized in Chapter 8: that Jakobson cannot be concerned, as I must, with distinguishing between similarity and equivalence, or between simile and metaphor, since both are ranged on poetry's side as the victor over prosaic contiguity or metonymy. His dependence on a generic linguistic distinction (between synchronic and diachronic) prevents him from worrying the distinction I have been worrying here. The consequences of this theoretical difference are pursued in the next chapter but needed to be mentioned here.

our common sense says it can be, given the way language operates generically) to the illusion of the self-sealing identity of poetic metaphor? One may begin, as we have seen, by pressing one aspect of similarity between two entities (preferably, from my point of view, with one of them—the vehicle—seen as but a part, a reduced version, of the other, the variegated and unmanageable tenor). Even though one can add other aspects of similarity, gradually shifting from the balanced awareness of tenor and vehicle (which always returns us to the tenor), toward an awareness of the vehicle and its terms only, the heterogeneity of the two is still left unchallenged. The similarities being accumulated probably are the most likely ones, those which are least liable to challenge the comparative procedure by forcing obviously unresolvable points of difference upon us. The poet appears to be working the path of little resistance, satisfying the minimal requirement that features dwelled upon in the vehicle can be translated back into features of the tenor which do not seem unreceptive to the terms of translation. (The literal and the figurative applications of the terms, seen separately and yet with points of union emphasized, constitute an obvious device, for example.) But so long as the obvious aspects conducive to the heterogeneity of the two entities are not challenged, nothing very special has happened. The analogy is partial, either partner can withdraw from it unscathed, and normal language behavior has not been undermined.

The opportunity to transform the discourse arises when the poet confronts the heterogeneity head on, attacking a point of obvious and insurmountable difference, and—perhaps by no more than a verbal trick—forces *it* to serve the transfer of terms as well, even though it should be clear that this is the one element of comparison he should have avoided, since it threatens the very possibility of comparing the two entities. Yet he forces this very element to serve, and to serve maximally. And this maximal service changes how the balance of his discourse must be seen as working. By manipulating his language until the vehicle is made to absorb this least likely element of the tenor, he has converted the gravest threat to his comparison into that which confirms it as total identity: the poet has provided the double-pointed words that prove and contain that identity, if the reader allows himself to be trapped in the poet's game of verbal sleight-of-hand.

As an obvious and brief example, it is no problem to claim that lovers are like saints in their unworldly involvement with the objects of their loves, and to extend this claim of similar unworldliness; but, as a potential difference and a grave one, it may also be obvious that the lovers' unworldliness may seem contemptible from the standpoint of worldly pursuits while the saints' may seem exemplary. One sort of love, the sensual, may be seen as but an inferior part, or earthy counterpart, of the spiritual love that is the other sort being compared in the poem. But what if, instead of continuing to move down parallel paths, emphasizing superficial sameness between the two sorts of love, the poet took on directly what is most outrageously different between lovers and saints: that the former find their consummation in a bestial delight and the latter in a spirituality that is never consumed? What if he tortured his duplicitous language into producing the impossible identity here by finding that the lovers—in doing the very physical thing that is most natural to them as lovers—are yet performing the uniquely saintly function after all, and so persuasively, that they themselves become examples for the world, thereby undoing the one point of difference granted at the start? If the poet does these things well enough, he seduces us into the lovers-saints identity, though one earned on the lovers' side and in the teeth of all the obvious and still reasonable claims that would find it absurd. If he does them well enough, he has written "The Canonization."

Again, there are many obvious ways to find similarities between a lover's valuing of his beloved and the merchant's valuing of his precious goods. Our language is full of words whose double meanings testify to the comparability of the two worlds that vie for the generic role of proper valuation. When the poet lists such similarities, however, he must be aware of the antibourgeois strain in our romantic tempers that insists on the differences between the two modes of valuing. Still, if analogy is all, he can suppress all but what blandly sees conjunctions between the two. But if, instead, he looks directly at the cruel manner in which one basis for valuing precludes the other from operating—the merchant's way precluding the lover's way—if he makes coincidences in the language of value serve to split the two and then reunite them within the now bitter terms that have reduced one to the other, then he has produced the remarkable "Farewell! thou art too dear for my possessing," which we examined in Chapter 6. The safety of analogy has been risked and lost; what has been gained is a new and equivocal structure of metaphor, transforming meanings and the very possibilities of meaning in discourse.

In this procedure the poet takes up the *a fortiori* challenge presented by the least likely point of comparison, the antagonist to his very attempt to compare. He forgoes the comfortable sequence of similarities that put up no resistance, since they blandly avoid all is there to threaten them, thereby keeping their meanings innocuously evasive. In submitting his work to that which most endangers a limited enterprise and forcing it to underwrite a far more ambitious one, he is committing himself to that tradition, treated in Chapter 6, which grades poetic value by the degree of resistance overcome. He has effected what Coleridge called for: "the balance or reconciliation of opposite or discordant qualities." In accord with those theorists with which I began this chapter, the poet demonstrates the willingness to challenge his work's unity by meeting a diversity that will either wreck it or deepen it, but must disrupt its facile unfolding: he commits himself to reveal its capacity to absorb what seems directed toward breaking it up. Further, in cultivating the *a fortiori* opposition, he is cultivating the casuistic extremity that he makes his own and ours, the lens through which diffuse and unpointed experience achieves visionary definition.[24]

Although we have, in Ransom's footsteps, been dealing with technical conceits, it has clearly been my intention in this chapter to move beyond the lyric and to treat as metaphor all complete transfers of terms and visionary structures. Even more, I mean to emphasize the transfer as casuistic—as moving from a broad and imprecise realm of experience to an extremely reduced and purified part of it, thereby joining metonym to metaphor. One could trace similar developments of analogical extensions transformed to metaphor in narrative and dramatic structures, with or without the word play we have just witnessed. For example, the comparisons, polarizings, and intermeshings of guilt as theological and guilt as legal in Kafka's *The Trial*, or of time as Christological and time as chronological (Christ's seasons and nature's) in Eliot's *Murder in the Cathedral*—these lend themselves to analysis like that which I have applied to the duplicity of "China's Earth" in "The Rape of the Lock."[25] In that poem, too, verbal analysis can be expanded to a broader view of two-faced metaphor: the two rapes—of body and

[24] Compare my earlier description of this process in *The Tragic Vision* (New York, 1960), p. 256. (I should point out that it comes in the concluding section of a book devoted to novels, so that it should serve as an indication of the extent to which these claims can be extended beyond the verbal play of the lyric to fictions generally.) "I have suggested that for the poet to formulate the extreme situation is indeed for him to play the casuist by purifying experience of the casual; that, through the narrow intensity of *a fortiori* controls, the extreme situation can manage to account for the total breadth of experience, for all that is less committed and more compromising—and compromised. This is in effect what Henry James means in speaking of actual life that 'persistently blunders and deviates, loses herself in the sand,' in his complaints against the 'stupid work' of 'clumsy' raw experience which, unpurified, not merely militates against art but obfuscates its own meaning, leaving to art the role of mining this meaning anew. The extreme, then, is both more pure and more inclusive—pure in the adulterations it rejects and inclusive in the range of less complete experiences it illuminates even as it passes them by. Thus at once the rarity and the density, the order and the plenitude."

[25] See *The Tragic Vision*, pp. 114–44, for my study of *The Trial*, and *The Classic Vision* (Baltimore, 1967), pp. 337–62, for my study of *Murder in the Cathedral*. All the works treated in both volumes I try to analyze as reductive metaphors of broad existence juxtaposed to narrow extremity. See my summaries of these metaphors in *The Classic Vision*, pp. 20–21, and the "Epilogue" (pp. 365–67).

of hair—one suggested as it is denied and the other explicitly enacted, are collapsed into a more inclusive version of the same metaphor, though it is now open to analysis that is not limited to word play.

Metaphoric identity is a captive of the willed moment of aesthetic intentionality. Secured only by the illusion produced by verbal, narrative, and dramatic powers, it cannot be submitted to the rigors of a propositional analysis that looks into the reasonability of its equations without being deflated at once. Yet, in its casuistry, that formal enclosure which traps the motion of its living reductions serves as a microcosmic emblem of existential forces in man and culture that are seeking definition and perceptible shape. At any cultural and psychological moment, there is, outside and before the poem, a broad and as yet undefined area of variegated experience, emotional and intellectual, which seeks to become an identifiable symbolic entity and which the poet—trying to identify it and make it available to himself and his culture—seeks through extremity to reduce to a manageable reduction.

This is, in effect, the description proposed by Eliseo Vivas, as he tries to follow these forces in experience and history as they move from "subsisting" in the culture to "insisting" in the poem.[26] Operating without name under the culture, as it were, but as a moving power within that culture, these forces achieve a symbolic identity only as the poet creates a metaphor for their metonymic representation. The subsistent influence of these forces is thus captured in their miniature "insistence" in the poem, as the poem, which is formally coextensive with its anthropological meaning. Having achieved this articulate identity, these forces have in effect been reduced to a new word (defined in and through the poem itself) in the poet's and his culture's vocabulary, which has now enlarged its capacity to speak. Of course, they can win this new "existent" status, in which they are ready to be extracted from the poem and more thinly applied to other contexts in order to serve their culture's discursive needs, only as they turn generic, becoming minimized into an old word like the others it joins. But the "new word" remains there, as the poem, for us to return to it in its metaphoric fullness to observe the forces in the full complexity of their operation.

The poem as total metaphor, then, is the self-enclosed formal fiction, clustered about the newly fashioned aesthetic center, transformed product of the several sorts of deviations we have observed. But, in indulging this fiction, we see what history has been formed into, under its aegis. Though a fiction, it helps us to see what the poet's conscious-

---

[26] In "The Object of the Poem," *Creation and Discovery* (New York, 1955), especially pp. 137–43. I adapt to my own purposes his distinctions among "subsistence," "insistence," and "existence" in *A Window to Criticism*, pp. 59–63.

ness is consciousness *of*: what its world is shaped like, or what the shape of that consciousness itself is. Thanks to the fixed object that has trapped us—as it has trapped the motions of life—within it, its vision becomes ours for now. At the same time, we must remain aware of its limited relation to reality, however it expands ours by rendering this version of it so precisely. For we must know the miracle to be self-induced, through being word-seduced—an aesthetic illusion, though one with anthropological consequences, if only tentative ones.

I suggest that the poem as metonymic metaphor functions much as does Erich Auerbach's conception of the *figura*. Like the *figura*, it is a part of historical experience that, though broken off from that sequence, serves as a purified reduction of it that takes on its own center of meaning. Yet, from the perspective of history, it remains just a part of that outside, unfigured totality while, from the internality of the *figura*, it gives that entire outside structure a meaning, *its* meaning. Just so the metonym-become-metaphor, as I have been conceiving it, must be only a figure of speech and yet the autonomous figure of experience itself, reducing (figuring) it to its own self-sufficient system of meanings while trying to picture (to figure) it all. It is the utterly fulfilled part that arrogantly subsumes the whole, except that we also know it remains but a part. Thus does it figure reality without losing the sense of reality's contingent movements (beyond figuring). For it must help us retain the doubleness of perspective that reminds us of its limited sway. It reminds us of the persistent realities of the diachronic even as it rivets our awareness to its own synchronic reduction. It can thus—while preserving experience unreduced—yet give that experience a typological structure, except that it does not, like Christian typology, rest on an external body of faith that would literally transfigure history. As in the case of all man-made books, with their authority that can be generated internally only, the figure as secular metaphor (at once figure of speech and of experience) must derive its power from its own form in collision (and collusion) with its reader's acquiescence.

Let me recapitulate the process with which this chapter has been concerned. This poem before me—as an alien "other," outside me and my consciousness—imposes upon me to make it no longer "other." My habitual willingness to indulge the myth of total interpretability makes me a willing subject for an experience that, restricted to appearance only, is properly termed "aesthetic." This experience would convert the object from "other" to part of myself. Under the aegis of this experience, the poem comes to me and my consciousness by using the distortions the poet works upon his medium (the words, the empirical sequence of events, common literary fictions, conventional generic practices) to produce a new and uncommon fiction beyond the language of my own consciousness until now. The need for it to remain a fiction is sustained by the peculiarities of language treated as a sensuous medium or the peculiarities of stage or of printed page, as any of these is the ground for the unempirical fictional occasion. But the poem works upon aesthetic habits derived from my experience with prior fictions, upon the way I worked upon them while working upon myself, in order for me to receive it in accordance with my aesthetic intentionality. If I am successfully responsive to what I see as its Gombrichian clues, I willingly reject my prior norms and follow the deviations to the new center, the new fiction, the new master metaphor of vision to which these point. Then the poem as "other" has become a form of consciousness that can alter my own. In short, I have (with all the phenomenological qualifications I have suggested) "discovered" a poem and, through it, momentarily, a new way of seeing that, after the moment, can become mine for good, so that its otherness is dissolved. And I "see" differently: my normal capacities (that is, those I had prior to this poem) have been expanded, as well as rendered more narrowly precise, as I face up to a new consciousness of "reality."

But there is no danger of solipsism: I have not ignored—indeed the poem's self-consciousness, its awareness of its unreality as but a fiction, prods me to remember—the grudging presence of those existential realities beyond the illusory categories of fiction, a presence that lurks and threatens. Still I reach for that next poem in order to help affirm what human consciousness can in its freedom shape for itself as *its* fixed version of the moving world, within the boundary existence that reality permits it. Against the fading fiction in my memory, as I return to the empirical sequence of fleeting moments which make up my existence, there stands the work's self-awareness: to be aware of itself as fictional only is also to be aware of its permanent and unchanging nature, potentially the object of an experience that is repeatable. It tells me that it is still there to be returned to, and *still* there, literally untrue to life and therefore always fixed—however dynamically its form captures life's movements—unlike my own moving, unrepeatable existence.

It would seem, then, that the post-Kantian vision which has illuminated the way of modern organic theory after Coleridge is not enough, though this may be as far as the tradition I traced in Parts One and Two of this study can bring us.[27] Or, rather than not enough, it is too much,

---

[27] Though I am claiming that the needed extension to this tradition arises out of the recent theorist's willingness to acknowledge the frailty of the verbal miracle and the ease with which reality dissipates it, I should repeat here my awareness that there is ample precedent in the tradition, before and after Kant, for this notion of

thanks to the literalism of its belief in man's word as transformed to flesh. It was this overstatement of the persuasive power of the word that became the self-mystification of the New Criticism. For, when the airiness of words has faded and the breath fails, there is the final summoning by existential fact that cannot be categorized away even by our form-making genius. As a result of all that the humanistic tradition has taught us, we must do justice to man's power to transform nature; but we must also beware of his solipsistic tendency to treat his forms as if they were the only terms on which nature can exist.

Once the traditional modernist is willing to accept the reality of nature's final dominion of fact—before and after his free verbal act of forming it—he is ready to accept the diminished conditions of the as-if on which his forms rest. He has thus abandoned the metaphysical gluttony of an all-inclusive monism (like the Coleridgean I AM or the Hegelian synthesis), while retaining, with modesty, a monistic poem. This modesty does not say less for his creations, now with their self-important claims balanced by their self-conscious fictionality. The visions of reality—the poet's and, through him, his culture's—are rendered manageable and even perceptible by the emblematic reductions of the poem as metonymic metaphor: the moments at which they force an identity, at once new and alien and recognizable, among their disparate elements provide equations that reveal the poet's semantics of imagination. And as these equations achieve metaphorical completeness, their forms provide their culture with the normative categories through which to grasp the variegated world, thereby unlocking an internal moment of anthropological vision.

But, as Wallace Stevens, the ultimate modernist, reminds us,[28] the presence of the world outside metaphor is suggested by the self-referential reminders of the poem's fiction built into the metaphor itself. The determinate matter of the world, other and indifferent, which man suffers, he tries to overwhelm with his free act of creativity, but not without knowing—sometimes to his panic—that matter persists, and

---

fictional self-consciousness. In Chapter 6 I referred to passages from Aristotle to Johnson that modify notions of poetic truth with notions of poetic illusion. Even the more ambitious claims made after Schelling and Coleridge are occasionally accompanied by skepticism. In Chapter 8 I shall, in my discussion of Paul de Man, treat a similar self-consciousness that arises in Romantic irony. But in the peculiarly modernist notions that I have associated with names like Wallace Stevens, Frye, Gombrich, Colie, and Burckhardt, this sense of the aesthetic as-if achieves a major systematic development.

[28] It is evident throughout this study that, for me, modernism is the ultimate realization (as well as the final retreat) of the humanist aesthetic tradition, while the postmodern represents at least the loss of faith in the word and at most the outright rejection of it.

in persisting undermines that freedom. As poet he forces his words to take on body, as we watch similarities become equivalences, analogies become metaphors, in violation of our normal sense of verbal property and propriety. Still, in the self-denial that is implicit in the metaphor, it reminds us also that all this occurs only within the limited domain of aesthetic intentionality, that—earth being but earth—words finally are only words, so that breath drifts off into air and can have no substance. Verbal miracles dissolve into the illusions in which we can believe only by knowing of their impossibility. But the aesthetic dream of body provides the substance on which human culture as the communal dream depends. It is the dream made into our substance that provides where we live, though it is the reality as an alien substance that kills us.

VIII
Poetics Reconstructed: The Presence of the Poem

These days it may seem quite daring, if not perversely reactionary, to proclaim the poem to be utterly and ultimately present, and, even worse, to proclaim it in the title of my concluding chapter. After all, news from abroad has been arriving almost daily for several years now proclaiming its absence: the emptiness of the word and of the verbal forms it pretends to constitute, the zero degree of writing.[1] We are to yield up the word to the hiatus that surrounds it.

Yet, from the earliest portions of this book, when I freely (though with running apologies to more recent and shrewder epistemology) used the term "object" to characterize the role of the poem, I have preferred to assume the physical presence of the poem before the reader as a phenomenological datum. In this I have been in accord with the implicit assumption of literary commentary from the time that, by writing literature down or printing it as pages and books, one began to look upon it as a physical thing. For indeed literature did begin to be looked upon rather than just heard: it was something out there that stayed rather than a passing fancy momentarily floating by the ear. But its presence was to move from physical to figurative reality: taking on spatial rather than just temporal characteristics, the poem became its own synchronic metaphor. In the Renaissance it took on the aesthetic dignity of a physically present art, and tried to earn its right to such dignity by manipulating its elements into becoming its own emblem, graphic symbol of itself. Air had indeed taken on body, the integral and inviolate body of the Burckhardtian "book," inheritor of the rights (and rites) of the sacred Books divinely authored. Here is the final reali-

---

[1] In rolling with this wave sweeping, with its negations, over poetic form, I shift advisedly (if, I confess, momentarily) from the word "poem" or even "literature" to the demythifying and deconstructing term "writing" (*écriture*). But this shift is for me no more than momentary, and justified only within this context of generalized reduction.

zation of the myth-making impulse toward the literal reification of the spoken word, as God had reified His creative Word. Such presence, with its illusion of physical immediacy, carries with it the sense of its present-ness, a forever-nowness that makes it a fixed form resisting—as Keats reminds us with his urn—the flow from past to future that denies the present as a possible category of thought. So, to the impressive here-ness of presence, the word adds the unmoving now-ness of the present.

In accordance with this impulse and its realization, formal criticism over the centuries has emphasized the spatial characteristics that it metaphorically imposes on the literary work's temporal nature as it tries to freeze its dynamics of movement into a fixed presence—and a perma-nent present. One could argue that, thanks to Aristotle, drama has a head start in formal analysis, perhaps because (as my discussion in Chapter 6 seeks to establish) the tangible, moving-picturelike quality of dramatic performance, so obviously a framed imitation of real-life experience, at once (and without metaphor) bestows a spatial quality upon itself. The conversion of mere temporal sequence into spatial "thing" is less immediately come by (aside from the notion of page and book as physical things) in lyric and narrative. Here the devices of form—repetition and juxtaposition as the most obvious of them—do what they can to spatialize the discourse, at their most extreme mov-ing toward the fixity of symbol or even emblem.[2]

Prior to the book, it might be argued, even the oral tradition strug-gled against the temporality of its medium, using the formulaic epithet or repeated sequences of parallel action to produce the echoes that permitted the evanescence of sound to spatialize itself.[3] The same im-pulse accounts for the dominance of verse: this need to turn mere dis-course, disappearing as it is spoken, into a terminal and precious object leads to the special cherishing of the role of meter and rhyme. More recently this became the tendency, traced in Chapter 2 from Words-worth and Coleridge through Ransom to Burckhardt, to make a special

[2] See my "The Ekphrastic Principle and the Still Movement of Poetry; or Laokoön Revisited," in The Play and Place of Criticism (Baltimore, 1967), pp. 105–28.

[3] This observation, hardly original, is supported by Lévi-Strauss, who gives it con-siderable importance: ". . . the question has often been raised why myths, and more generally oral literature, are so much addicted to duplication, triplication, or quad-ruplication of the same sequence. If our hypotheses are accepted, the answer is obvious: The function of repetition is to render the structure of the myth apparent. For we have seen that the synchronic-diachronic structure of the myth permits us to organize it into diachronic sequences . . . which should be read synchroni-cally. . . . Thus, a myth exhibits a 'slated' structure, which comes to the surface, so to speak, through the process of repetition" ("The Structural Study of Myth," Structural Anthropology, trans. Claire Jacobson and Brooke Grundfest Schoepf [New York, 1963], p. 229).

case for phonetic effects in verse. The primary insistence on the sensory property of words, apart from their conceptual property, is to remind us, we saw, that the poem has a physical medium to be regulated and manipulated, almost like that of the plastic arts: that the poem literally shouts its physical presence, its here-ness and now-ness, to us, and does not pass away. Thus such theorists may have it both ways: using the fact of the written page *and* the sensory stimuli of sound to announce the poem's presence.

It is this character of word as sensory medium, forced upon our awareness—as Burckhardt claims—by the poet, that persuades us to bestow "corporeality" itself upon the poem, indulging the momentary myth of making this word flesh. With language leading us to allow this subversive fusion of metaphor and pun to reflect—just this once and for this frozen moment—onto substance and concept, we indeed accept the poem as present, as the present, and as *a* present, a miraculous gift that seems to exclude all else, to turn everything else into absence, what is past or outside, next to its persistent inside "now." It is a "now" which never becomes "then," for it has a presentness and a presence that—unlike the flowing moment of sound—have become fixed. If, skeptically, we ask which moment this "now" is, among the many moments or hours consumed in the act of reading, we are returned to the diachronic reality that undercuts our mythic projection of that sacramental moment of aesthetic experience, when the entire poem suddenly becomes ours and we are its.

Critics who argue against conventional verse usually attack the use of meter and rhyme as no more than meaningless play; but those who would defend verse-making accept this very assumption of meaninglessness and make it central to their own argument as they turn it around to serve the defense of meter and rhyme. Further, in what they thus reveal about the poetic medium, they can, by broadening their argument, make it serve to characterize the aesthetic workings of non-verse as well. As we recall that Ransom made a special case for the "arbitrary" nature of meter (a determinate structure of sound totally "out of relation to" the structure of meaning), it may occur to us to treat meter or rhyme as an extreme gesture to the arbitrary nature of all the elements of language which the poet must convert into inevitability. Seen thus, verse-makers go to such self-irritating lengths in imposing arbitrary structures of sound upon their discourse in order to call attention to its sensory—and thus corporeal—nature, but also to reveal that, when a proper poem domesticates all its elements, not even the most arbitrary of signifiers can remain arbitrary for long. It is as if we can thus use verse as our emblem of the poet's continual need to defy the structuralist view of discourse, forcing his discourse to become a proper aesthetic medium, at once the source and mouth of his expressive act—and also its form. All elements at the disposal of the poet—conventions of plot, character, conceit, ideology, as well as language—are for him arbitrary in that they are generic and thus "out of relation to" the needs of his poem, which are unique. What the verse-maker does to the phonetic level of his language, making it serve his need as its inevitable instrument, is emblematic of what, in less spectacular and less easily marked ways, all poets do to the materials they subject to their transforming powers which convert the arbitrary into *their* inevitable instruments. And the claim to a medium that—no longer arbitrary—has been forced to take on body is expanded to cover any form produced by a true *poesis*.

In their concern with the mythic sacramental moment, is it that theorists of presence have been taken in like the primitive religious man sympathetically described by Mircea Eliade? With his notion of "sacred time" and "sacred space," Eliade clearly plays the role of mythologizer, with Burckhardt perhaps appearing to be his secular shadow in the realm of poetics. Not that I am about to attack Lévi-Strauss with Eliade, whose nostalgia leaves him insufficiently critical and himself open to attack; but Eliade's language of sacramental presence—for all its mythologizing—seems at times embarrassingly similar to that of those fictionalizing skeptics who, like me, defend the illusionary presence of the poem. So, despite embarrassment, that language is also comfortably familiar, leading him to seem ranged on the side of "presence" against the structuralists and their emptying of language, their unsubstantializing it.

Since Eliade so nakedly pronounces in behalf of both presence and presentness, it is useful briefly to examine his formulations in order to see the extent to which the tradition that defends poetic presence can use this language without being trapped by its consequences. Eliade uses his notion of "hierophany" (the manifestation of the sacred) to arrive at definitions of the discontinuities, or breaks, in both space and time for "religious man," as he terms him. Once any ordinary object is invested with the sacred, it "becomes *something else*, yet it continues to remain *itself*." A sacred stone is thus a stone like all the others and yet "its immediate reality is transmuted into a supernatural reality."[4]

---

[4] *The Sacred and the Profane: The Nature of Religion*, trans. Willard R. Trask (New York, 1959), p. 12. It is almost too obvious to need pointing out that this double awareness, which claims entities that are discrete and yet that fuse by overrunning the bounds of property and propriety, is here stated in language all too similar to that used by critics trying to describe the behavior of functional metaphors in poetry. See my analysis of the metaphors in Shakespeare's *Sonnets*

A sacred place is intruded upon the space continuum of man's experience, having been set aside as a break in that experience, though in another sense it seems (to the profane consciousness) only a part of that formless continuum. Only it has meaning for religious man, a resting place for the structure of his thought, and one capable of giving meaning to the rest, in its light having the world turn sacred.

Similarly, the sacred intrudes upon the linear continuity of time for the religious man, causing time to be stopped by what I have elsewhere termed "eschatological punctuations," which can always be returned into the present through ritual.[5] We can observe that such an intrusion is, in effect, an invasion of time by the metaphors of sacred space—by a revered and structured point, always retained to permit one's return to it. For one cannot give shape to time without spatializing it. Thus sacred time is characterized by Eliade by adjectives like reversible, recoverable, repeatable, reactualized, identical—and, most significant of all, circular.[6] The favorite adverb is "indefinitely," as a forceful alternative to the profanely temporal necesssity of "once only"—and that "once" in a flurry of befores and afters that obscure the identity of the now. What permits him to describe sacred time with all these spatial attributes is "that properly speaking, it is *a primordial mythical time made present.*" Hence to repeat a religious festival periodically is to return each time to "find the same sacred time."[7] The chunk of sacred time on each occasion is found and cut apart from the rest of time just as that sacred place was set aside from the rest of space: sacred time *is* space, capable of being made present in the present, here and now.

---

throughout *A Window to Criticism: Shakespeare's Sonnets and Modern Poetics* (Princeton, N.J., 1964). The key point in both cases is the insistence that the two entities must at once remain separate and become one, the one state not requiring the undoing of the other. As the similarity to Erich Auerbach's *figura* reminds us, the tradition in poetics has inherited its language from the miraculous defiance of number in Eliade's sense of religious psychology.

[5] The phrase is from *"Murder in the Cathedral:* The Limits of Drama and the Freedom of Vision," *The Classic Vision* (Baltimore, 1971), pp. 337–62. In this play, I argue, the separate and intertwining calendars of nature and Christ—with the permanent intrusion of Christmas and Easter (Becket's as well as Christ's) seen as "eschatological punctuations" upon the routine calendar of the Chorus of the Women of Canterbury—are mysteries aimed at unlocking formal and metaphorical problems in the play as well as the theological ones.

[6] I should point out here the necessary dependence of the tradition of presence on the prefix "re," just as I later point out the structuralists' equal but opposed dependence on the prefix "de." Need I mention the appearance of "re" in my title to this chapter?

[7] *The Sacred and the Profane*, pp. 68–69. Each periodic repetition of a festival is just like each reading or performance of a literary work as viewed by a critic committed to the poem as sacred text—that is, as a Burckhardtian book.

As the marked-out repository of meaning, it bears the metaphors of space as religious man's attempt to isolate and formalize it. We have seen that the language of space is the language of form, the molds into which we cast our experience to catch it as it flies. And the need for both presence and presentness characterizes the critic who, alas, must sanctify his object—reify it out of his experience of it— in order to keep it wholly and steadily before him as itself. The poem must be plucked out of all discourse as its own closed system, composed at once of ordinary words (part of that endless hum, the continuum of words used by and available to us all), but with its own meaning emanating from within. Though written and experienced in time, it is endlessly recoverable with a presence ever renewed.

I have purposely subjected the theoretical tradition of presence to the extreme language used by Eliade to mythologize, out of his nostalgia, the reading of the world by the primitive mind that believes it saturated by a divine presence. But I do so not, as others do, in order to convict these theorists of confounding religion with literary study through creating and falling prey to a myth that the poem is a sacred object; rather in order to emphasize, despite the similarity of language, the crucial difference between an arbitrarily chosen sacred object or moment and a purposefully crafted work of art. In calling the object or moment of faith arbitrary, I mean that its being chosen is determined by fiat from outside and not by any elements intrinsic to its own make-up. It is like other objects or moments, except that it has been singled out; and the act of faith makes that singling out enough, by itself and without any resonance within the object or moment, to make it forever special, and specially present. Whether or not anyone believes in that specialness depends wholly on his having or not having the faith on which the arbitrary choice rests. The object or moment cannot earn its role: it hardly has that within itself which can persuade one to accept its privileged status. One either accepts the literalized metaphor or he does not.

The poem whose unique system persuades the critic of its presence, on the other hand, has bent its verbal forces toward literalizing its metaphor. He accepts and reacts to the privileged status of the *parole* as *micro-langue*,[8] not in response to the arbitrary command of an outside faith, but in response to the internalizing directions through which, by deviation and transformation, the verbal construct has worked its way to presence from the open-ended flow of generic discourse. If he puts teleology into the poem as object, it is because this ob-

---

[8] For my use of *micro-langue*, see Chapter 7, p. 188, above.

ject seems to have wrestled with its teleology to make it its organizing principle. So he is forced to reify this experience into a privileged object because he is convinced that it has earned its way from within, with a system of internal relations that seems to have shaped itself into substance. His faith in it, then, rests upon what he sees it as doing rather than what has been done to it (by anyone, that is, except the rapt and overzealous critic). Lest he also should be literalizing his metaphor, however, he must remind himself to believe in what the poem does rather than in what it explicitly says. And what it does he must remind himself in the end to see as only a verbal act—an act of playful illusion, of make-believe, of counterfeiting. What is finally present is no more than air, but what a present body it shadows forth!

In our faithless age, then, without arbitrary interruptions of our experiential flow in the name of the sacred, any claim to presence will have to persuade us all on its own. It is this claim that allows the contextualist definition of aesthetic experience and of the aesthetic object—of a self-sufficient intramural system—that traditional criticism in our time has argued for. As modern semiology tirelessly reminds us, the function of meaning in usual discourse (considered naïvely) is utterly arbitrary, with signifiers claiming attachment to signifieds for none but casual and externally imposed reasons. Those seeking presence in the poem must see all elements that are potentially arbitrary as transformed by its creator into elements of internal necessity. Forced by modern skepticism to accept a language made up of none but empty signifiers, they see the poet as torturing his words into fullness in spite of what they were when he came upon them before the poem. Without disagreeing with semiologists about the arbitrary nature of normal signification, then, they can insist upon the poetic conversion that makes the signifier the inevitable container of this special signified. And this is a marriage that permits no exchanging of partners. This persuasion of unity and embodiment, however alien to our sense of how language ought to behave, is within the powers of the poem. It is what has enchanted theorists in this tradition to invent the extravagant metaphor of the poem's iconicity, as if it would—as even Lessing suggested—provide the occasion for language to violate its role as arbitrary sign and, through a sort of incarnation, become a natural sign, a signifier forced into the shape of its signified. But this persuasiveness, as "aesthetic," is by definition related to appearance only (mere *Schein*), so that we have faith in it as a fiction only. We literalize no myth, though we trace so carefully the letters that make it up. For what they make up they firmly contain, and they contain us as well.

Eliade's concept of the sacred, like the I AM of post-Kantian idealism, springs from the dream of destroying the subject-object opposition, the dream of investing the object with an inspirited meaning that turns reality into something responsive to the subject's desires. If we literally believe the myth, then nature is no stranger, but we expose ourselves to the demythifying action of a skeptical science. The doctrine of presence seems so exposed, even in those modern organic theorists who, with the nurturing of illusion, have tried to exempt themselves from the charge of myth-making. It is at once clear that an anthropologist like Lévi-Strauss can have little difficulty in exposing the mythifications of Eliade. But even the critic's self-conscious awareness of the poem's fiction, together with his detailed analysis of the source of its power, has not, as he might have hoped, immunized his theory of presence from the structuralist challenge. He must face up to this challenge if his claims for aesthetic presence are to seem more than wishfully visionary.

To speak of the structuralist challenge to the doctrine of fictional presence, we must make clear the fact that we are referring to what most commentators think of as main-line structuralism, that which is interested more in the homologous relations among "the sciences of man" than in distinguishing poetic structures from other linguistic structures. As is invariably pointed out, this structuralism derives from Saussure's original "binary opposition" between the "signifier" and the "signified" in language, together with the insistence on the arbitrary nature of the relationship between the two.[9] Out of Saussure's concentration on the "signifier" arises the further distinctions between *langue* and *parole*: the system of language (that universal structure which controls and essentially contains all individual speeches in the language without itself ever speaking) and the individual speech act (which stumbles forth, apparently spontaneously, in time, as the only thing we hear, though always in accord with the noumenal language system). Out of this distinction other distinctions flow, all of them central to structuralist theories. Of especial importance is the one I have referred to before between the "synchronic" and the "diachronic," which, referring to the spatial and systematic model on the one hand and the temporal or empirical sequence of experience on the other, are simply descriptions of the way the *langue* and the *parole* work. This dichotomy we can trace everywhere in structuralist work—importantly, for example, in Jakobson's distinction between metaphor (the spatial sense of similar-

[9] Ferdinand de Saussure, *Cours de linguistique générale* (Paris, 1916). As we have seen, this insistence on the arbitrariness of the relationship requires the two to be kept apart, while theorists of presence wish to explore ways in which poets force them—"esemplastically," Coleridge would say—together: a visible incarnation. Thus the structuralist systematizing among emptying signifiers at once confronts the alternative of poetic presence as one it must obliterate.

ity) and metonymy (the temporal sense of contiguity).[10] Through all these runs the central Saussurean (and, consequently, structuralist) principle of binary opposition, of definitions based on mutually dependent differentiations. This movement, which in literary study turns the critical into the "diacritical," leads to the treating of each subject by virtue of what it is not—a methodological tactic that is, as we shall see, exploited to the extreme by Derrida, who uses it to turn structuralism against itself.

From the standpoint of what I have presented as the tradition of humanistic literary theory, this sequence of distinctions presents a major difficulty (as spokesman for the humanist tradition, I would say a major *weakness*): the terms in which their binary alternatives are set are invariably controlled by the framework of *general* linguistics, which is all that Saussure pretended to. However new the terms he invented, the distinctions themselves, which structuralist after structuralist acknowledges he owes to Saussure, were hardly new when he introduced them—as, in some ways, a retrograde Platonism—to nascent linguistic theory. But, as distinctions applicable to all language behavior, they cannot confront the theoretical possibility that literary works are unique and privileged systems—different from general linguistic systems—so that these distinctions are *not* applicable to them. For structuralists this possibility cannot exist because the nature of their analytical instrument precludes it. Yet all the variations of "the structuralist activity," as they expand by way of "semiology" to become "the sciences of man"—linguistic, anthropological, historical, and psychoanalytic—make claims that mean to apply to literary issues, and they make them while still wedded to those original rather primitive distinctions of Saussure and his general linguistic method.[11] It may well be, then, that —for all the demythifications that structuralist method may have produced—they are themselves guilty of the grossly naïve myth of reifying their own terms, of confounding their language with reality, projecting the former upon the latter: that is, they limit what can exist (in this case the kinds of operations of which language is capable) by what their terms, and the system of differentiation permitted by their terms, permit to exist.

The demythifications that structuralists—led by Lévi-Strauss—

---

[10] Yet we shall see that Jakobson, despite his indispensable role as father figure to structuralism, is off the main line in his concern—consistent with his adherence to Russian formalist and Prague School principles—for the distinction between poetic and general linguistic structures.

[11] I am, obviously, referring, between the dashes, to writers like Barthes, Lévi-Strauss, Foucault, and Lacan, respectively.

have produced in many areas of study, as these smoothly translate into one another, derive from the concentration upon the signifier and, within that, upon the invisible synchronic system to which the contents of actions and beliefs can be reduced. For such structuralists homology is all. Searching for the generative grammar of mind, they are after the key that will unlock the universal syntactical powers with which man, as speaking subject, generates and controls all that his mind, by way of languages, touches and organizes. He is only the "I" of the sentence generating and controlling its variety of predicates. The method demythifies in that it cleanses its object of study of all content, what it *seems* to be about, in the interest of reducing its apparent signifieds to systematic relations among signifiers. Yet, obviously, structuralist method, in its uniformity of claim, must not be allowed to seem open to the charge of concealing a Platonic ontology, so that, as a "totalization," it would stand in need of being demythified itself. Structuralists try to preclude this need in advance, in effect by demythifying their method themselves. They must of course try to keep it from sounding as Platonic as it does, for example, in my own formulation, by insisting (and demonstrating) that they are talking only about mutually related and disposable functions within systematic sets, and not at all about ontological entities. It is a series of arrangements of moves rather than of things; and what is moved about, within the system of rules, are counters that—for structuralist purposes—are devoid of content. In emptying the sentence or the belief system of content, they are demythifying it by revealing how, once transferred into the kinetics of the system as one of its elements, it really behaves and for what reasons.[12]

As literary criticism, such a procedure would seem to reintroduce the form-content dichotomy, restricting its interest to pure, contentless structures. And these structures are of interest by virtue of their being homologous to the structures that underlie all the "sciences of man." Not only can this method be reduced to a narrow, life-denying formalism, but the forms with which it deals—as generic to the discourse that constitutes all the human sciences—reveal nothing about the exclusively poetic manipulations of language. We may well worry, as Ransom used to about science, whether "the world's body," with its messy contingencies, has been overlooked in the interest of the skeleton; but we must worry also about what has happened to the poem's body— world-freighted as it is—provided it *has* any substantial presence (as

[12] In the extreme form that structuralism takes in Barthes's "semiology," for example, all texts are transformed into anonymous codes that are part of a single system of writing (*écriture*).

it is the purpose of this chapter to argue). It is the case, then, that the narrowly scientific objectives of modern structuralists, with their un-differentiated Saussurean dichotomy, have blurred some of the distinctions and purposes that characterized the Russian formalists and the Prague School theorists from whom in other respects they seem to have sprung.[13]

Some nominal structuralists, the Russian formalist Jakobson chief among them, have continued to press their interest in the specialness of poetic structures, showing a concern that runs counter to the main line of structuralism as I have been describing it. Their efforts may seem similar to my own emphasis on deviation and transformation as the poet seeks to turn a generic language into unique poem. We have seen that Jakobson begins, in the usual Saussurean manner, with the opposition of synchronic and diachronic elements, and that for him this translates into the distinction in all discourse between metaphor and metonymy, which together—as the elements of "selection" and "combination" in interaction—make up, respectively, the verbal members of discourse and their organization into sentences. Thus selection and combination must represent equivalence on the one hand and contiguity on the other. But poetry (in Jakobson) and, through him, myth (in Lévi-Strauss) claim equivalence as their governing character, which moves to control the combining as well as the selecting elements. The various similarities among words chosen, referring in poetry to equivalence in phonetic as well as grammatical functions, reach out to affect semantic relations as well,[14] creating equivalences in them. With the pressure of poetry forcing the elements toward equivalence—metonymy toward metaphor, contiguity toward similarity—the ten-

---

[13] Russian formalism itself, in its self-conscious dedication to technique, at times was charged with aestheticism, the aridly formalistic neglect of the world and its values. Such charges of craft-conscious escapism, from which the best of them worked to protect themselves, usually arose from the parochial Marxism that demanded obvious social relevance; but they helped give formalism as a generic term the bad name that is still indiscriminately applied to any in the post-Aristotelian, post-Kantian, or post-Coleridgean fraternity—members of the tradition treated most sympathetically in this book. However unjust the charge of worldly irrelevance, the point to emphasize is that Russian and Prague versions were originally dedicated to distinguishing poetic from nonpoetic language, how the former dislocated (deviated from) the latter. It would seem that, as Jakobson generalized his interest in language, so did the structuralism to which, as transmitting agent, he led the way.

[14] For a forceful expansion of this call for new applications to semantics of elements before limited to generative syntax, see Nicolas Ruwet, "Linguistics and Poetics," in *The Languages of Criticism and the Sciences of Man,* ed. Richard Macksey and Eugenio Donato (Baltimore, 1970), pp. 296–313. See also the discussion that follows this essay, especially p. 316.

sion between the diachronic and synchronic is clearly to be resolved on the side of the latter.

It all, of course, sounds a good deal like Burckhardt's method of building toward verbal corporeality. But there are differences. Jakobson's sort of formalism would seem to leave in the poem no residue of contingency, of unabsorbable temporal difference, after the spatial structure has completed its work. In effect, one might argue, these are proponents of a presence that is too unqualified. Their essential faith in the victory of spatial form does not permit the necessary skepticism that perceives its illusory basis and, consequently, the nagging persistence of existential contingencies which aesthetics cannot finally wish away, however persuasive its symbolic reductions. For if, as this sort of structuralist must also insist, man is conceived only as speaking subject, then the language form is adequate to itself and cannot point beyond, to its insufficiency. For what can the "beyond" be, except further sentences? On the other hand, there is in Burckhardt (as I have expanded upon him in the spirit of Gombrich), an existential assumption behind the fictional self-consciousness—and the self-reference to which it leads—that can open to temporality the poems whose forms it apparently seeks to close off.

It is also the case that the procedure of Jakobson and (when he is most clearly his ally) Lévi-Strauss, however complete the homage they mean to pay to poetic structure, tends to restrict its words to generically grammatical activities, whose significance is measured almost statistically.[15] Nor can they distinguish adequately between similarity and equivalence or follow the movement in poetry from the first to the second, as does Ransom's pseudo-religious procedure, for example, with its dependence on the secular miracle that half-denies itself. Such a procedure—however unscientific—is necessary, as Burckhardt has shown us, if the claim to verbal corporeality is to be earned. To return to my earlier lament about the structuralists at large, I find that the exclusivity of Saussure's binary oppositions extends its limitations even to so profoundly humanistic an enterprise as is intended by the Russian formalist and Prague School traditions as they operate as a minor voice within structuralism. Consequently, a theorist like Jakobson cannot reach to such radically deviant behavior of words—with a doubleness beyond grammars and glossaries—as Burckhardt allows for, or as I have suggested, for example, in my discussion, in Chapter 6, of "dear"

---

[15] See Jakobson and Lévi-Strauss, "Les Chats de Charles Baudelaire," L'Homme, 2 (1962): 5–21, and the criticism of this essay in Michael Riffaterre, "Describing Poetic Structures: Two Approaches to Baudelaire's Les Chats," Yale French Studies, 36–37 (1966): 200–42.

in Shakespeare's Sonnet 87 or the passage on "China" in Pope's "The Rape of the Lock." These are ways in which the poem outdoes its grammatical possibilities. One would have to undo the *langue* itself, and not merely permit it to be deviated from, before a *parole* could be permitted to work this way. And not even so aesthetically sensitized a structuralism as Jakobson's can give such license. So what structures such a formalist sees he sees exclusively, unable to conceive either less generically descriptive forms or an existence beyond them, a reality in which these forms dissipate like the airy things they are.

But we have seen that the main line of structuralism is not diverted by any such challenge to its uniform applicability to the ever-homologous sciences of man, of which poetics happens for them to be a coordinate and unprivileged one. Instead, demythifying all claims to such privilege, it guards its capacity to reduce varieties of contents to structural sameness, thereby disabusing us of our illusions about the specialness of those contents. It is to this structuralism we now return to see its consequences. The cost of demythification, as we would expect, is the denuding of our existential world, along with its language: the washing away of diachronic sequence, with all the (now unmasked) significance we gave to it as it collided with our consciousness. But such a denuding is precisely what was intended, for surely one of the objectives of many who picked up structuralism was to undo the mystifications of some existentialists and phenomenologists. In the area of literary criticism and theory it was the "consciousness critics" of the Geneva School who were to be undone. The rapt obsession with temporality, the defiance of space and form as destructive, by a Poulet or a Richard, represented a celebration of subjective consciousness, a consciousness before language and superior to it. Because such critics saw language as an unavoidable mediating element that, based on its principle of differentiation, kept selves and their objects separate, the self-conscious subject had to achieve a breakthrough beyond such separateness, as the literary work faded into the blend of reader and author, reader-*as*-author. If the subject-object opposition was overwhelmed in the act of reading, it all melted onto the subject's side, while the object disappeared. Thus far "consciousness criticism." But the structuralist, committed to a method in which differentiation—indeed, "binary opposition"—was all, would be only fortified in reaction to such a notion of a consciousness prior to language, and—worse—a notion of a multiple and undifferentiated co-presence of consciousness. These notions would present themselves to his shearing tools as romantic mystifications of a speaking subject seeking to escape his grammatical function.

The structuralist has done his work by swinging as his ax a series of words to which he has attached the ubiquitous prefix, *de*, from *de*-mythification to the audacity of total *de*construction, almost—at times —in worship of that which is *not*, the spirit of deprivation. He means to lay the conceptual and verbal world bare and barren, a blank, white, phantom universe, filled only with "traces." But this is to verge— beyond the main march of structuralists—on Derrida, who presses the principle of differentiation to an extremity that, returning diachronic awareness at the expense of the synchronic, outdoes structuralism, and perhaps undoes it as well. Troubled by interpretations of Lévi-Strauss that saw him as exclusively synchronic and, consequently, that left him open to the charge that he was a myth maker himself—covertly reifying differential structures into deep structures—Derrida tries to "de-center" Lévi-Strauss (claiming that Lévi-Strauss, to his credit, really is at crucial moments decentering himself), showing how his terms, as functional only, can undercut the attempt to ontologize them, or to have them serve any myth about origins that such a metaphysical center would require.[16] As we shall see, Derrida's commitment to de-centering, to the introduction of "free play," to the Heideggerian aware-ness of the co-presence of what is absent with each thing present, all help him conspire to the deconstruction—and ultimately the destruc-tion—of metaphysics, although he must first deconstruct our sense of the presence of the word.

It is probably a mistake to press Derrida's brilliantly chilling anal-ysis of language functions, both a means to and a major portion of his metaphysical (or rather antimetaphysical) quest, into literary theory, which may seem rather trivial in light of his monumentally ambitious undertaking. Yet what I might term his "critical structuralism" has had discernible consequences on poststructuralist or modified structuralist attitudes to the presence of the poetic word (and world) and of the "book" constituted by poetic words. In the shadow of Derrida's "nega-tive way," a follower might well be concerned with the pied variety of history that structuralism, in its synchronic flights, tends to leap over. Without returning quite to "consciousness criticism" in the spirit of phenomenology, but more in the spirit of Heidegger than of Lévi-Strauss, such a critic sees that negative way as leading toward the re-sistant stuff of an uncentered temporality, the duplicitous experience that structuralism would gloss into a universal sameness. He is led to resist the ontological presumption that would press the thing or word

---

[16] He softens on Lévi-Strauss, trying to bring him into his own corner, in "Struc-ture, Sign, and Play in the Discourse of the Human Sciences," in *The Languages of Criticism and the Sciences of Man: The Structuralist Controversy*, pp. 247–65.

(better yet, thing *as* word) beyond the modesty of its diachronic contingency to the mythical totality, the corporealization, that used to be called both "logos" and "cosmos."

Explicitly writing under the influence of Derrida, Joseph Riddel, in a recent study of William Carlos Williams, seeks to create a postmodernist poetics based on the acknowledgment of what the word *cannot* do (in contrast to the modernist's idolatry of the word).[17] It comes as no surprise that his conclusion to that book bears the title of "The Poetics of Failure," which, aping Derrida's habit, we might reverse into being a claim for "The Failure of Poetics." Far from remaking itself into a sufficient and integral word, the poem's language proclaims its insufficiency: instead of at once encompassing and constituting its object, it acknowledges the inevitable gap between itself and all that it would be and say.

This is in some ways similar to what Paul de Man, at times in accord with this spirit, has observed. As student of early Romantic poets and thinkers, he seems ready to yield up the presumption and the "mystification" of the would-be symbol and to accept the limited accomplishment and the pathos of poetic allegory.[18] This dwindling of presumption is the poet's realistic acceptance of the metaphysical (or antimetaphysical) consequences of "the disappearance of God."[19] Nor will he resort to the myth of the man-god expressed in the I AM of absolute idealism, with its identity of subject and object. Rather the distance between them is acknowledged—a distance that neither the subject nor his forming word can overcome, as the world remains "other," irrecoverably outside himself and his language. His poem is to reflect this duality in his experience. No longer pretending to the delusion of verbal wholeness in its spatial form, the poet retreats to the reduced security of the diachronic, with its gaps and discontinuities, conceding that his language is only an imperfect *parole,* no longer mystifying himself with the total design of a noumenal *langue.* As de Man describes it, "in the

---

[17] *The Inverted Bell: Modernism and the Counterpoetics of William Carlos Williams.* See my reference to this work and its polar relation to Burckhardt's hermeneutic assumption about the interpretable Book in note 47 to Chapter 5.

[18] This discussion is based on his influential essay, "The Rhetoric of Temporality," in *Interpretation: Theory and Practice,* ed. Charles S. Singleton (Baltimore, 1969), pp. 173–209.

[19] This phrase is meant to refer to the book of that title by J. Hillis Miller, from time to time theoretically allied to de Man. The loss of God remains an undercurrent in structuralist and near-structuralist thought, stimulating it to keep its signifiers empty. It is as if such theorists are playing their part in fulfilling Foucault's historical version of human "archaeology."

world of the symbol" the relationship between "image" and "substance"

is one of simultaneity, which, in truth, is spatial in kind, and in which the intervention of time is merely a matter of contingency, whereas, in the world of allegory, time is the originary constitutive category. . . . The secularized allegory of the early romantics thus necessarily contains the negative moment which in Rousseau is that of renunciation, in Wordsworth that of the loss of self in death or in error.

Whereas the symbol postulates the possibility of an identity or identification, allegory designates primarily a distance in relation to its own origin, and, renouncing the nostalgia and the desire to coincide, it establishes its language in the void of this temporal difference. In so doing, it prevents the self from an illusory identification with the non-self, which is now fully, though painfully, recognized as a non-self.[20]

The symbol, nourished by the dream of identity, is yielded up to allegory, which contents itself with the inevitability of difference. Consequently, the Romantic reduces his hopes to the demystified dimensions of his metaphysical condition.

This negation, which undoes the "tenacious self-mystification" that elevates symbol over allegory, affects poetic hopes. Confronting his incapacity to overcome the subject-object opposition, de Man's early Romantic poet—in ways paradigmatic of the modern poet generally—responds with irony as he yields to his diachronic fate in spite of his mythic, synchronic hope. But his irony emphasizes this paradoxical existence of gap within a failed language: it acknowledges the absence of the elusive unity that would overwhelm distance and discontinuity—a unity he knows better than to seek any longer.[21] Thus de Man can define "the act of irony": it

reveals the existence of a temporality that is definitely not organic, in that it relates to its source only in terms of distance and differ-

---

[20] "The Rhetoric of Temporality," pp. 190–91. Here and elsewhere in de Man, the sense and tone are, properly, reminiscent of the sense of loss and distance and temporal incompleteness—of the subject's return on himself—which we find in the study of Wordsworth by de Man's cohort, Geoffrey Hartman: *Wordsworth's Poetry 1787–1814* (New Haven, 1964). It is a view of the Romantic imagination profoundly at odds with my view of Coleridge's unqualified organicism in Chapter 5.

[21] This irony is as different from the unifying irony of the New Critics as is his submission to allegory, with its modest dualism, from their all-inclusive symbolism. For his irony, like his allegory, is desperately (and despairingly) antiorganic.

ence and allows for no end, for no totality. . . . It dissolves in the narrowing spiral of a linguistic sign that becomes more and more remote from its meaning, and it can find no escape from this spiral. The temporal void that it reveals is the same void we encountered when we found allegory always implying an unreachable anteriority. Allegory and irony are thus linked in their common discovery of a truly temporal predicament. They are also linked in their common de-mystification of an organic world postulated in a symbolic mode of analogical correspondence or in a mimetic mode of representation in which fiction and reality could coincide. It is especially against the latter mystification that irony is directed. . . .

What de Man is here formulating is the subject's failure to realize the Goethean humanistic dream, his blotting it out as a mystification. The subject cannot after all unite with its object; man cannot remake the world in accordance with his forms. Matter in its resistance rather goes its own way and eventually reduces him to *it*: "Nature can at all times treat him as if he were a thing and remind him of his factitiousness, whereas he is quite powerless to convert even the smallest particle of nature into something human." The Lucy poem of Wordsworth, "A Slumber did my spirit seal," according to de Man, uses its allegory and irony to turn death into the ultimate act of demystification, into the annihilation of human—as verbal—presumption. It leads to the presence only of emptiness, of blankness, as the final denial of the dream of fullness, of symbolic totality, thus the denial of the word as it is the denial of life: "The actual now, which is that of the moment of death, lies hidden in the blank space between the two stanzas."

The sequence of life is reflected in the sequence of language: both are studded with spaces separating the befores from the afters. Both suffer the sense of distance and the fact of "anteriority," though they become one in bowing before the existence of death at the far end. De Man thus crosses from the temporality of existence to that of verbal syntax, signifier succeeding signifier, separated from one another at a distance from each signified. The terminology of a linguistics made familiar by structuralism is forced to serve an existential thematics, in spite of the usual antagonism structuralists display toward existentialism. Is it that de Man is using linguistic terms no more than metaphorically, masking claims that have only thematic significance? This crossing from the nature of existence to the nature of language enables him to insist that the Romantic consciousness of the world and the void expresses itself in poems whose verbal form has the limitations of existence impressed directly upon it. As de Man sees these poems, verbal emptiness is a necessary reflection of metaphysical absence. He has—perhaps unfaithfully, but only perhaps, as we shall see—used the spirit of Derrida to reinforce his own commitment to existential alienation.

As de Man sees it, then, Wordsworth's Lucy poem expresses an awareness of death as the ineluctable reality that "unmetaphors" (as Rosalie Colie would put it) the verbal aggrandizement that seeks to enclose and contain the world. This claim should be familiar to those who have followed my own attempts to find affirmation and denial as co-present in the metaphorical thrust of the poem.[22] The poem links organic presumption with its impossibility, links the finality of its verbally contained vision with the open contingencies of external awareness that relegate it all to the play of words, mere words—breath after all, and not substance. But for me (as for Colie) verbal presence outshouts the "blank space" that surrounds it. If the metaphor undercuts its totalizing power to reduce and contain a world, it does so only while it retains its illusory power that for now contains us and transforms our world. The poetic word overcomes existential and linguistic difference and distance with its power to create a momentary sense of identity. It is not that the metaphor works partially only, but rather that it works all the way, though it also makes us aware of the conditions under which it cannot work at all.[23] The organic impudence of the word is something I must defend, so long as I add its self-conscious sense of the fiction of its workings, which reminds us of its ultimate impotence, and our death, revealing its organicism and our forming power to be a fond dream, realized for now without lulling our skepticism. But any sense of ultimate verbal absence is shadowed and postponed by our overwhelming sense of its living presence.

In the case of de Man, it may be an error for us to extrapolate a

[22] In each of my books I have argued that the metaphor works wholly and miraculously (as a substantive transfer of properties) only while reminding us that, as verbal play, it cannot finally work at all: from the earliest pages of *The New Apologists for Poetry* (Minneapolis, 1956), pp. 17–18, through the treatment of Mann's *Doctor Faustus* in *The Tragic Vision* (New York, 1960), pp. 87–102, until it becomes the informing principle of *A Window to Criticism*. By *The Classic Vision*, pp. 31–32, I concede that "all poems must covertly contain their anti-poems," at once committing themselves to their metaphorical reduction and seeing its miracles broken up and dragged to earth. This is, finally, my theme in Chapter 7, above.

[23] This paradoxical notion of all-and-none, of simultaneous identity and polarity in which only synthesis is impossible, is one that I pursue in constructing an anti-Hegelian model in the diagrams and accompanying discussion in *The Classic Vision*, pp. 24–27. This positing of a model whose identities feed on permanent oppositions-without-synthesis has obvious similarities to Derrida's method.

universally applicable "rhetoric of temporality"—based on an allegory and an irony that constitute a flight from organicism—out of a single group of historically bound poets and thinkers responding to what might be seen as a momentary crisis in sensibility.[24] It may be a history lesson we are being given rather than a general theoretical claim. And the retreat to which those sensibilities resorted may have been, not an act of demystification, but a failure of nerve that prepared for new ways of mystifying themselves: the Romantics' discovery of the Fall, and with it the alienation from nature of the now isolated and distanced ego, converted the ego into exclusively temporal terms, thus preparing the way for the myth of existentialism, with its worship of the diachronic.[25] Despite the concern for difference and the concentration on blankness, this would suggest a movement quite antagonistic to structuralism, although not out of accord with moments in a "critical structuralist" like Derrida.

To see the clear consequences of these tendencies stated with the force of a universal method, we must look at Derrida himself (or at least the slim segment within his work that touches most directly on our problem) even though—as I have said—his weapons are trained upon the normal uses of language out of which metaphysics grows. For it is

[24] It must be pointed out that de Man takes other positions on other subjects, and even on Rousseau he takes one that puts him at some distance from Derrida. See *Blindness and Insight: Essays in the Rhetoric of Contemporary Criticism* (New York, 1971). Since de Man is mainly concerned with general questions of interpretation, and thus the use made of texts by critics, he may give us reason to see his treatment of early Romanticism only as his discrete reading of an historically conditioned series of texts. But what he tells us of critics generally, the role of their blindness in their interpretation, may prompt us to wonder about the general use to which his own predilections lead him to put these texts—in which case this essay must be treated as more than a local observation, and may be seen as a clue to his own critical sensibility.

[25] The theorist of verbal presence could argue that, despite the Romantic's ironic self-consciousness and his sense of alienation from nature, he can write a poem whose present structure can sustain his irony in its linguistic form. In contrast to de Man, he would argue that a dualistic vision, with its lingering Cartesianism, need not preclude a Coleridgean poem, whose I AM overwhelms the *cogito* it contains. Keats's "Ode to a Nightingale" is a striking example of the verbal-dramatic triumph fashioned by the Romantic self-consciousness over the visionary doubts it contains and does not dispel: it becomes a symbolic metaphor for the allegorical concessions of the spirit that fills it. I see examples of such verbal sustenance in Wordsworth himself (in my analyses, for example, of "To the Cuckoo" and "Elegiac Stanzas" in "William Wordsworth and the *Felix Culpa*," *The Classic Vision*, pp. 149–95), so that my Wordsworth is not altogether de Man's (or Hartman's), except in his weaker poems, for which theirs becomes a persuasive "explanation," as Burckhardt would put it. The stronger ones, as formally monistic, are open to "interpretation," whatever their thematic insufficiency.

Derrida who, without existential pathos showing at the methodological level, carries the Saussurean principle of difference to its extreme.[26] Beginning with it as the basis of linguistic structure, he presses it to invade the "blank space" on the page with the actualities excluded by the words that do appear: hence the absent invades the present, supplementing and replacing—if not quite effacing —it. And the center of the discourse, the principle of inclusion (and exclusion) that in the most elementary sense is to unify what's there by keeping out the rest (what "doesn't belong"), is dislodged from its place as the ruler of discourse who governs admissions: in effect it is—to us the prefix *de* yet again in a metaphorical, though hardly mythic, way of my own—dethroned.

It is the case, then, that for language and for the metaphysics that a mythified doctrine of language encourages, Derrida protectively asserts what others have lamented: that "the center cannot hold." Retrograde organicists might charge that he is following through with Yeats's sequel, loosing "mere anarchy" upon us. The centripetal relationship between parts and whole, on which organic unity depends, is exploded once words turn duplicitous and centrifugalism is licensed as an elementary linguistic principle. Such would seem to be the price of the negative way, the undoing of discourse and thought as we have known it. But we must remind ourselves again that Derrida is explicitly attacking philosophical rather than poetic discourse—attacking, that is, a common-sense notion of centering and presence in language rather than the special case I have been making on the basis of transformed deviations from discourse that create a new center and a new presence. That such teleological assumptions may be myths is a charge I have several times tried to answer, so I still claim that it is worth asking whether deconstruction of metaphysics need deconstruct the poem. If Derrida's notion of *écriture* seeks to make all discourse subject to his deconstructive critique, need we be prevented from seeking special dispensations for poetry as the mode of discourse that subverts the others? The blanket term *écriture* does not eliminate distinctions within writing—if we can make them stand up—unless we want naïvely to reify the word, allowing it to solve our problems by confounding them a priori in the coverall term invented for the purpose.

---

[26] Even Derrida seems at times to use linguistic absence as a cover for the metaphysical disappearance of God (the transcendental Signified). He tries to convert nothingness from an ontological emptiness to a linguistic function, but the existential sense of loss remains beneath, though hidden by his concentration on an austere methodology of negations. It is a consequence of the Heideggerian influence that he cannot shake. As in Foucault, the concept and function of words follow from what history has done to our sense of the life in them.

Derrida's case against our normal sense of language assumes that it has ontological implications: if our normal sense of language assumes that it contains as much reality as it signifies, eliminating the rest as it eliminates all the signifiers that do not display themselves as present, then the principles of similarity and presence are assured. But these would violate the differential basis on which the functions of language, and the structures of those functions, are built. Let us go back to recapitulate the several enunciations of difference in the operations of language, as these multiply in Derrida to corroborate the decentering impulse. Five rather obvious ones occur at once. There is, first, as Saussurean phonology reminds us, the identity of a signifying sound that is achieved only by its distinctness from (and so, indirectly, by its negative reference to) the other sounds in the system: there is, second, the graphic form of the word, composed of letters that, only arbitrarily related to the phonemes, are differentiated from the sound; third, the graphic form of the word becomes an entity through its differential relations to the other written forms in the system; fourth, either the phonological or graphic form, as signifier, is also arbitrarily related to the signified concept and thus at a distance from it;[27] and fifth, the signified has its meaning derived by negative reference to other concepts differentiated from itself.

In each of these cases the present and visible is defined by virtue of the absent and invisible (represented by the blank [*blanc*] whiteness of the page), in accordance with the relationship originally established by Saussure between the *parole* and the unspoken *langue* that controlled and made possible every element in the *parole*. So it is, as the sounds we do not hear give meaning to those we do, as unheard sounds give meaning to the silent printed page, as the words we do not see frame the meaning of those we do, as concepts that have no natural words light up the arbitrary graphic patterns before us, and as the meanings excluded from the signifiers before us help shape what *is* signified. According to Derrida, the not-there asserts its presence, despite its absence, by imposing its "trace" upon what is apparently there. It is the felt presence of this "trace," ghostly mark of the absent, that fills the

---

[27] Many structuralists, Derrida among them, make a great deal of Saussure's characterization of the relation between signifier and signfied as an arbitrary one (like the relation Derrida also stresses between the phonological and graphic form of the word). The obvious fact should be noted that the distinction between natural and arbitrary signs has been an accepted one in theory—and a philosophically fruitful one—from Plato's *Cratylus* through Addison, du Bos, Burke, and Lessing to Gombrich. See Lévi-Strauss's suggestion that Saussure is responsible for the "principle of the *arbitrary character of linguistic signs*" in "The Structural Study of Myth," *Structural Anthropology*, p. 209.

blank space with a presence as marked as its black-print neighbors. And these present words, conversely, are the less present for their self-sacrificial gestures to what is external to the writing. Obviously, no instance of *parole* can win exemption from its self-abnegating obligations to the *langue,* the absent-present dynamic field of differentiation that controls all its operations. Any notion of a *micro-langue,* with its implication of presence, would be a mystification indeed.

The climax to Derrida's obsession with the Saussurean principle of difference occurs in the reflexive negations of his essay "Differance."[28] In order to avoid affirming difference as a single privileged metaphysical universal (though a universal that denies all others), Derrida invents the term that, in denying others, denies itself as well, so that its deconstructive effects do not stop short of being reflexive. Through his willfully errant spelling of the word (in French), he emphasizes its duplicity and the consequence that it is, in effect, deprived of existence. We can think of three ways in which the word *"différance,"* in effect, is *not.* It does not seem to exist aurally since, obviously, we cannot—listening to the French—hear that it is being spelled with an *a* rather than an *e;* it does not seem to exist as a proper written word (say, in the dictionary) since it is a willful and erroneous variant that can only remind us of the form from which it varies; and it does not seem to exist as a concept since, because of the nature of its double meaning, it "seems to differ from itself." The essay thus proceeds out of a decentering of differ*a*nce itself. Through the unspoken and unheard *a,* available only on the page,[29] the word becomes false to itself: it becomes an impossible juncture of the synchronic and diachronic, each denying itself for the other. Such self-denial is built into the very nature of difference—but, still more, of differ*a*nce. The key to the argument is the pun on the French verb *différer,* which means both "to differ" and "to defer." Derrida seizes upon this distinction (I almost said "difference") between simul-

---

[28] "Differance," in *Speech and Phenomena, and Other Essays on Husserl's Theory of Signs,* trans. David B. Allison (Evanston, Ill., 1973), pp. 129–60.

[29] Derrida's central interest in writing (not the "book," of course, but *écriture*) rather than in speech is in obvious contrast to Saussure. It is curious that, while Derrida uses the conditions of the blank and silent page spotted with words as a preferred means to turn writing away from presence, those representing the tradition of the centered book—as we have seen—found in the physical reality of the written word, the page in hand, a step toward the aesthetic of presence. But we have also seen that they came to require the sensory presence of meter and rhyme, as sounds, to give poetry the physical ingredients of a plastic medium, capable of being manipulated, so that air could be converted to substantive body—the body reposing in the book of printed pages. So, as I suggested earlier, they end up having it both ways—written and spoken—as mutually reinforcing, while Derrida sees the two as canceling one another out. Did the theory of presence not have an illusionary basis, the charge of mythic reification could be justly lodged against it.

228

taneously present entities seen in contrast (differing) and similar entities, one present and one absent, separated by a temporal gap (deferring). And to have a noun that reflects the temporal as well as the spatial meaning, he develops "differance" out of the present participle of the two-edged verb as the alternative to "difference," an alternative that allows the word to carry out its meaning through its function—by being (doubly) differant from itself.

Here, out of the pun that permits the self-conscious play on the *a* and through it the written alphabet, Derrida has the word that is symbol of his principle of deconstruction. The phonetic coincidence, turning the word into the butt of its own joke, leads to his decentering of any teleology in language. But Derrida's case against normal discourse as present is one with which I would agree, though only in order to strengthen my case for poetic discourse. It is surely odd that the device of the pun, which for Burckhardt was the dominating, indeed the enabling, act of presence, is for Derrida the instrument to undo any such notion as presence. For Derrida verbal ambiguity is seen essentially as Burckhardt claimed Empson saw it: as one word having several meanings (hence for Derrida its presence evaporating into its functions). We recall that Burckhardt, on the other hand, preferred the converse as his definition of ambiguity: as several meanings *having one* word. Hence, for Burckhardt, the word takes on the corporeality that confers substantive presence. (This is the methodological assumption behind my treatment of "dear" in Shakespeare's Sonnet 87 [Farewell! thou art too dear for my possessing"] in Chapter 6.)[30] The word that makes a passage work (even, perhaps, such a one as "differance," which Derrida has, as momentary philosopher-poet *malgré lui*, given us) is surely there irreplaceably, and it doubtless calls attention to itself in its duplicity.[31]

---

[30] Of course, this corporeality is a perceptual illusion, related to the nature and intentionality of the aesthetic experience, as I have continually insisted—an illusion made conscious of itself in the object as we are expected to interact with it.

[31] I have myself, for my very different purposes from Derrida's, spoken of "duplicity" and even of "systematic duplicity." It was for me the use of difference to multiply and cross-fertilize genres and, consequently, to produce a new and complex presence. In speaking of the overwhelming resolution achieved by Pope's "The Rape of the Lock," I suggest, in language that by now should be familiar, "that Pope required the double-edged quality built into the mock-heroic in order to bring off the controlled or systematic duplicity that can give us the now-you-see-it-now-you-don't vision whose airiness comes to have body." But the duplicity, I insist, must be systematic to bring off his brilliantly ambiguous relation to the genre he uses, adapts, half-parodies—half-converting the mock epic "to a new genre of pastoral-epic fabricated for the occasion." I add that where duplicity is less than systematic, as in "Eloisa to Abelard," it fails to achieve total presence and the poem is less than wholly successful. (See *The Classic Vision*, pp. 103, 105–106.) Here, in the spirit of Burckhardt, I am emphasizing a use of doubleness opposite to Derrida's.

The question remains whether it does so to dissipate its meanings or to gather them into itself. Burckhardt sees the gathering-in as the way it proves its irreplaceability, and, by inversion, Derrida sees the dissipation as the way it demonstrates its nonexistence.

What is the nature of the word's property and when (or where) does either verbal usury or self-depreciation begin? These are questions we may see the two of them answering in opposite ways, the one seeing an aggrandizement and the other a stripping away—the one a self-inflating Henry IV and the other a self-undoing King Lear. To some extent, I would claim, the answer depends on whether we are speaking of the word as functioning in a poetic or a philosophic text, as mystic accretion or as skeptical deprivation of meaning.[32] It is as if Burckhardt (or I) and Derrida represent, respectively, the positive print and the negative of a photograph, both seeming to have the same reality (or unreality) but with reverse emphases, the lights of one being the darks of the other.

It would be unjust to see the two within the framework of a simple opposition between the claim to total presence and the claim to total absence, though some element of opposition exists. My consciousness of miracle-as-illusion requires that I, though a theorist of presence, deny the substantive affirmations of poetic metaphor by declaring it a fiction —air after all and not body, though perceived as body in the intentional act of aesthetic contemplation: so in presence there is absence. Conversely, Derrida must admit that since, after all, those *are* words present before us which have their meanings evaporate into their differential functions, they are there even if they are constituted (as functions) by all that is not there: so in absence there is presence.[33] The concen-

---

[32] Again I am holding out for the treatment of poetry as privileged discourse (whose existence depends on its being distinguished from metaphysics), despite Derrida's structuralist habit of collapsing all discourse under the rubric of *écriture*. It is worth noting the subtitle of Derrida's essay, "White Mythology: Metaphor in the Text of Philosophy," trans. F. C. T. Moore, *New Literary History*, 6 (1974): 7–74. With all his play, he must yet work to denude the metaphor, as a positivist would. In this essay Derrida proceeds from puns on the French *usure* and "property" (the words I stress in my next-to-last sentence) as, through these, he relates the growth and conversions of verbal meanings to the growth and conversions of economic value (see esp. pp. 14–17 and 49–52). Once again, as with "systematic duplicity," there is a coincidental play on these very words in my own work, this time as early as *A Window to Criticism* (1964): see pp. 94–96 and 108–11 on "usury" as both self-aggrandizement and giving oneself away and pp. 150–54 on "property" as that which one owns in relation to that which, properly, one is. In my case, as with Burckhardt's, the difference is obvious between my interest in the substantive metaphor that accumulates and fuses meanings and Derrida's intention—by un-metaphoring them—to reduce them and break them apart.

[33] Defending himself after his essay, "Structure, Sign, and Play in the Discourse

tration on presence (against an acknowledged background of absence) may seem to be only a quibbling difference from the concentration on absence (against an acknowledged foreground of presence), but its consequences for critical practice make it as grave a difference as we can conceive. The two positions themselves may well turn out to be binary oppositions, as mutually dependent as the positive and negative photographic prints, except that the poet—and the critic dedicated to exposing his power—must develop from the absent shadows the present light that draws and focuses and holds our vision.

Let us return to Derrida's spatial-temporal double sense of differance to bring forth a final consequence from the way he uses this term to symbolize and constitute the operation of language. The insistence on deferral as a diachronic mode of difference is meant to allow Derrida the final displacement of the word—moving off from itself now in time as well as in space—from its own place in the printed (and blank) context. The two meanings are to justify the self-effacing function of words as they both take and yield their place in their differantial structures. As we have seen, what enables Derrida to perform his "systematic play" of differance is the pun on *différer* in French, a pun that does not occur in English. The doubling of meanings allows him to see the word— while it performs its divergent function within a synchronic structure of differences—as postponing the performance of the needed function until a later moment, by an agent acting similarly within the diachronic system of functions. In this way the entity within the system doubly *points to* (that is, away from itself) instead of being a *point*: in a system without origins, it clearly can initiate nothing but can only keep the game moving.

---

of the Human Sciences," at the Johns Hopkins symposium, Derrida insists that he did not mean, by dwelling on "decentering," to deny the existence of a center: "First of all, I didn't say there was no center, that we could get along without the center. I believe that the center is a function, not a being—a reality, but a function. And this function is absolutely indispensable. The subject is absolutely indispensable. I don't destroy the subject; I situate it. That is to say, I believe that at a certain level both of experience and of philosophical and scientific discourse [sic] one cannot get along without the notion of subject. It is a question of knowing where it comes from and how it functions. Therefore I keep the concept of center, which I explained was indispensable, as well as that of subject. . . ." Earlier in the discussion, Derrida admits, "The concept of structure itself . . . is no longer satisfactory to describe that game. How to define structure? Structure should be centered. But this center can be either thought, as it was classically, like a creator or being or a fixed and natural place; or also as a deficiency, let's say . . ." It is this sense of center as "a deficiency" that leads him to conclude, "So, I think that what I have said can be understood as a criticism of structuralism, certainly." Hence my designation of Derrida as a "critical structuralist." See pp. 271–72 and p. 268, respectively, in the Macksey and Donato volume.

The playing down by the word of its own presence is clearly enhanced by this act of deferring, the sacrifice of its own differentiating performance in favor of what is temporally external to its appearance, following it. But I would point out that, thanks to the accidents of the development of the two languages, this act suggests a pun in English on "defer" that does not occur in the French *différer*: the act of deferring implies the act of *deferring to*.[34] It is an act of deference, a willingness to yield up one's own rights by acknowledging the superior claim of another. If one defers action because he is deferring *to* another—showing deference to his rights by citing difference from him—then the self-abnegation and the effacement of one's function are complete. One has joined a social or even perhaps a moral justification for elevating the absent entity over the present one.

I believe—despite the fact that, in French, *déférer* is a separate verb—that Derrida's use of difference carries the sense of deference (as well as deferral) in it. Shall I say, using Derrida on himself, that there is a "trace" of being deferential that invades and further complicates differance? This "trace" is significant because it carries the notion of differance to the extreme—pointed to by Derrida's own discourse—that the words of a discourse, by their behavior, claim they are altogether without rights, and bow to the rights of others. By continual and systematic acts of differantial deference to what is outside the discourse, lurking beyond the blank space and seeking to emerge into that space as "traces," the words in their centrifugal self-deprecation would undo the very possibility of language as we see it operating in poems. In Derrida's own discourse, the very word "differance," with or without my emendation, is surely and in a profound sense a word behaving most *un*deferentially.[35] The decentering use to which he puts it does not alter our sense of the need he has for the word's capacity to contain its divergent meanings. How much more undeferential—how much more self-assertive—would it be if it was serving a Burckhardtian poem!

The theorist of verbal "presence" must be grateful to Derrida's sense of the word as differantial and, by implication, as deferential, for showing us, in so extreme a fashion, how inadequate this description of sign behavior in normal discourse is to describe what happens in poems. The self-abnegation of the decentered word becomes a *reductio ad ab-*

---

[34] One might well argue that the pun in English on "defer" has a more inevitable relationship between its two meanings than does the pun in French on *différer*.

[35] I might have given similar treatment to his word *supplément*, which he also finds to yield a double, synchronic-diachronic meaning, on the one hand completing a pattern by filling in a gap and on the other hand breaking a pattern by adding a new element that has no place in it. I find some similarity in my Bergsonian interest in the duplicitous relations between the instance and the instant or instantaneous (see *The Classic Vision*, pp. 13–14).

surdum of the way we can denature language that lacks the character to fight for presence. Derrida's persistent denial of verbal presence in writing generally can thus be converted into a forceful argument *for* presence in poetry-as-fiction. And Derrida becomes his own persuasive example. Very likely Burckhardt would have smilingly endorsed Derrida's use of *"différance"* (or, elsewhere, *"supplément"*), enjoying the ironic attempt by Derrida to use the pun as a self-conscious device to demystify the very idolatry of the word for which Burckhardt fought. And the more self-consciously involuted and reflexive Derrida was seen to be, the more he would satisfy the fictional and illusionary requirement that Burckhardt and those I have treated as his theoretical allies believe the poem needs to undercut itself and prevent its being projected externally into a metaphysical myth.

The theorists of presence, adapting Gombrichian principles to literary interpretation (as Colie did), are also concerned with gaps in the poem's structure. But they distinguish these gaps from those in normal discourse which they may acknowledge can best be described in Derrida's way. They are concerned with the poet's capacity to remake the words he finds, and it is this remaking that reveals precisely the lack of presence in normal language that makes Derrida's a useful description. Dedicated to presence, they see the gaps in poems as that which, as they are filled, reinforce verbal fullness; and they address themselves to filling them in ways imposed by the poet. There are indeed "traces" of elements not present that are to guide them, but these are the generic patterns mixed and mastered by the poet—patterns perceptible to those who know how to follow the poet's clues in searching them out. For it is he who limits our applications of their meanings. These "traces" thus become present, derivable from the words used and in turn helping to pack those words with substance that makes them irreplaceable: these "traces" reinforce presence rather than undermine it. This method of gap-filling differs profoundly from the invasion of gaps by Derrida's "traces" that are uncontrollable by the words now present—indeed, that are uncontrollable except by the universally differential behavior of the invisible language structure. His differentiation forces present words to defer to what is absent, to what is as unseen as the *a* in the excluded word "differance" is unsounded. Perhaps we should ask where the mystification really lies: with my self-conscious claim of presence— an admittedly illusionary presence—in language that gives to "traces" "a local habitation and a name" or with Derrida's beckoning to "traces" as absent ghosts or an absent structure inhabiting blankness, which undermines the present by replacing its graphic, visible agents with shadows.

As just a single brief example—and yet an allegory—of what I am claiming here, I choose a poem that should be a most difficult witness for me, for it is a poem of rather direct statement, by that splendid poet of direct statement, Ben Jonson. "Why I write not of Love." Further, it is a negative poem, a demythifying poem about absence, thus requiring a diminished and unpresumptuous language, minimizing itself in its unpretentious monosyllables as it affirms only what it lacks:

> *Some act of* Love's *bound to rehearse,*
> *I thought to bind him, in my verse:*
> *Which when he felt, Away (quoth he)*
> *Can poets hope to fetter me?*
> *It is enough, they once did get*
> Mars, *and my* Mother, *in their net:*
> *I wear not these my wings in vain.*
> *With which he fled me: and again,*
> *Into my rimes could ne'er be got*
> *By any art. Then wonder not,*
> *That since, my numbers are so cold,*
> *When* Love *is fled, and I grow old.*

The statement of loss—loss of love and youth—seems unambiguous enough, and the treatment of the routine mythological instruments of the poets is clearly harsh and prosaic. But let me ask the reader to be disturbed by two things and to examine their significance: first, the un-questioning acceptance—despite the harsh tone—of the mythological metaphor and, second, the sharp break that separates the last two and a half lines from the rest of the poem.

The conventional machinery of love's divinity—Cupid with wings, Mars and Venus—far from being demythified, seems to be accepted with a matter-of-factness that reduces it to being a part of the poet's prosaic world of present deprivation. Indeed, Cupid is the only other acting, speaking character in the drama he shares with the poet, and a literalized character he is, literalized and almost domesticated. The name "Cupid" is not itself mentioned, since it is assumed that he and his name are identical with *Love,* not merely the generic noun but a proper name that becomes personified once "him" is used in line 2. That love in the poem remains both Love and Cupid is consistently made clear by his speech and action, by reference to the other gods, by his wings and the use he makes of them to flee. Love, as love and Cupid, may begin as a conventional metonym, but, without any seeming effort by the poet, it is also a totally embodied metaphor. Here, then, is reifica-tion without a blush, within a tough-minded, realistic framework that accentuates the distance between prosaic reductions and myth even as that distance is collapsed.

Yet the projection of myth is clearly tied to poetic invention: it is Jonson's poet—a would-be lover, to be sure, but a lover as a mythifying poet—who seeks to capture the free-flying god in his verse, tying him up in his words. Words, then, are to enclose and hold and give solid presence to the elusive (mythic) reality to which they refer—just as the word "Love" in this poem *is* Cupid and holds Cupid, though it does so while dragging along its less corporeal, unpersonified meaning. But, alas, the word and poem hold Cupid only to announce—in the title and argument of the poem—that they cannot do so, that he is "fled," leaving an empty, unmetaphored and uncorporealized sense of language for a poet "cold" and "old." Cupid, we see, is reacting against the more successful act of reifying captivity performed by the words of another poet ("It is enough, they [the poets] once did get / *Mars,* and my *Mother,* in their net"). Thanks to his wings, Love will not be bound as Mars and Venus were by Homer. He is obviously referring to the net thrown over them by the jealous Hephaestus (Vulcan) to trap the lovers there, unmoving, forever to be exposed to the gaze of the mocking gods. What is striking about this glancing and yet telling reference is Cupid's charge that it is the poet's net that bound Mars and Venus, despite the fact that, of course, in the story as related in the *Odyssey,* the net is the angry husband's. This discrepancy serves to make his charge the clearer: it is the net of the poet's words that does the work that enables the god's net of forged metal to do its work. It is the poet, not the actor, who is responsible for the capturing, for the tale is the poet's, and it is all a story, a myth. In the world of myth, and youth and love (themselves myths), the poet is the ultimate actor, just as the present poet (as a conventional Renaissance poet-lover), seeking to capture Love in his poem, would use the heated poem to capture love in his life.

The poet's verbal network entwines its immortal objects and, like Vulcan's, fixes them in a permanent display for those invited to gaze. His initial interest in binding Cupid, we remember, was to recount ("rehearse") an act of love's limitation or confinement ("bound"). So his role *is* like Vulcan's in Homer's tale. For the poet to capture the gods is for him to claim their immortality at his own. But his poem is also to be seen to be as mortal as he is, emptied of the fleeing god, left at the end to announce only its own emptiness and his aging mortality that leaves him without love, upper and lower-case. For the lower *is* the uppercase love, human love becoming the god himself; to have it is to have him, to be the mythologized lover as poet, immortal and ever young.

Thus, after the one full stop that disrupts the poem's octosyllabic couplets, Jonson can conclude with the straightforward resignation of the final two and a half lines, with not a drop of explicit mythology left in them, except for the obvious fact that "Love" and "fled" in the final line are to carry with them—if only nostalgically—their previously earned meanings in the literalized metaphor. Love is unmetaphored in these final lines as a logical consequence ("Then wonder not") of his own previous action, in which he used his metaphorical wings to flee the poet's verbal net. So love has, in effect, unmetaphored both itself (no longer *himself*) and the poet—but not the poem altogether: for the action is intelligible only if we too accepted the literalness of its previous metaphorical existence. The domain of the poem has demonstrated that love is Love, an immortal and mythified reality, so that one cannot be lost without the other.

The simple assertion of fact in the final four words of the poem startles the reader in a way that belies their deceptive conjunction with the first half of the last line. "And I grow old" speaks to us with a voice from outside the fiction. There is a flat and unelevatable literalness in these words that can in no way be absorbed into the modest metaphorical action that has gone before. The opening of the line, "When Love is fled," can and should—as I have said—be read by way of what has gone before. But the stark intrusion of the plain fact of mortality ("and I grow old") makes us, in retrospect, wonder whether the first half of the line should not be taken just as plainly, with "Love" now seen only in its unmetaphored dimensions. Well, these "cold" "numbers" of the poet, abandoned by the warm myth of love, really warrant by this time only the flat, unresonant reading, in which the clause "Love is fled"—despite verbal coincidence—is just as prosaically and even physiologically factual as its companion clause, "I grow old." And the love that is fled may be someone more mortal and literal than Cupid, someone the poem also could not hold. The previous extravagance, in which the mythic drama seemed simply literal in *its* way, is dissipated by the final statements of absence and decline. Are these final four words—with their impact upon the four words before them, making us rethink their meaning—the consequence of the poem and its mythological workings, or are they the cause of the poem, retroactively inventing it and its mythology as their rationalization?

Is this, then, a poem that shows us the action leading to the poet as old man or is this poem the lying and self-mocking invention of the poet as old man? Is it the dead result of a once-living myth or a futile game disguising the make-believe of a false language that never lived? The poet must be seen as both effect and cause. Clearly, the precedent of Homer that is cited indicates that it is the poet who casts the net of words, so that, in this case, it is he who has done the casting on his own and, thanks to the facts of aging life, has come up empty. But the poem is present, even if love (and Love) win their absence from it. The poem

236

makes use of the myth in the act of unmaking it.[36] Its net of words has caught the god, if only to chronicle his escape and its own consequent emptiness. The poem acknowledges the myth-making power of poetry and displays that power itself by showing its mythic drama as if it is a drama between real persons, before giving up that past fullness of power for the present emptiness of impotence. The poem's pretense at immortality, in its attempt to capture the god—immortal Love—in its net of words, as immortal Homer did, gives way to its confession that, in the demythified world, it is no more than a reflection of the poet's mortality. To the extent that these words are but his, and limited by the world of fact that limits him, they are in their aging modesty at odds with that older arrogance of the word that sought to create and contain the gods. This poem, in its recital of history, does so yet, despite the confessed absence that has taken over the momentary present of the poet who is growing old. Strangely, existential absence only reinforces aesthetic presence, though at the cost of compelling that presence to doubt itself. The poem, in short, describes man's story in a way that may echo Derrida's negations, but the description is itself a magnificently present affirmation of verbal form. The word "Love" becomes metaphor and myth, rebounding even upon the poem's title, and yet escapes from the net that, as the poem, has captured it.

I have repeatedly been using the fictional or illusionary element in the poem—and its self-conscious employment—as the guard against our falling into the temptation of believing literally in the mythic capacity of the poetic word to contain its meaning. As the metaphor, functioning aesthetically, takes on substance, as if in imitation of the miraculous word that takes on flesh—air become body—it assumes this total presence only as it reminds us of how we have been taken in, that, like any miracle, it is impossible to believe in except as a myth. Though its vision—as a reduction of reality—is one we must momentarily accept, we reduce reality to it only as we acknowledge its own awareness of its insufficiency once it relaxes its magical dominion.

Gombrich and, after him, Colie have reminded us that formal devices of self-reference function in visual as well as verbal arts to remind us of the work's illusionary status and, thus, to keep us from reifying it into a chunk of reality. But the literary work, because of the nature of its ambiguous medium, has a greater need than the work of plastic art to emphasize—through self-referentiality—its illusionary status. For, we must remember, we are more likely to treat words as if they

---

[36] Jonson similarly makes and unmakes his mythic metaphor in his well-known "Drink to me only with thine eyes." See my discussion of this poem, in some of the same terms, in *The Classic Vision*, pp. 69–71.

were occurring in normal discourse without essential deviation: we have a tendency, only enforced by structuralist theory, to respond automatically to all words similarly within the common-sense opposition of signifier and signified. The physical materials of the plastic arts are obviously not to be confused with the materials of the world. As I have suggested elsewhere, no observer is likely to try to eat the oranges off a still-life canvas, hanging in the frame that sets it off from the surrounding reality, although many readers will take the speech of a character in a play as if it were a straightforward proposition stated by the discourse, or a line of a lyric as if it were a direct plea or claim or confession of its composer, or a sentence of narration from a novel as if it were historical exposition. Clearly, the poet, forced to use the words used before by others, has a need beyond that of his fellow artists to work for the reverberations in the poem and its turnings on itself that constitute form and its protective shield of illusion.

Using another example, I can make a direct assault on the notion of absence by an assault on the very word, as Derrida attacked difference-deferral with an attack on differance. Appealing once more to a coincidence of interests between Derrida and me, I cite an earlier passage of my own, seemingly written (though in 1962) as if in anticipation of this chapter. Looking for an example to illustrate my claim of "incarnation in the word" (what I am terming "presence" here), I came upon—of all things—John Donne's play upon "absence" in the lines from "A Valediction Forbidding Mourning,"

> Dull sublunary lovers' love,
> Whose soul is sense, cannot admit
> Absence, because it doth remove
> Those things which elemented it.

My comments on this passage then,[37] relating to Donne's poem about a love that would transcend sense and absence alike, apply to my argument here. I suggested that the word "absence" is to be read as if, thanks to a playful etymology, the root of the word is sense (repeated from the previous line), so that "absence" means, in effect, "away from sense." We discover that the word itself, like the dull sublunary lovers, has a soul of sense. Sense is precisely the thing that elements the word, so that when it is removed, as in absence, so is their love. With the notion of admitting absence, these lines allow entrance to negation— an affirmative act—a conferring of presence on a lack, on a deprivation.

---

[37] See A Window to Criticism, pp. 15–16.

Yet the entire possibility is couched in the negative ("cannot admit / Absence") since only true lovers can manage so disheartening a contradiction. Further, admitting absence "doth remove / Those things which elemented" the dull sublunary love, which is just the reverse contradiction, the negation of an affirmative: the taking away (thus producing the absence) of that which is responsible for sense's presence. So taking away sense equals *ab*sence in letter as in concept, in letter *as* concept. It is this removal—precisely the "ab" of "absence"—which forces us to realize "absence" as a deprivation of sense, thus remaking our awareness of the word's very form—and love's. But the true lovers' love, which *can* manage the contradiction and admit absence, is an eternal present, and so is this language whose presence gives that love substance within the philological confines of the poem.

Working from mere phonetic coincidence, the poet forces the word to deny its emptiness and behave in a way that leaps the bounds of ordinary discourse, turning signs into things. Unlike what structuralists teach us to expect, this signifier, having turned its arbitrary relation to its signified into an inevitable one, has constituted itself as a signifier filled with meanings it alone has created. Though words have no business appearing to behave this way, we cannot read them fully in cases like this unless we permit them to behave just this way. As it functions here, the word as entity ("absence") overcomes its own meaning since (much as with Derrida's "differ*a*nce") the word is irreducibly there, denying absence. It can defer to no other word or linguistic function or meaning since its presence is indispensable to its function and meaning. In this "absence" there is presence indeed, though we must remember also that it is only an outrageous play on the word that brings it about and sustains it.

Yet I mean to claim that the manipulations I speak of are not only the verbal ones on which Burckhardt has dwelled and upon which this example depends. Though the manipulation of language is for Burckhardt the primary means to achieve corporeality for the poem—through the substantive fusions of pun or metaphor—whatever the poet treats as his medium can become the basis for deviation and hence can be manipulated into an apparent presence. We must remember that, as founder of the formal tradition, Aristotle himself did not treat language as a formative element in poetic creativity; he rather, as we have seen at length in earlier chapters, treated the structure of the action as his manipulable element, distorting and shaping historical sequence into the teleology of the successful plot. Dramatists, Aristotelians or not, may manipulate the imitated but transformed happenings they recreate into a play, as well as the intricacies of speeches, and their ordering.

Similarly, a novelist may manipulate the deviated-from imitations of historical narration or (if first-person novelists) of autobiographical narration or journal commentary—in each case instead of or in addition to the manipulations of the language he found which must be transformed into the language he must have.[38] Out of such manipulations must arise the sense of a special presence beyond the absent-present that Derrida may persuade us we have in normal discourse. But it is a special presence aware of its presumption and wary of asking us to take it literally.

The sense of form, at once creating body and denying its more than illusory nature, is affirming a present structure while it acknowledges a sequence of fleeting words. This is in accord with my earlier definition of form in poetry as the imposition of spatial elements on a temporal ground. We are not allowed to forget that what we are witnessing (on stage or page) is an imitation of the purely diachronic which, in accord with Derrida, disappears off the page as we watch. It is *as if* it were an unrepeatable series of real-life occurrences or references whose beginning, middle, and end—like its words—make up an always changing flow that resists all echo, all pattern. Whether an as-if happening, an as-if history or autobiography or confession, or some other, the real-life model sequence that is being counterfeited is to remain a part of our conscious awareness as we respond aesthetically, even while the work helps remind us of that counterfeit quality, its crucial as-ifness. And it is by means of the formal imposition of spatial elements—devices of repetition, juxtaposition, or other forms of self-reference—that our aesthetic habits of perception are encouraged to disrupt the temporal flow, imposing pattern upon the discrete entities sliding by, out of diachronic differences creating at least similarity, and at most identity and simultaneity, in order to turn fleeting sequences into present art. But, unless we victimize ourselves with some static, neoclassical myth about the total absorption of spatial form, we remain aware that what the pattern seeks to capture is in motion, that if the pattern is reversible the motion is not. The aesthetic presence of the poem may persuade us toward perceiving identity, though our sense of its fiction reminds us that

---

[38] It may well be argued that the concern for "point of view" in the novel was originally brought to the fore by aesthetically self-conscious novelists like James and Conrad, because they sought to invent a discipline—peculiar to the medium of prose fiction—that would emphasize those self-referential elements that would put the work on its own. The use of artificially limited and controlled perspectives, manipulated in response to formal-thematic needs, was to give it a self-awareness that cut it off as an illusionary world not easily confused with the diffuse presentation of chronicle history or biography.

identity itself is a fiction in the empirical and linguistic world of differences.

So we must read or watch doubly: as if the beginning, middle, and end are chronological only, as irreversible and unrepeatable as the passing moments of our lives, *and* as if the beginning, middle, and end are as circular in their mutually implicative nature as Aristotle has taught. We witness as if what is before us is there for the first time and will not come again, and yet we know it to be a fictional occasion created by the familiar and fixed sequence we with many others have out there to witness again and again—and a sequence that reminds us of its fixed (and, as sequence, counterfeit) nature through the clues it provides to point us within it to the patterns of artifice, the illusory simultaneities and identities, we are to find. Since its sequential appearance is innocent, we can—through aesthetic blindness—persist in reading it temporally only, as if we can read it but once, ignorant of its as-ifness and refusing all clues that suggest self-reference. In effect, it is the reader's equivalent of eating the oranges off the painted canvas—except that it is so much more easily and commonly done with words. The illusion has been too persuasive, so that the myth of the work's reality has been literalized. If, on the other hand, we ignore the passing before-ness and after-ness, converting all contingency into teleology, we become victims of our own patterns, at the expense of the primary presupposition of literature as a temporal art. There is a victimization by illusion in this as in the other extreme: if those who see only the passage of words and action fall prey to art's illusion, converting it to the delusion that would confuse it with life, those who see only the formal patterns, which they have imposed as their structure to undo the chronological sequence, fall prey to the illusion of formal presence, which, however encouraged by the poet, still distorts through mythification the diachronic reality of human history.[39]

I repeat, then, that we must read or watch doubly. Thanks to our previous experiences with this and other poems, but thanks also to our submissive attitude to the present experience of this poem, we must both be surprised and expect to be surprised. The remarkable character of

[39] I trust that this paragraph has clarified the extent to which the sort of doubleness I have been proposing is distinguished from the apparent doubleness of those structuralists who derive from Russian formalism. I am speaking for a synchronic structure that requires us at each moment to remain conscious of the unabsorbable diachronic facts, so that we retain the double awareness of both; but I see them (whether Jakobson on poems or Lévi-Strauss on myths) as having the diachronic finally fully absorbed—without remainder—by the synchronic. Hence my sense that theirs is an apparent doubleness only.

aesthetic experience is such that the surprise we get (the surprise in action, in verbal manipulation, or any element in between) must be the surprise we expect—and must remain a surprise nevertheless, though, of course, an aesthetically distanced surprise. And, however paradoxical this double illusion, it must appear to us as such each time we read or watch: our synchronic sense is to coexist in harmony with our diachronic sense while the *micro-langue*, which is a *parole* too after all, works its paradoxical—if illusionary—magic upon us. So long as this double illusion holds, the illusion of a temporal sequence without form and the illusion of a spatial pattern without contingency may seem to cancel one another out, so that each is prevented from victimizing its witness into literalizing a mythic metaphor, as it can do acting singly. What remains is the sense of a moving presence or a present motion as our aesthetic illusion, a fiction we know to be such, though an always present fiction. This doubleness in our reading intentions, then, is the only appropriate response to the doubleness in the work before us. As in the Jonson poem, the words we read enclose their object and they do not: they become an all-embracing spatial symbol of their experience and they leave it intact in its ever-contingent temporality. So the thematic double relation between the words-as-aesthetic-work and their object is an existential reflection of the aesthetic double relation between us as reader-interpreters and the words as *our* object.

Let me now review some of the alternative positions I have touched on. The main-line structuralists, with their emphasis on the synchronic, helped expose, in so-called phenomenological critics, the self-indulgent myths arising out of an antiformal emphasis on the temporal, founded on the prelinguistic consciousness as a point of origin and return. But a critical structuralist like Derrida in turn exposes the mythic consequences of the excessive emphasis on the synchronic, common to many structuralists. He is concerned that some of them have not sufficiently pressed to the negative consequences of the differential functions of language—that, instead, they can stumble into a notion of discourse that has a center and an origin, at the expense of the diachronic and of free play. Instead of words being treated as elements in a unified central system, Derrida would have them treated as differential, decentralizing functions.

Now, this negative critique in some fundamental ways turns out to be the enemy that would overturn the humanist poetics and the dominant poetic forms it fostered, emptying both of content and justifying instead only a "poetics of failure" and poems of verbal insufficiency, based on self-abnegation. Yet, in what this critique reveals about structuralism, as in what structuralism revealed about "consciousness criticism," it can—despite its objectives—help renew the prospects for the more positive alternative I have represented here. This is a defense of verbal systems that affirm presence instead of putting up with absence, provided those systems do not preclude the diachronic realities of a *parole* while they manage to blur the generic opposition between signifier and signified that limits the operations of normal language. Even more crucially, the defense requires that each system be a self-conscious fiction, and be seen as such, so that it anticipates and undercuts any temptation to literalize the achieved verbal myth of presence. This is the alternative I have been suggesting in my attempt to justify man's myth-making power as poet, though not as philosopher. For the myth is a fiction, and our poetic fictions protect it as such without catering to its latent presumption upon reality.

It may seem that I am doing little more than, in a retrograde neo-Kantian fashion, raising the ghost of Ernst Cassirer against the living, though negative, power of Derrida. But, unlike an idealist, I do insist that one must see around the categories of vision to existential fact, since it is fact that wins in the end. It *is* man's humanistic triumph that he is a myth maker—so long as he sees the myth as myth and does not so reify it that he makes it his only reality. In its own way, the assault by Derrida is a newer version of that oldest attack on the poet as myth maker by Plato, who struck that gravest blow, in the name of the demythifying reason, in that ancient war between the poets and the philosophers. Of course, as ontologist, Plato raised his own myth in the place of the poet's; and his myth was less self-conscious in that, unlike the poet's, it was not aware of its own fictional nature. So the reified myth of the ontologist we may have done well to deconstruct. But the myths of the poet, as fictions that turn out to be less self-deluded than those of the metaphysicians, we do well to keep—and can afford to do so without arousing the demythifying ire of that sleeping skeptic in each of us as modern man, conscious of our ontological losses and wary of our unconscious nostalgia.

Yet these myths are not just an escapist game, for they do possess "visionary power," though in a way more limited than is suggested by most users of that phrase. It is as if we are all at the play of life and are asked not to err, as did those seventeenth-century French protectors of "verisimilitude," by mistaking delusion for illusion: we are not to take the metaphor for life, but we see life the more acutely for the metaphor and through it—though always tentatively and without any final commitment to belief, beyond subjecting ourselves to its power. Our acceptance of the self-conscious myth-as-fiction, filled with illusion and artfully displaying that illusionary power (at times almost with a trace of exhibitionism), allows us to grasp the metaphoric equations that have shaped our culture's changing sense of its worlds. In a way this may be a knowledge (or, really, a not-quite-knowledge) before science or a prophecy for the knowledge of science—thus adding *prescience* (pre-science) to *presence*—though science itself may well end up as the myth (prescience) being taken too literally.[40]

The poet's metaphoric reductions, reality as vision present and prescient, are the brilliantly fashioned hobby-horses (both Laurence Sterne's and Gombrich's) on which we canter off for a spin into the countryside built to the horse's dimensions. We believe him to be our horse and we don't, for we can change horses. But we know we must finally dismount, intimidated by the death-on-horseback who pursues us through a staccato sequence of successive minutes that can neither be transformed nor redeemed—pursues us all as pedestrians and runs us down. We can recall de Man's reminder, as he justifies man's retreat from the worship of his verbal form, of how the early Romantic lived with the awareness that his humanistic claim to power was a delusion: "Nature can at all times treat him as if he were a thing and remind him of his factitiousness, whereas he is quite powerless to convert even the smallest particle of nature into something human."[41] Man may not be able to remake nature into his forms, despite the arrogant I AM of post-Kantian idealism; but he can still choose to live, in part anyway, in accordance with what his creative vision of nature provisionally allows. If he insists on living *only* with the reified products of that vision, then he may visit upon us all the post-Nietzschean horrors described by Thomas Mann; but he must create forms beyond nature's "given" if he is, even momentarily, to be more than a driven and determined thing, part of nature's "given," himself. Within his sphere man transforms the nature and the time he suffers, and lives in the light of the forms that work his inventive miracles. But his final (continually final) incredulity before all but the fact of death unmasks the miracle for what it is—an illusion that could not have been and that has asserted its power while it acknowledged its impossibility—though it shines the more brilliantly for what it was. Even as the poet raised it up as his

---

[40] So prescience has its puns too. In its prescience the metaphor-as-poem is a before-knowledge rather than knowledge itself: rather than being burdened by positivistic criteria that determine whether its knowledge is true or false, its foreknowledge is subject only to the self-limiting terms of its fictional casuistry. As prescient it sees far, though its vision is illusive only and its modesty must not have us take it for a circumscribed (scientific) knowledge that has its own illusions. So this foreknowledge—prescience—is at once less than knowledge and free from its bonds.

[41] "The Rhetoric of Temporality," in *Interpretation: Theory and Practice*, p. 196.

244

metaphor, he managed to keep it in touch with earth, unmetaphoring it as it soared, making and unmaking his illusion.

So there is no need to demythify it: it demythifies itself in the constructing. Its construction is viewed as at once total construction and mere construction, with an awareness in which one eye borrowed from Coleridge is balanced with one eye borrowed from Derrida. But so delicately balanced an illusionary construct can never, like the airy onticspheric myths of the metaphysician, be deconstructed. For the body of the myth-as-fiction, as its own voice, has substance that survives its creator's extinction because, though an object for now and later, it has anticipated its own unreality from the start. Its very existence, though an ambiguous existence as fiction, proves that to demythify need not be the same as to deconstruct. So, thanks to the peculiar presence of the poem and its word, the deconstruction of metaphysics can be made to serve the *re*construction of poetics. Still, this is too dramatic a claim: in the long tradition I have "traced,"[42] from the early use of this term to this last one, poetics—like the poem—has been present all along, constructed and constructing. May it continue.

---

[42] I of course use the verb *trace* advisedly, in hopes that, in the manner of semiology according to Derrida, every term and concept in my theory exists only in relation to the "traces" of the absent-present terms and concepts in the traditional system that has been my subject and object—and my point of departure.

Index

THE JOHNS HOPKINS UNIVERSITY PRESS

This book was composed in Linotype Palatino text and display type by Monotype Composition Company, Inc., from a design by Susan Bishop. It was printed on 60-lb. Warren 1854 Regular paper and bound in Holliston Roxite vellum by The Maple Press Company.